THE JOURNAL OF THE JOINT COMMITTEE OF FIFTEEN ON RECONSTRUCTION

39TH CONGRESS, 1865–1867

BY

BENJ. B. KENDRICK, Ph.D.,

Instructor in History, Columbia University
Sometime Schiff Fellow in History

THE LAWBOOK EXCHANGE, LTD.
Clark, New Jersey

ISBN 9781584774433 (hardcover)
ISBN 9781616192730 (paperback)

Lawbook Exchange edition 2005, 2012

The quality of this reprint is equivalent to the quality of the original work.

THE LAWBOOK EXCHANGE, LTD.
33 Terminal Avenue
Clark, New Jersey 07066-1321

Please see our website for a selection of our other publications and fine facsimile reprints of classic works of legal history:
www.lawbookexchange.com

Library of Congress Cataloging-in-Publication Data

Kendrick, Benjamin B. (Benjamin Burks), 1884-1946.
   The journal of the Joint Committee of Fifteen on Reconstruction: 39th Congress, 1865-1867 / by Benj. B. Kendrick.
     p. cm.
   Originally published: New York: Columbia University, 1914.
   (Studies in history, economics, and public law; v. 62 = whole no. 150)
   Includes bibliographical references and index.
   ISBN 1-58477-443-6 (cloth: alk. paper)
    1. United States--History--Civil War, 1861-1865--Sources. 2. Reconstruction--Sources. I. United States. Congress. Joint Committee on Reconstruction. II. Title. III. Studies in history, economics, and public law ; no. 150.

H81.K46 2004
973.8'1--dc22
                                            2004040734

Printed in the United States of America on acid-free paper

STUDIES IN HISTORY, ECONOMICS AND PUBLIC LAW

EDITED BY THE FACULTY OF POLITICAL SCIENCE
OF COLUMBIA UNIVERSITY

Volume LXII]   [Whole Number 150

THE JOURNAL OF THE JOINT COMMITTEE OF FIFTEEN ON RECONSTRUCTION

39TH CONGRESS, 1865–1867

BY

BENJ. B. KENDRICK, Ph.D.,

Instructor in History, Columbia University
Sometime Schiff Fellow in History

New York
COLUMBIA UNIVERSITY
LONGMANS, GREEN & CO., AGENTS
LONDON: P. S. KING & SON
1914

Copyright, 1914
BY
BENJ. B. KENDRICK

To

My Father and Mother

WM. T. AND LAVICIE M. KENDRICK

TO WHOSE INFLUENCE IS DUE MY FIRST
INTEREST IN THE HISTORY OF THE
RECONSTRUCTION PERIOD

PREFATORY NOTE

THE primary object of this volume is to make available to students of American history and constitutional law an important document, hitherto not easily accessible. This document is the journal of the joint committee of fifteen on reconstruction (39th Congress, 1865-67). Though it relates principally to the genesis of the fourteenth amendment, it throws some light on the five or six less significant matters with which the committee was concerned. Since there is only one printed copy of the journal known to be extant, its value as an historical source would seem to justify its being reprinted. Therefore, with the exception of a brief introductory chapter, it occupies all of Part I of this book.

In this introductory chapter, there will be found (1) a short account of how the journal came into existence; (2) the story of how the manuscript copy of the journal was discovered; (3) a discussion of the influence which it had on the Supreme Court in determining that tribunal's interpretation of the civil rights clause of the fourteenth amendment. Though no one of these matters bears a very intimate relation to the rest of this volume, yet it seems that each is of sufficient interest to merit the space given it.

In Part II, the first two chapters deal with the origin and personnel of the committee, while in the remaining six I have endeavored to give a history of the measures that were evolved by the committee, together with an interpretation of these measures and an analysis of the motives of the men who championed or opposed them.

In the preparation of my manuscript, I have been greatly assisted by my kinsman, Mr. Thomas Shields, to whom I wish to acknowledge my appreciation. My colleagues, Professors C. A. Beard and R. L. Schuyler, have kindly given me the benefit of their criticism in regard to the introductory chapter. To Professor Wm. A. Dunning, at whose instance this work was begun, and who has read all the manuscript and made many helpful suggestions, I desire to express my indebtedness and gratitude.

BENJ. B. KENDRICK.

COLUMBIA UNIVERSITY, NEW YORK, JULY, 1914.

CONTENTS

PAGE

PART I

INTRODUCTION AND THE JOURNAL OF THE JOINT COMMITTEE ON RECONSTRUCTION

A. INTRODUCTION 17
    How the journal came into existence 17
    The author's discovery of the manuscript journal 18
    The journal's influence on the Supreme Court in its interpretation of the fourteenth amendment 22
B. THE JOURNAL OF THE JOINT COMMITTEE ON RECONSTRUCTION. 37

PART II

THE HISTORY OF THE JOINT COMMITTEE

CHAPTER I

ORIGIN OF THE JOINT COMMITTEE

Presidential reconstruction 133
Opposition to the President's policy 136
Thaddeus Stevens' initial movements against the President. . . . 138
Stevens and the radical caucus. 139
The Republican caucus 140
Meeting of the 39th Congress 141
The House resolution creating the committee 142
Four groups of political opinion in the Senate 144
The Senate's amendment of the House resolution 145
Attitude of various senators toward a committee 146
Newspaper comments on the committee 148
Political situation in December, 1865 152
Position of the conservatives 153

CHAPTER II

MEMBERS OF THE COMMITTEE

	PAGE
Thaddeus Stevens	155
Stevens' early life	155
Beginning of his political career	156
First election to Congress (1847)	158
His attitude toward slavery	158
Second election to Congress (1858)	160
Attitude toward secession	161
Stevens' criticism of Lincoln	162
The "conquered province" theory of reconstruction	163
Stevens' plan of confiscation	166
Estimates of Stevens	167
Why the Republicans accepted his leadership	168
William Pitt Fessenden	169
Fessenden's early life	170
His service in the House of Representatives (1841–1843)	170
Election to the Senate	172
Fessenden as a financier	173
His position in regard to reconstruction	173
Fessenden and the impeachment of Johnson	180
Estimates of Fessenden	182
John A. Bingham	183
Roscoe Conkling	185
George S. Boutwell	187
J. W. Grimes	190
George H. Williams	191
Minor members of the committee (Howard, Morrill, Washburne, Blow, Harris)	192
The Democratic members (Johnson, Grider, Rogers)	195

CHAPTER III

REPRESENTATION AND CIVIL RIGHTS

The problem of readjusting the basis of representation	198
Representation according to voters	199
First report of the committee on representation	200
Defeat of the committee's proposition in the Senate	201
Discussion of the proposition in the House	202
Radical opposition in the Senate	205
Reduction of Southern representation *versus* negro suffrage	206
Attitude of the Democrats	207

	PAGE
Opinions of the press	210
Why a civil-rights amendment appeared necessary in the North	213
The first civil-rights amendment	214
Practical defeat of the measure in the House	215
Conservative and Democratic opposition	216
Bingham's speech advocating the civil-rights amendment	217

CHAPTER IV

Uniting the Republican Congressmen Against the President

An excursus into the reconstruction of Tennessee	221
Testimony taken by the sub-committee on Tennessee	225
The sub-committee recommends the admission of the Tennessee members	226
Recommendation not adopted by the joint committee	226
Importance of Tennessee's admission in the struggle between Johnson and the radicals	227
Radical attempts to break with the President	230
President's veto of the Freedmen's Bureau bill tends to alienate the Conservatives	233
Declaratory resolution of the power of Congress over reconstruction	234
Why Johnson vetoed the Freedmen's Bureau bill	235
Press comment on the veto	237
Action of the House on the declaratory resolution	239
Johnson's 22nd of February speech	242
The declaratory resolution before the Senate	243
Its passage	249
Johnson fails to grasp the situation	250
Stewart's compromise plan of reconstruction	252
An estimate of the plan	253
Stewart's advocacy of his plan	254
The question of Tennessee's admission again becomes important	256
Stevens' attack on the President	260
Johnson vetoes the Civil Rights bill and the breach with the conservatives becomes complete	263

CHAPTER V

Raison d'Etre of the Fourteenth Amendment

Northern interest in Southern conditions	264
An estimate of the evidence given by the various witnesses	265
What the Republicans wished to prove by the testimony	266

Evidence showing necessity for a civil rights amendment.	267
The Committee satisfies itself that an amendment in regard to the National and Confederate debts is necessary	282
Why Confederate leaders were disqualified from holding office	285
The disloyalty of the Southern people justified the diminution of their representation	290

CHAPTER VI

THE FOURTEENTH AMENDMENT

Demand for a congressional plan.	292
Consideration of a modification of the Stewart plan.	293
The Robert Dale Owen plan.	296
Owen's recital of the reception of his plan by the committee.	298
Owen's plan rejected	301
The committee's first draft of the present fourteenth amendment.	303
The fourteenth amendment before the House	304
Debate in the Senate on the original form of the fourteenth amendment	309
Modification of the amendment by the Republican senators in caucus	316
Hendricks' denunciation of the Republican program	317
Final passage of the amendment.	319

CHAPTER VII

DID CONGRESS HAVE A PLAN OF RECONSTRUCTION?

Four matters throwing light on the question.	320
(1) Fessenden's report	321
Ambiguity of the report.	325
(2) Congressional action on the restoration bill.	327
Temporary postponement of the bill	327
Stevens' first reconstruction bill	330
Amendments to and discussion of various restoration bills.	332
Why the radicals refused to pass any restoration bill.	333
Debate on the restoration bill in the House	335
The bill laid on the table	336
Stevens' plea for his reconstruction bill	337
Conclusion.	337
(3) Restoration of Tennessee	338
Ratification of the fourteenth amendment by the Tennessee legislature	338
Radical opposition to admitting Tennessee.	339

	PAGE
Attitude of the conservatives	342
Action of the Senate	345
The President's message on Tennessee	347
(4) Opinion of politicians as to the Congressional plan.	348
The four matters summarized	348
Conclusions.	352

CHAPTER VIII

The Reconstruction Act

Why the Republican party was ready to forsake the fourteenth amendment as a basis of reconstruction	354
Influence of disorder in the South	356
Stevens' second reconstruction bill	358
The bill debated in the House	361
Commitment of the bill.	379
A military bill offered in the committee	380
The military bill adopted by the committee	382
Debate on the military bill in Congress	383
Refutation of the radical argument as to the prevalence of disorder in the South	387
Effect of the Southern states' rejection of the fourteenth amendment	391
Embarrassing position of the conservatives.	392
The Blaine amendment	397
A special bill for reconstruction of Louisiana passed by the House.	398
Plans of the conservatives.	399
Stevens' final plea against the Blaine amendment	403
Defeat of the Blaine amendment in the House	405
The military bill before the Senate.	406
The bill changed so as to incorporate the Blaine amendment	407
The first Reconstruction act as a finality.	408
Sumner's opposition to the first Reconstruction act.	408
Differences between the House and the Senate	409
Motives of Stevens and the radicals	410
The Reconstruction bill further amended in the House.	411
The bill becomes law	414
End of the joint committee	414

PART I

INTRODUCTION
JOURNAL OF THE JOINT COMMITTEE

INTRODUCTION

(1) When the Southern Confederacy collapsed in April, 1865, those state governments which were regarded as having been in allegiance to it were not recognized by any Federal official as legal. They were forbidden to continue in existence, and for at least a few weeks seven of the late Confederate states were entirely without civil governments and were subject to the Federal military authority alone. In four states, however, Virginia, Tennessee, Louisiana, and Arkansas, loyal civil governments had been instituted during Lincoln's administration and these President Johnson, in harmony with the reconstruction policy of his predecessor, recognized as regular and legal. Moreover, in pursuance of that policy, he caused loyal civil governments to be established during the summer of 1865 in the other seven states. By December most of these Lincoln and Johnson governments were performing nearly all the regular functions of state governments, and so far as the Federal executive department was concerned, they were recognized as having resumed their normal position as states in the Union.

Though they had formally accepted the abolition of slavery and the invalidity of secession as the accomplished objects of the war—and certainly few people were saying at that time that the war had been waged for any other purpose—yet when the 39th Congress met in December of 1865, it at once became evident that the majority of its members were in no mood to accept unconditionally the reconstruction policy that had been developed by the executive department of the Government. There was no consensus, however, as to a substitute for the executive policy. Hence all were determined not to act precipitately on the reconstruction question, but to delay—some with the hope of coming to an understanding with the President, others with the idea ultimately of carrying out a thorough overhauling of southern political, economic, and social conditions. These latter persons, therefore, determined upon the expedient of appointing a joint committee to which all matters pertaining to reconstruction should be referred. Since the object of the radical group in desiring the appointment of this committee was delay, and since delay was also the object of the more conservative group, the latter readily acquiesced in the scheme. It was the members of this committee who, from December, 1865, to March, 1867, determined the principles of reconstruction that finally were carried into effect in the South.

The chief measure that was evolved within this committee was the fourteenth amendment to the Constitution, and the journal kept by the committee's clerk is by far the most important source of information concerning the process by which the framers of that amendment arrived at the conclusions which they submitted to Congress. Since the manuscript copy of this journal has come recently into my possession, my experience in finding it calls for a few words of explanation.

(2) In the spring of 1910, I was engaged in preparing an essay on the report of the reconstruction committee. In examining some of the secondary material, I found that both Dr. Rhodes in Volume V of his History of the United States, and Dr. Horace Flack in his work on the fourteenth amendment, referred to a printed copy of the journal; but upon making inquiry I discovered that both of them had used a copy that was then, and still is, in the Government

Printing Office at Washington. None of the larger city or university libraries of the country possessed a copy. This I considered strange, and so decided to look up the order for printing. After some search I found that it was not until February of 1884 that the Senate of the United States had ordered six thousand copies to be printed. From the fact that the journal was published by the order of a body of men who could have had but little interest in its contents, together with the fact that no copies were to be found even in the library of Congress or in the House and Senate libraries, I concluded that the six thousand copies were never distributed. This conclusion I later ascertained from the gentleman who in 1884 was director of the printing office, was correct.

When Senator Morrill of Vermont, who had been a member of the reconstruction committee, introduced, on February 5, 1884, the resolution for printing the journal, he exhibited the manuscript copy, and said: " At the decease of Senator Fessenden, this book, containing a very well-kept, clear journal for a year, was transferred to Portland, Maine, and not until recently has it been ascertained that it was in existence. It must be a document of too much importance to remain out of print."

This gave me a clue and I determined if possible to find that manuscript copy which Morrill then exhibited. I already knew that a grandson of Senator Fessenden, Mr. James D. Fessenden, of the New York bar, had been the literary executor of the illustrious Maine statesman. To him I accordingly wrote, and ascertained that the manuscript journal had been in his possession, but at an auction sale of his grandfather's autograph letters in 1908, it had been disposed of; to whom he did not know. I then had recourse to the books of the auction company which had charge of the sale, and after considerable difficulty located the purchaser. This proved to be a well-known collector of autograph letters and original documents, but upon reaching his house, I was dismayed to find that he had recently sold out his entire collection and departed for Europe. His sale had been conducted by a different auction company from that which had conducted the Fessenden sale. From an examination of their books, I discovered that they had disposed of the journal to an autograph dealer. Fortunately, he had not sold it before I reached him, and I succeeded in obtaining it for the Columbia University library which had commissioned me to purchase it.

It should be stated, however, that the journal is one made up from the notes kept by the clerk of the committee at its various sessions. It is in the handwriting of the second clerk of that committee, George A. Mark, who was a native of Portland, Maine, and was appointed to his position on the motion of Senator Fessenden. While in Washington in the summer of 1910, I had Mr. Mark's handwriting verified both by his son, who is now living in that city, and by a clerk in the library of Congress, where Mr. Mark was subsequently employed. The genuineness of the journal is also testified to by the fact that in it were several loose sheets containing the various propositions that were offered by several members of the committee for amending the Constitution in regard to the apportionment of representatives. Each of these resolutions is in the handwriting of the individual member who offered it. Moreover, one of these sheets contains Robert Dale Owen's suggestion for a fourteenth amendment, which is discussed in Chapter VI. This is in the hand of Owen himself, with annotations in the hand of Thaddeus Stevens.

How the journal which had been in Portland, Maine, came to be in Washington in 1884, I have not been able to determine with entire satisfaction to myself. I have found, however, that Roscoe Conkling, who represented the defendant in the case of San Mateo County *versus* the Southern Pacific Railroad,[1] which was pending before the Supreme Court from the fall of 1882 to the spring of 1885, referred to the journal of the committee. In his oral argument Conkling not only quoted from the journal, but definitely stated that he had it in his possession. Unfortunately, he did not tell how he came by it. He said that he had consulted some of those whose opinions it preserved. This certainly meant Morrill, who was then the only ex-member of the committee in Congress, though two other ex-members—Boutwell and Williams—were probably then in Washington. Conkling also said: " It seems odd that this journal has never been printed by order of either house. It has never been printed, however, or publicly referred to before, I believe."

From the two facts that Conkling consulted Morrill and thought the journal ought to be printed, it almost certainly follows that it was from Conkling that Morrill obtained it when he secured the passage of the order to have it printed. Conkling, in turn, had doubtless borrowed it from the son and biographer of Senator Fessenden, General Francis Fessenden, who, I learned from Mr. James Fessenden, was then in possession of all the Senator's public and private papers. After the case was decided in 1885, Conkling evidently returned the manuscript journal to General Fessenden. When it was ordered to be printed, not the original, but a copy was sent to the printer, for the manuscript now in the Columbia University library shows no signs of ever having been in a printer's hands. The printed copy in the Government Printing Office, however, is identical in contents with the manuscript journal. It is not likely that Conkling

---

[1] See *infra*, p. 28.

would have been willing to let the original copy, which he was under obligation to return in good shape, go out of his hands for the purpose of having it printed, and so a copy was doubtless made for that purpose.

(3) As said before, this document whose history has been sketched briefly above was the very one which Roscoe Conkling used with such telling effect in one of the crucial cases in the process by which what has been termed a "revolution in our constitutional law," was accomplished.[1] By "revolution" is meant that change whereby the states, which since the death of Marshall had been substantially independent of Federal judicial control, were again, and even more completely than ever, subjected to the Federal judiciary by the interpretation that the Supreme Court finally gave to section 1 of the fourteenth amendment. This revolution was not made by the adoption of the fourteenth amendment itself nor indeed by the earlier interpretations of that amendment, but was brought about partly by the change in the personnel of the Court and partly by a change in the minds of the judges under the stimulus of powerful counsel—a change which a layman might reasonably regard as a flat reversal, but which the trained lawyer, by pointing out differences and discriminations, may exhibit as orderly progressions of judicial reasoning.

The first time the Court was called upon to interpret section 1 of the fourteenth amendment was in 1872 in the famous Slaughter-House cases.[2]

Mr. Justice Miller stated in the following words the opinion of the majority of the Court as to the purpose and scope of all the war amendments and particularly of section 1 of the fourteenth amendment:

[1] Beard, *Contemporary American History*, ch. III.
[2] 16 Wallace, 36

On the most casual examination of the language of these amendments, no one can fail to be impressed with the one pervading purpose found in them all, lying at the foundation of each, and without which none of them would have been even suggested; we mean the freedom of the slave race, the security and firm establishment of that freedom, and the protection of the newly-made freeman and citizen from the oppressions of those who had formerly exercised unlimited dominion over him. It is true that only the fifteenth amendment, in terms, mentions the negro by speaking of his color and his slavery. But it is just as true that each of the other articles was addressed to the grievances of that race, and designed to remedy them as the fifteenth.

Speaking specifically in regard to the first section of the fourteenth amendment, Justice Miller continued:

We doubt very much whether any action of a state not directed by way of discrimination against the negroes as a class, or on account of their race, will ever be held to come within the purview of this provision. It is so clearly a provision for that race and that emergency, that a strong case would be necessary for its application to any other. . . . .

We do not see in those amendments any purpose to destroy the main features of the general system. Under the pressure of all the excited feeling growing out of the war, our statesmen have still believed that the existence of the states with powers for domestic and local government, including the regulation of civil rights—the rights of person and of property—was essential to the perfect working of our complex form of government, though they have thought proper to impose additional limitations on the states, and to confer additional power on that of the Nation.

From the tone of this opinion it is clear that in 1872 the majority of the Court believed that section 1 of the fourteenth amendment was to be invoked primarily for the protection of the freedmen in their civil rights. The judges were unwilling to give that section an interpretation which would render corporations wholly or partly immune from state regulation by narrowly restricting the state's police power. Again in 1876, the Court refused to interpret the fourteenth amendment in such a way as to hold invalid a state statute regulating corporations. In the case of Munn v. Illinois,[1] it was called upon to determine whether the legislature of Illinois could fix by law the maximum charge for the storage of grain in warehouses. Chief Justice Waite, in delivering the opinion of the court, said:

It is insisted, however, that the owner of property is entitled to a reasonable compensation for its use, even though it be clothed with a public interest, and that what is reasonable is a judicial and not a legislative question.

As has already been shown, the practice has been otherwise. In countries where the common law prevails, it has been customary from time immemorial for the legislature to declare what shall be a reasonable compensation under such circumstances, or, perhaps, more properly speaking, to fix a maximum beyond which any charge made would be unreasonable. . . . .

We know that this is a power which may be abused; but that is no argument against its existence. For protection against abuses by legislatures the people must resort to the polls, *not* to the courts.

At a later period, however, this position in large measure was abandoned. In a series of cases extending from 1889 to 1898, the Court, by virtue of that section of the fourteenth amendment which denies to a state the right to " deprive any person of life, liberty, or property, without due process of law," has undertaken to declare null and of no effect state laws which seemed to fix the fares and freights

---

[1] 94 U. S. 113.

of railroads and the charges of other public corporations unreasonably low. As Professor Beard says, "The Court has moved from the doctrine of non-interference with state legislatures to the doctrine that it is charged with the high duty of reviewing all and every kind of economic legislation by the states."[1]

In the case of Chicago, Milwaukee and St. Paul Railroad Company *v.* Minnesota, the Court said:

The question of the reasonableness of a rate of charge for transportation by a railroad company, involving as it does the element of reasonableness both as regards the company and as regards the public is eminently a question for judicial investigation requiring due process of law for its determination. If the company is deprived of the power of charging reasonable rates for the use of its property, and such deprivation takes place in the absence of an investigation by judicial machinery, it is deprived of the lawful use of its property, and thus in substance and effect, of the property itself without due process of law and in violation of the Constitution of the United States.

In the foregoing case, it happened that the rates which the Court declared unreasonably low, were not fixed directly by the state legislature, but by a railroad commission. The climax of "judicial supremacy" was reached in 1898 in the case of Smyth *v.* Ames,[2] in which the Court held a Nebraska statute unconstitutional, because it fixed the maximum rates to be charged by railroad companies so low as to be practically confiscatory. The Court held that the following principles were settled law:

1. A railroad corporation is a person within the meaning of the fourteenth amendment declaring that no state shall de-

---

[1] *Contemporary American History*, p. 73.
[2] 169 U. S. 466.

prive any person of property without due process of law, nor deny to any person within its jurisdiction the equal protection of the laws.

2. A state enactment, or regulations made under the authority of a state enactment, establishing rates for the transportation of persons or property by railroad that will not admit of the carrier earning such compensation as under all the circumstances is just to it and to the public, would deprive such carrier of its property without due process of law and deny to it the equal protection of the laws, and would therefore be repugnant to the fourteenth amendment of the Constitution of the United States.

3. While rates for the transportation of persons and property within the limits of a state are primarily for its determination, the question whether they are so unreasonably low as to deprive the carrier of its property without such compensation as the Constitution secures, and therefore without due process of law, cannot be so conclusively determined by the legislature of the state or by regulations adopted under its authority, that the matter may not become the subject of judicial inquiry.

It is clear that the Supreme Court in the decade from 1889 to 1898 did depart from its earlier position as announced in 1872 and 1876 in the Slaughter-House cases and in Munn v. Illinois respectively. This change in the attitude of the Court toward the fourteenth amendment has given rise to the opinion that "although it was a humanitarian measure in origin and purpose, and was designed as a charter of liberty for human rights, it has become the Magna Charta of accumulated wealth and organized capital." [1]

In making the change to the broad doctrine that the Court should exercise judicial control over all kinds of legisla-

---

[1] Collins, *The Fourteenth Amendment and the States*, p. 138.

tion, two fundamental doctrines were necessary. One was that the power to regulate corporations could not be exercised in such a manner as to deprive them of the right to earn a fair return on the capital invested. With that we are not concerned here. The second doctrine, just as fundamental, is that which was laid down as settled law in Smyth v. Ames, "that a corporation is a person within the meaning of the fourteenth amendment." In 1886, twelve years before this case was decided, this principle was first stated by Chief Justice Waite. The Court was ready to receive arguments in the case of Santa Clara County v. The Southern Pacific Railroad,[1] when the Chief Justice said: "The Court does not wish to hear arguments on the question whether the provision in the fourteenth amendment to the Constitution, which forbids a state to deny to any person within its jurisdiction the equal protection of the laws, applies to corporations. We are all of the opinion that it does."

This announcement, which may be regarded as a *dictum*, was affirmed in 1888 as a part of the decision in the case of Pembina Mining Company v. Pennsylvania,[2] in which the court said:

The inhibition of the fourteenth amendment that no state shall deprive any person within its jurisdiction of the equal protection of the laws was designed to prevent any person or class of persons from being singled out as a special subject for discriminating and hostile legislation. Under the designation of "person" there is no doubt that a private corporation is included. Such corporations are merely associations of individuals united for a special purpose, and permitted to do business under a particular name, and have a succession of members without dissolution.

[1] 118 U. S. 394.   [2] 125 U. S. 181.

In 1889, in the case of Minneapolis and St. Louis Railroad Company v. Beckwith,[1] the Court decided that a corporation was a person within the meaning of both the "due process of law" and the "equal protection of the laws" clauses of the fourteenth amendment. "These cases, considered together as one opinion," says a recent writer,[2] "mark one of the most important developments in our constitutional history. In an address before the University of Berlin in 1908, President Hadley, of Yale University, declared them to rank with the Dartmouth College case in their restraining effects upon the states in relation to the corporations. They opened the door for organized capital to contest whatever laws of the states it considered disadvantageous."

How the Court was induced to abandon the attitude of non-interference and assume judicial control in the widest sense has never been made the subject of historical inquiry. When that study is made, first rank will be given to a dramatic episode which occurred in the argument of the San Mateo case, when Roscoe Conkling, a member of the committee which drafted the fourteenth amendment, produced in the court room a copy of the journal of his committee and revealed for the first time what purported to be the real intention of those who framed the fourteenth amendment. It is to point out the part played by the journal of the committee in the beginning of this legal revolution that the foregoing digression into the realm of constitutional law has been made.

In the case of San Mateo County v. The Southern Pacific Railroad Company,[3] the defendant maintained that the state

---

[1] 129 U. S. 26.
[2] Collins, *op. cit.*, pp. 128, 129.
[3] 116 U. S. 138.

of California in assessing the value of its property had violated that section of the fourteenth amendment which forbids a state to deny to any person within its jurisdiction the equal protection of the laws. The San Mateo case was argued on December 19, 1882, by which date railroad companies, especially in the West, were coming to be the objects of what they considered invidious state legislation, and subjected to an unequal and exorbitant rate of taxation. Under these circumstances the companies determined to appeal to the Supreme Court for protection. Collis P. Huntington, a well-known railroad magnate of the old school, was at that time president of the Southern Pacific. His principal attorney as well as personal friend was Roscoe Conkling, a recently resigned senator from New York, who was then devoting his entire time to his legal profession. Huntington selected Conkling as his chief counsel, and upon the latter devolved the onerous task of convincing a majority of the members of the Supreme Court that the opinion of Justice Miller in the Slaughter-House cases was based upon a misconception of the intent of the framers of section 1 of the fourteenth amendment. Conkling undertook to show that the reconstruction committee, of which he had been a member, had designed that section as much for the protection of white people as negroes against discriminating state legislation. Having accomplished this, his next purpose was to prove that though the word *person* was placed in juxtaposition with *citizen,* the two were not synonymous; that the former in this section had its ordinary juristic meaning, and hence included artificial persons (i. e., corporations) as well as natural persons. There is no doubt that Conkling's argument at this time marks the beginning of that important revolution in our law which has been briefly sketched above.

In the earlier decisions which involved the fourteenth

amendment, the Court seems to have been unusually prone to take into consideration the intention of the framers of that amendment. Since Conkling had been a member of the committee which drafted the fourteenth amendment, he may have been presumed to have been in an excellent position to interpret the intentions of himself and his colleagues. But that was not all. He occupied a still stronger strategic position in that he was armed with the very journal of the committee, and with it proceeded to show that the committee did not expect that the operation of the amendment would be confined merely to the protection of the freedmen. Because of the importance of Conkling's speech in the history of our jurisprudence, I will venture to give rather copious extracts from it.

I come now to say that the Southern Pacific Railroad Company is among the "persons" protected by the fourteenth amendment. . . . .

The idea prevails—it is found in the opinion of the Court in the Slaughter-House cases; it has found broad lodgment in the public understanding; that the fourteenth amendment—nay I might say all three of the latter amendments were conceived in a single common purpose—that they came out of one and the same crucible, and were struck by the same die; that they gave expression to only one single inspiration. The impression seems to be that the fourteenth amendment especially was brought forth in the form in which it was at last ratified by the states, as one entire whole, beginning and ending as to the first section at least, with the protection to the freedmen of the South.

Conkling then criticized Justice Miller's opinion in the Slaughter-House cases as to the "pervading spirit" of all the war amendments.

It may shed some modifying light on this supposition, to

trace the different proposals, independent of each other, originating in different minds, and at different times, not in the order in which they now stand, which finally, by what might be called the attrition of parliamentary processes in the committee and in Congress, came to be collected in one formulated proposal of amendment.

These originally separate, independent propositions, came from a joint committee of the two Houses. The committee sat with closed doors. A journal of its proceedings was kept by an experienced recorder from day to day.

It seems odd that such a journal has never been printed by order of the two Houses. It has never been printed, however, or publicly referred to before, I believe.

Having consulted some of those whose opinions it preserves, and having the record in my possession, I venture to produce some extracts from it, omitting names in connection with votes.[1]

From these skeleton entries—a journal is only a skeleton—your Honors will perceive that different parts of what now stands as a whole—even parts of the clauses supposed to relate exclusively or especially to freedmen and their rights—were separately and independently conceived, separately acted on, perfected, and reported, not in the order in which they are now collated, and not with a single inspiration or design. You will perceive also that before what now constitutes part of the first section was perfected, or even considered, the committee had reported, and lost all jurisdiction and power over, the portion of the amendment which did in truth chiefly relate to the freedmen of the South. The subject of suffrage, the ballot, and representation in Congress, was disposed of before the committee reached the language on which to-day's argument proceeds.

Conkling then quoted at length from the journal in order

[1] Conkling had good reason to omit the names; he indeed might have been embarrassed by them, for he himself voted consistently against the civil rights amendment. See *infra*, ch. iii.

to show that the civil rights section of the fourteenth amendment as originally considered in committee constituted by itself a whole, separate amendment to the Constitution. Moreover, he asked why, if the end to which the mind of the author, Bingham, was reaching out was simply to bespeak protection for the black man of the South, he should choose such general and sweeping words, when he could so easily and briefly have expressed exactly the idea on which his thoughts were bent. These words were taken almost bodily from the Constitution as follows:

The Congress shall have power to make all laws which shall be necessary and proper to secure to the citizens of each state all privileges and immunities of citizens in the several states; (Art. 4, Sec. 2) and to all persons in the several states equal protection in the rights of life, liberty, and property (5th amendment).[1]

Conkling then continued:

Now, may it please your Honors, obviously the object of the draughtsman of this last referred to amendment in making reference on the face of his resolution to article 4, section 2, and to the fifth amendment, was to remind the committee of the established meaning and universally accepted import and force of the words which there stood.

At the time the fourteenth amendment was ratified, individuals and joint stock companies were appealing for congressional and administrative protection against the invidious and discriminating state and local taxes. One instance was that of an express company, whose stock was owned largely by citizens of the state of New York, who came with petitions and bills seeking acts of Congress to aid them in resisting what they deemed oppressive taxation in two states, and oppressive and ruinous rules of damages applied under state laws. That

[1] See *infra*, p. 61.

complaints of oppression in respect of property and other rights, made by citizens of northern states who took up residence in the South, were rife, in and out of Congress, none of us can forget; that complaints of oppression, in various forms, of white men in the South,—of "Union men," were heard on every side, I need not remind the Court.

Conkling, after arguing further that the fourteenth amendment was intended as much for the protection of white men as negroes against discriminating state legislation, then undertook to prove to the Court that the amendment was designed to operate upon associations of individuals (i. e., corporations) as well as upon individuals singly.

The defendant here, in respect of its property is in law and in fact but the business style of individual owners united and co-operating in a common undertaking, and who, as mere method and convenience, conduct business through corporate agency. Be it a church, a hospital, a library, a hotel, a mill, a factory, a mine, or a railroad, the property and assets of a corporation belong to no one save the creditors and the shareholders.

Suppose, in South Carolina, a society of colored men should incorporate themselves and acquire a church or a college, and this property should, by statute be confiscated, either by discriminating taxation or otherwise, can it be supposed that the fact of their having formed a corporation, rather than a joint-stock company or a partnership, would exclude them from the protection of the fourteenth amendment? Could such a cramped construction be given to the amendment, even if the rule of its construction restricted its operation to only the cases known or foreseen by those who chose the language?

I have put the case of colored men. Let me transpose the illustration. In several states, colored men outnumber white men. Suppose in one of these states laws should be contrived by the colored majority, or a constitution set up, under which the property of white men should be confiscated, surely the Court would not say the Constitution is dumb, but would speak, if only the parties to the record were reversed.

I have sought to convince your Honors that the men who framed, the Congress which proposed, and the people who through their legislatures ratified the fourteenth amendment, must have known the meaning and force of the term "persons."

. . . . .

Those who devised the fourteenth amendment wrought in grave sincerity. They may have builded better than they knew.

They vitalized and energized a principle as old and as everlasting as human rights. To some of them, the sunset of life may have given mystical lore.

They builded, not for a day, but for all time; not for a few, or for a race, but for man. They planted in the Constitution a monumental truth, to stand foursquare whatever wind might blow. That truth is but the golden rule, so entrenched as to curb the many who would do to the few as they would not have the few do to them.

Though the points argued by Conkling were not decided by the Court in the San Mateo case, yet his speech in that case marks distinctly the point at which the Supreme Court ceased to interpret section 1 of the fourteenth amendment as having reference almost wholly to negroes, and began to regard it as having a much broader application. In order to show that Conkling's argument had a most profound effect upon the minds of the judges, the three following incidents are related.

Justice Miller, who had delivered the opinion of the Court in the Slaughter-House cases, was still on the bench when the San Mateo case was argued. He listened to Conkling's refutation of his own opinion, and when another of the defendant's counsel began to argue the same points which Conkling had made, Miller interrupted him and said: " I have never heard it said in this Court or by any judge of it that these articles [i. e., the fourteenth amendment] were supposed to be limited to the negro race. The purport of the general discussion in the Slaughter-House cases on this subject was nothing more than the common declaration that when you come to construe any act of Congress, you must consider the evil which was to be remedied in order to understand fairly what the purpose of the remedial act was." To this statement, Conkling's associate replied, "I understand, then, that so far as your Honor is concerned, the color line has disappeared from American jurisprudence." To this, Miller did not dissent, from which we may fairly conclude that he was ready to abandon what had been generally regarded as a very narrow interpretation of the civil rights clause of the fourteenth amendment.

In the spring of 1883, Justice Field was sitting in the circuit court in California, when he was called upon to decide the Santa Clara case, which involved the same general principles as the San Mateo case. His decision is remarkable in that he adopted the same attitude toward the purport of the civil rights section of the fourteenth amendment which Conkling had enunciated in his San Mateo speech. In fact the justice quoted several passages from that speech, a notable one being the concluding paragraph of it in which Conkling laid down what he considered the true method of interpretation.

But an appeal from Justice Field's decision of the Santa Clara case in the California circuit, was taken to the Supreme Court. As has been seen, the case was argued before that tribunal in 1886. Again the Court refused to decide the question raised under the fourteenth amendment, but in his dictum quoted above, the Chief Justice committed himself and the Court to the doctrine that the " equal protection of the laws " clause should be interpreted as extending to persons other than members of the colored race, and that "persons" in this sense included corporations. The dictum as to both these matters followed Conkling's view, and the door was opened for organized capital to contest, often-times successfully, before the highest Court in the land, whatever laws of the states it considered disadvantageous to its own interests. And what gave greatest force to Conkling's argument was his ingenious use of the journal of the joint committee on reconstruction.

THE JOURNAL OF THE JOINT COMMITTEE OF FIFTEEN ON RECONSTRUCTION.
39TH CONGRESS.
1865–1867.

IN THE HOUSE OF REPRESENTATIVES,
December 4, 1865.

On motion of *Mr. Stevens*:

Be it resolved, by the Senate and House of Representatives in Congress assembled: That a joint committee of fifteen members shall be appointed, nine of whom shall be members of the House, and six members of the Senate, who shall inquire into the condition of the States which formed the so-called Confederate States of America, and report whether they, or any of them, are entitled to be represented in either House of Congress, with leave to report at any time, by bill or otherwise; and until such report shall have been made, and finally acted on by Congress, no member shall be received into either House from any of the so-called Confederate States; and all papers relating to the representation of said States shall be referred to the said Committee without debate.

Attest,
EDW'D MCPHERSON, *Clerk*.

December 12, 1865.

Amended in the Senate, on motion of Mr. Anthony, so as to read,

Resolved by the House of Representatives, (the Senate concurring) That a joint committee of fifteen members shall be appointed, nine of whom shall be members of the House, and six members of the Senate, who shall inquire into the condition of the States which formed the so-called Confederate States of America, and report whether they, or any of them, are entitled to be represented in either House of Congress, with leave to report at any time, by bill or otherwise.

Attest,
J. W. FORNEY, *Secretary.*

Dec. 13, 1865.

In the House of Representatives, on motion of *Mr. Stevens*, the amendments of the Senate were concurred in.

Attest,
EDW'D MCPHERSON, *Clerk.*

Members on the part of the Senate.

Mr. William P. Fessenden of Maine.
" James W. Grimes, " Iowa.
" Ira Harris, " New York.
" Jacob M. Howard, " Michigan.
" Reverdy Johnson, " Maryland.
and " George H. Williams, " Oregon.

Members on the part of the House of Rep's.

 Mr. Thaddeus Stevens, of Penn'a.
 " Elihu B. Washburne, " Illinois.
 " Justin S. Morrill, " Vermont.
 " Henry Grider,   " Kentucky.
 " John A. Bingham, " Ohio.
 " Roscoe Conkling, " New York.
 " George S. Boutwell, " Massachusetts.
 " Henry T. Blow   " Missouri.
and " Andrew J. Rogers, " New Jersey.

Saturday, January 6th, 1866.

The Joint Committee on Reconstruction met (in the room of the Senate Committee on the Pacific Railroad) pursuant to the call of Mr. Fessenden, its chairman.

Present—The Chairman, Messrs. Grimes, Harris, Howard, Johnson and Williams, of the Senate, and Messrs. Stevens, Washburne, Morrill, Conkling, Boutwell and Blow, of the House.

On motion,

Ordered, That Mr. Wm. Blair Lord (of New York City) be appointed clerk and stenographer of this Committee; and that the Chairman be instructed to obtain from the Senate the necessary authority for his employment.

On motion of *Mr. Stevens:*

Ordered, That a sub-committee, to consist of three members, be appointed to wait on the President and request him to defer all further executive action in regard to reconstruciton until this Committee shall have taken action on that subject.

On motion,

Ordered, That the Chairman, and Messrs. Johnson and Washburne constitute said sub-committee.

Adjourned to ten A. M. on Tuesday next.

Tuesday, January 9, 1866.

The Committee met pursuant to adjournment: all the members present.

The Chairman submitted the following resolution, which was unanimously agreed to:

Resolved, That all the resolutions submitted to or adopted by this Committee, the views expressed in Committee by its different members, all votes taken and all other proceedings in Committee of whatever nature, be regarded by the members of the Committee and the clerk as of a strictly confidential character, until otherwise ordered.

The Chairman, from the sub-committee appointed at the last meeting of the Committee, to wait on the President, reported orally,

That the Committee had waited on the President and expressed to him the views of the Committee as set forth in the resolution appointing the sub-committee; that the Committee desired to avoid all possible collision or misconstruction between the Executive and Congress in regard to the relative positions of Congress and the President, and that they thought it exceedingly desirable that, while this subject was under consideration by the Joint Committee, no further action in regard to reconstruction should be taken by the President, unless it should become imperatively necessary, and that they thought mutual respect would seem to require mutual forbearance on the part of the Executive and of Congress. To which the President replied substantially that while he considered it desirable that this matter of reconstruction should be advanced as rapidly as might be consistent with the public interest, still he desired to secure harmony of action between Congress and the Executive, and it was not his intention to do more than had been done for the present.

Mr. Stevens submitted a joint resolution, upon which he asked immediate action by the Committee, proposing to submit for ratification to the several States the following amendment to the Constitution of the United States:

Representatives shall be apportioned among the several States, which may be included within this Union, according to the number of their respective legal voters; and for this purpose none shall be considered as legal voters who are not either natural born or naturalized citizens of the United States, of the age of twenty-one years.

Congress shall provide for ascertaining the number of said voters. A true census of the legal voters shall be taken at the same time with the regular census.

After discussion.

Mr. Conkling moved to amend by inserting the word "male" between the word "naturalized" and the word "citizens."

The amendment was adopted.

Mr. Morrill moved to further amend by inserting after the words "of the age of twenty-one years" the words "and who can read and write."

The amendment was not agreed to.

The further consideration of the subject was postponed till this evening.

The Chairman submitted the following:

Resolved, That, in the opinion of this Committee, the insurgent States cannot, with safety to the rights of all the people of the United States, be allowed to participate in the Government until the basis of representation shall have been modified, and the rights of all persons amply secured, either by new provisions, or the necessary changes of existing provisions, in the Constitution of the United States, or otherwise.

On motion of *Mr. Stevens,* the further consideration of the resolution was postponed for the present.

On motion of *Mr. Stevens*, the Committee took a recess till 7½ o'clock this evening.

The Committee reassembled at 7½ o'clock P. M.—absent Mr. Blow.

The consideration of the joint resolution submitted by *Mr. Stevens* was resumed.

Mr. Williams moved to further amend the same by striking out the words, " and for this purpose none shall be considered as legal voters who are not either natural-born or naturalized male citizens of the United States, of the age of twenty-one years."

After discussion.

Mr. Johnson moved to postpone the further consideration of the joint resolution until the next meeting of the Committee.

The motion was agreed to.

Mr. *Stevens* and *Mr. Howard* submitted propositions for the future consideration of the Committee.

Ordered, That the same be placed on file for future consideration.

On motion of *Mr. Harris,* the Committee adjourned till Friday next at 10½ o'clock A. M.

Friday, January 12, 1866.

The Committee met pursuant to adjournment; absent Mr. Rogers.

The consideration of the joint resolution submitted by *Mr. Stevens* was resumed.

The pending question was upon the amendment proposed by *Mr. Williams.*

Mr. Williams withdrew his amendment.

Mr. Morrill moved the following as a substitute for the original proposition:

Representatives and direct taxes shall be apportioned among the several States, which may be included within this Union, according to their respective numbers of persons, deducting therefrom all of any race or color, whose members or any of them are denied any of the civil or political rights or privileges.

Mr. Williams gave notice that at the proper time he should move the following substitute:

Representatives and direct taxes shall be apportioned among the several States of the Union according to their respective numbers, excluding negroes, Indians, Chinese, and all persons, not white, who are not allowed the elective franchise by the Constitutions of the States in which they respectively reside.

Mr. Conkling gave a similar notice in regard to the following substitute:

Representatives and direct taxes shall be apportioned among the several States, which may be included within this Union, according to their respective numbers, counting the whole number of citizens of the United States; provided that whenever in any State civil or political rights or privileges shall be denied or abridged on account of race or color, all persons of such race or color shall be excluded from the basis of representation or taxation.

Mr. Boutwell gave a similar notice in regard to the following substitute:

Representatives and direct taxes shall be apportioned among the several States, which may be included within this Union, according to the respective number of citizens of the United States in each State; and no State shall make any distinction in the exercise of the elective franchise on account of race or color.

After discussion.

Mr. Bingham, in order to test the sense of the Committee, submitted the following resolution:

Resolved, That, in the opinion of this Committee, the amendment to the Constitution of the United States submitted by Mr. Stevens, ought to be amended or modified.

Mr. Johnson moved as a substitute for the resolution of Mr. Bingham, the following:

Resolved, That, in the opinion of this Committee, the apportionment of representation in Congress, as now provided by the Constitution, ought to be changed.

Mr. Bingham accepted the substitute.

The question was then taken, by yeas and nays, on the resolution as modified, and it was decided in the affirmative, yeas 13, nay 1, not voting 1, as follows:

Yeas—The Chairman, Messrs. Grimes, Harris, Howard, Johnson, Williams, Stevens, Washburne, Morrill, Bingham, Conkling, Boutwell and Blow—13.

Nay—Mr. Grider—1.

Not voting—Mr. Rogers—1.

The resolution as modified was accordingly adopted.

Mr. Johnson submitted the following resolution:

Resolved, That, in the opinion of this Committee, representatives should be apportioned among the several States according to their respective numbers of legal voters.

The question was taken, by yeas and nays, and it was decided in the negative, yeas 6, nays 8, absent and not voting 1, as follows:

Yeas—Messrs. Grimes, Johnson, Stevens, Washburne, Bingham and Blow—6.

Nays—The Chairman, Messrs. Harris, Howard, Williams, Morrill, Grider, Conkling and Boutwell—8.

Absent and not voting, Mr. Rogers—1.

So the resolution was not agreed to.

Mr. Morrill submitted the following:

Ordered, That a sub-committee, to consist of five members, including the Chairman of the Committee on the part of the Senate, and the Chairman of the Committee on the part of the House, (Messrs. Fessenden and Stevens) be appointed, to which shall be referred the various propositions submitted by members of this Committee in relation to apportionment of representatives in Congress, with instructions to prepare and report to this Committee a proposition upon that subject.

The motion was agreed to.

Mr. Bingham submitted the following proposed amendment of the Constitution of the United States, and moved that the same be referred to the sub-committee just authorized:

The Congress shall have power to make all laws necessary and proper to secure to all persons in every state within this Union equal protection in their rights of life, liberty and property.

The motion was agreed to.

Mr. Stevens submitted the following proposed amendment of the Constitution, and moved that the same be referred to the sub-committee just authorized:

All laws, state or national, shall operate impartially and equally on all persons without regard to race or color.

The motion was agreed to.

On motion of *Mr. Stevens*.

Ordered, That the remaining members of the sub-committee, authorized at this meeting, be appointed by the Chairman of the Joint Committee.

The motion was agreed to.

The Chairman announced the following as members of the sub-committee:

Messrs. Fessenden and Stevens (named in the order of the Joint Committee) and Messrs. Howard, Conkling and Bingham.

On motion of *Mr. Stevens:*

Ordered, That the Chairman be instructed to introduce into the Senate a concurrent resolution authorizing the Joint Committee to send for persons and papers.

On motion of *Mr. Bingham:*

Ordered, That sub-committees, each composed of two members, be appointed to examine and report upon the present condition of the States composing the late so-called Confederate States of America, and not now represented in Congress; what has been their action in relation to any amendments of the Federal or State Constitutions; what may be the present legal position of the freedmen in the respective States; in what manner the so-called ordinances of secession have been treated; whether the validity of debts contracted for the support of the rebellion is acknowledged; and generally as to all evidence, documentary or otherwise, of the present loyalty or disloyalty upon the part of the people or governments of said states. That is to say, committees embracing

1st. Tennessee.

2nd. Virginia, North Carolina and South Carolina.

3rd. Georgia, Alabama, Mississippi, and Arkansas, and

4th. Louisiana, Florida and Texas.

On motion of *Mr. Howard:*

Ordered, That the sub-committees above authorized be appointed by the Chairman of the Joint Committee.

On motion of *Mr. Harris:*

The Committee adjourned to 11 A. M. on Monday next.

Monday, January 15, 1866.

The Committee met pursuant to adjournment; absent, Messrs. Johnson and Blow.

On motion of *Mr. Morrill:*

Ordered, That the various sub-committees authorized on motion of Mr. Bingham, at the last meeting of the Committee, shall consist of three members each instead of two members.

The *Chairman* announced the following as the members of the sub-committees ordered at the last meeting:

No. 1. Messrs. Grimes, Bingham and Grider.

No. 2. Howard, Conkling and Blow.

No. 3. Harris, Boutwell and Morrill.

No. 4. Williams, Washburne and Rogers.

Mr. Stevens submitted the following resolution of the House of Representatives:

Ordered, That the same be spread upon the Journal.

"On motion of Mr. *James F. Wilson:*

Resolved, That all papers which may be offered relative to the representation of the late so-called Confederate States of America, or either of them, shall be referred to the Joint Committee of fifteen without debate; and no members shall be admitted from either of said so-called States until Congress shall believe such States, or either of them, entitled to representation."

Adjourned to meet on call of the Chairman.

Saturday, January 20, 1866.

The Committee met pursuant to call of its Chairman; absent, Mr. Johnson.

The Chairman laid before the Committee the following papers, which were ordered to be entered upon the Journal of the Committee:

IN THE SENATE OF THE UNITED STATES,
January 8, 1866.

On motion of *Mr. Fessenden:*

Ordered, That the Joint Committee to inquire into the condition of the States which formed the so-called Confederate States of America, be authorized to employ a stenographic clerk.

IN THE SENATE OF THE UNITED STATES,
January 12, 1866.

On motion of *Mr. Fessenden:*

Resolved, by the Senate, the House of Representatives concurring, that the Joint Committee appointed to enquire into the condition of the States which formed the so-called Confederate States be authorized to send for persons and papers.

Attest,
J. W. FORNEY, *Secretary.*

IN THE HOUSE OF REPRESENTATIVES,
January 16, 1866.

On motion of *Mr. Stevens:*

Resolved, That the House concur in the foregoing resolution of the Senate.

Attest,
EDW'D MCPHERSON, *Clerk.*

The Chairman, from the sub-committee on the basis of representation, reported that the sub-committee had directed him to report the following for the action of the Joint Committee; the first two as alternative propositions, one of which, with the third proposition, to be recommended to Congress for adoption:

"*Resolved,* by the Senate and House of Representatives of the United States of America in Congress assembled, two-thirds of both Houses concurring, that the following Articles be proposed to the Legislatures of the several States, as amendments to the Constitution of the United States, which, when they, or either of them, shall be ratified by three-fourths of the said Legislatures, shall be valid as part of said Constitution; viz:

Article A.

Representatives and direct taxes shall be apportioned among the several States within this Union, according to the respective numbers of citizens of the United States in each State; and all provisions in the Constitution or laws of any State, whereby any distinction is made in political or civil rights or privileges, on account of race, creed or color, shall be inoperative and void.

Or the following:

Article B.

Representatives and direct taxes shall be apportioned among the several States which may be included within this Union, according to their respective numbers, counting the whole number of citizens of the United States in each State; provided that, whenever the elective franchise shall be denied or abridged in any State on account of race, creed or color, all persons of such race, creed or color, shall be excluded from the basis of representation.

Article C.

Congress shall have power to make all laws necessary and proper to secure to all citizens of the United States, in every State, the same political rights and privileges; and to all persons in every State equal protection in the enjoyment of life, liberty and property."

The Joint Committee proceeded to consider the report of the sub-committee.

Mr. Stevens moved that the last article be separated from whichever of the other two should be adopted by the Committee, and be considered by itself.

The question was taken by yeas and nays, and decided in the affirmative, yeas 10, nays 4; absent and not voting 1, as follows:

Yeas—Messrs. Grimes, Williams, Stevens, Washburne, Morrill, Bingham, Conkling, Boutwell, Blow and Rogers. —10.

Nays—The Chairman, Messrs. Harris, Howard and Grider—4.

Absent and not voting—Mr. Johnson—1.

So the motion was agreed to.

Mr. Stevens moved that the Committee take the second named of the alternative proposed articles as the basis of their action.

The question was taken by yeas and nays, and it was decided in the affirmative, yeas 11, nays 3, absent and not voting 1, as follows:

Yeas—Messrs. Grimes, Harris, Williams, Stevens, Washburne, Morrill, Bingham, Conkling, Boutwell, Blow and Rogers—11.

Nays—The Chairman, Messrs. Howard and Grider—3.

Absent and not voting—Mr. Johnson—1.

So the motion was agreed to.

Mr. Stevens moved to amend the proposed article by adding the following:

"And whenever the words 'citizen of the United States' are used in the Constitution of the United States, they shall be construed to mean all persons born in the United States, or naturalized, excepting Indians."

Pending the consideration of which

Mr. Conkling moved to amend the proposed article by striking out the words "citizens of the United States in each State," and inserting in lieu thereof the words, "persons in each State, excluding Indians not taxed."

The question was taken by yeas and nays, and it was decided in the affirmative, yeas 11, nays 3, absent and not voting 1, as follows:

Yeas—Messrs. Grimes, Harris, Howard, Williams, Washburne, Morrill, Grider, Conkling, Boutwell, Blow and Rogers—11.

Nays—The Chairman and Messrs. Stevens and Bingham—3.

Absent and not voting—Mr. Johnson—1.

So the amendment was adopted.

Mr. Morrill moved to further amend by striking out the word "creed" wherever it occurred in the proposed article.

The amendment was adopted.

Mr. Stevens withdrew his amendment.

The question was upon agreeing to the proposed article as amended, which was as follows:

" Representatives and direct taxes shall be apportioned among the several States which may be included within this Union, according to their respective numbers, counting the whole number of persons in each State, excluding Indians not taxed; provided that whenever the elective franchise shall be denied or abridged in any State on account of race or color, all persons of such race or color shall be excluded from the basis of representation."

The question was taken by yeas and nays, and it was decided in the affirmative, yeas 13, nay 1, absent and not voting 1, as follows:

Yeas—The Chairman, Messrs. Grimes, Harris, Howard, Williams, Stevens, Washburne, Morrill, Grider, Bingham, Conkling, Boutwell and Blow—13.

Nay—Mr. Rogers—1.

Absent and not voting—Mr. Johnson—1.

So the proposed article as amended was agreed to.

Pending the call of the yeas and nays

Messrs. *Howard* and *Grider* each said, that although they voted in the affirmative, they desired to be understood as retaining their right to support, in their respective Houses, some proposition more in accordance with their views, should they deem it advisable to do so.

On motion of *Mr. Bingham* it was

Ordered, That the Chairman of the Senate portion of the

Joint Committee (Mr. Fessenden), and the Chairman of the House portion of the Joint Committee (Mr. Stevens), be instructed to report as early as practicable to their respective Houses, the proposed amendment to the Constitution of the United States, this day agreed upon by the Joint Committee, and recommend its adoption by the same.

Mr. Rogers asked and obtained leave to submit to the House of Representatives a report setting forth the views of the minority of the Joint Committee upon the proposed amendment.

Adjourned to meet on call of the Chairman.

Wednesday, January 24, 1866.

The Committee met pursuant to call of its Chairman; absent Messrs. Harris and Johnson.

The Chairman laid before the Committee the following resolution of the Senate which was ordered to be entered upon the Journal:

"*January* 22, 1866.

Resolved, That until otherwise ordered, all papers presented to the Senate relating to the condition and title to representation of the so-called Confederate States shall be referred to the Joint Committee upon that subject."

The Committee proceeded to the consideration of the following amendment to the Constitution proposed by the sub-committee on the basis of representation:

"Congress shall have power to make all laws necessary and proper to secure to all citizens of the United States in each State the same political rights and privileges; and to all persons in every State equal protection in the enjoyment of life, liberty and property."

Mr. Howard moved to amend by inserting the words "and elective" after the word "political."

The question was taken by yeas and nays, and decided in the negative, yeas 2, nays 10, absent and not voting 3, as follows:

Yeas—Messrs. Howard and Rogers—2.

Nays—The Chairman, Messrs. Williams, Stevens, Washburne, Morrill, Grider, Bingham, Conkling, Boutwell and Blow—10.

Absent and not voting—Messrs. Grimes, Harris and Johnson.

So the amendment was not agreed to.

Mr. Boutwell moved to amend by striking out to and including the words "political rights and privileges," and inserting in lieu thereof the following:

"Congress shall have power to abolish any distinction in the exercise of the elective franchise in any State, which by law, regulation or usage may exist therein."

The amendment was not agreed to.

Mr. Blow moved to refer the proposed amendment to a select committee of three to be appointed by the chairman, with instruction to carefully review the same.

The question was taken by yeas and nays, and it was decided in the affirmative, yeas 7, nays 5, absent and not voting 3, as follows:

Yeas—The Chairman, Messrs. Morrill, Grider, Conkling, Boutwell, Blow and Rogers—7.

Nays—Messrs. Howard, Williams, Stevens, Washburne and Bingham—5.

Absent and not voting—Messrs. Grimes, Harris and Johnson—3.

The motion to refer was accordingly agreed to.

The Chairman appointed as the sub-committee Messrs. Bingham, Boutwell and Rogers.

On motion of *Mr. Stevens* it was

Ordered, That the injunction of secrecy be removed so far as to allow any member of the Committee to announce in his place in Congress the substance and nature of the proposed amendment to the Constitution of the United States, under consideration by the Committee this morning.

Adjourned to meet on call of the Chairman.

Saturday, January 27, 1866.

The Committee met pursuant to the call of its Chairman; absent Messrs. Blow and Rogers.

Mr. Bingham from the sub-committee on the powers of Congress, reported back the proposed amendment of the Constitution, referred to them, in the following form:

"Congress shall have power to make all laws which shall be necessary and proper to secure all persons in every state full protection in the enjoyment of life, liberty and property; and to all citizens of the United States in any State the same immunities and also equal political rights and privileges."

The Chairman moved to strike out the word "also" in the last clause.

The motion was agreed to.

Mr. *Johnson* moved to amend the last clause by striking out the word "any" and inserting the word "every" before the word "state."

The motion was agreed to.

Mr. *Johnson* moved to strike out the word "all" before the word "laws."

The motion was agreed to.

Mr. *Johnson* moved to strike out the last clause of the proposed amendment.

The question was taken by yeas and nays, and it was decided in the negative, yeas 4, nays 6, absent and not voting 5, as follows:

Yeas—Messrs. Harris, Johnson, Grider and Conkling —4.

Nays—The Chairman, Messrs. Williams, Stevens, Morrill, Bingham and Boutwell—6.

Absent and not voting—Messrs. Grimes, Howard, Washburne, Blow and Rogers—5.

So the amendment was not agreed to.

Mr. *Stevens* moved that the Chairman be instructed to report the joint resolution as amended to the Senate, and recommend its adoption by Congress.

The question was taken by yeas and nays, and it was decided in the negative, yeas 5, nays 5, absent and not voting 5, as follows:

Yeas—The Chairman, Messrs. Williams, Stevens, Morrill and Bingham—5.

Nays—Messrs. Harris, Johnson, Grider, Conkling and Boutwell—5.

Absent and not voting—Messrs. Grimes, Howard, Washburne, Blow and Rogers—5.

So the motion was not agreed to.

On motion of *Mr. Stevens,* the further consideration of the joint resolution was postponed until the next meeting of the Committee.

Adjourned to meet on call of the Chairman.

Washington, January 31, 1866.

The Committee met pursuant to the call of its Chairman; absent Mr. Washburne.

Mr. Stevens laid before the Committee the joint resolution heretofore reported by the Committee proposing an amendment to the Constitution of the United States in relation to the basis of representation, which together with all propositions upon the same subject offered by members of the House were by order of the House again referred to this Committee without instructions.

The Committee proceeded to consider the joint resolution.

After discussion,

Mr. Stevens moved to amend the same by striking out the words " and direct taxes."

The motion was agreed to by yeas and nays, as follows:

Yeas—The Chairman, Messrs. Grimes, Harris, Howard, Johnson, Williams, Stevens, Morrill, Bingham, Conkling, Boutwell and Blow—12.

Nays—Messrs. Grider and Rogers—2.

Absent and not voting—Mr. Washburne—1.

Mr. *Johnson* moved to amend the proviso so that it should read:

" Provided that whenever the elective franchise shall be denied or abridged in any state, on account of race or color, in the election of the members of the most numerous branch of the State legislature, or in the election of the electors for President or Vice-President of the United States, or members of Congress, all persons therein of such race or color shall be excluded from the basis of representation."

The motion was not agreed to.

Mr. *Johnson* submitted the following in order to obtain the sense of the Committee:

Resolved, That the proposed amendment to the Constitution of the United States, in relation to the basis of representation, should be so modified as to include among the grounds of disqualification therein referred to in relation to the elective franchise, one in regard to former condition of slavery.

The question was taken by yeas and nays and it was decided in the negative, yeas 6, nays 7, absent and not voting 2, as follows:

Ayes—The Chairman, Messrs. Howard, Johnson, Williams, Grider and Blow—6.

Nays—Messrs. Grimes, Harris, Stevens, Morrill, Bingham, Conkling and Boutwell—7.

Absent and not voting—Messrs. Washburne and Rogers —2.

So the motion was not agreed to.

Mr. *Stevens* moved that the joint resolution as modified

be reported back to the House of Representatives, with a recommendation that the same do pass.

The question was taken by yeas and nays, and it was decided in the affirmative, yeas 10, nays 4, absent and not voting 1, as follows:

Yeas—Messrs. Grimes, Harris, Howard, Williams, Stevens, Morrill, Bingham, Conkling, Boutwell and Blow—10.

Nays—The Chairman, Messrs. Johnson, Grider and Rogers—4.

Absent and not voting—Mr. Washburne—1.

The motion was accordingly agreed to.

Adjourned to meet on call of the Chairman.

Saturday, February 3, 1866.

The Committee met pursuant to call of its Chairman; absent Messrs. Johnson and Blow.

The Committee resumed the consideration of the proposed amendment of the Constitution of the United States, reported from the sub-committee on powers of Congress; the same having been amended, when last under consideration by the Committee (January 27, 1866) to read as follows:

"Congress shall have power to make laws which shall be necessary and proper to secure to all persons in every State full protection in the enjoyment of life, liberty and property; and to citizens of the United States in every State the same immunities, and equal political rights and privileges."

Mr. Bingham moved the following as a substitute by way of amendment:

"The Congress shall have power to make all laws which shall be necessary and proper to secure to the citizens of each state all privileges and immunities of citizens in the several states (Art. 4, Sec. 2); and to all persons in the several States equal protection in the rights of life, liberty and property (5th Amendment)."

After discussion,

The question was taken by yeas and nays, and it was determined in the affirmative, yeas 7, nays 6, absent and not voting 2, as follows:

Yeas—Messrs. Howard, Williams, Washburne, Morrill, Bingham, Boutwell and Rogers—7.

Nays—The Chairman, Messrs. Grimes, Harris, Stevens, Grider and Conkling—6.

Absent and not voting—Messrs. Johnson and Blow—2.

So the amendment was agreed to.

The question was upon agreeing to the proposed amendment of the Constitution as amended.

The question was taken by yeas and nays, and it was determined in the affirmative, yeas 9, nays 4, absent and not voting 2, as follows:

Yeas—The Chairman, Messrs. Grimes, Howard, Williams, Stevens, Washburne, Morrill, Bingham and Boutwell—9.

Nays—Messrs. Harris, Grider, Conkling, and Rogers—4.

Absent and not voting—Messrs. Johnson and Blow—2.

So the proposition as amended was adopted.

The question was upon ordering the same to be reported to Congress for adoption.

On motion of *Mr. Boutwell,* the further consideration of the same was postponed for the present.

Mr. Howard submitted the following proposed amendment to the Constitution of the United States, for future consideration by the Committee:

" That the payment of every kind of indebtedness arising or growing out of the late rebellion, contracted or accruing in aid of it or in order to promote it, is forever prohibited to the United States and to each of the states; such indebtedness and all evidences thereof are hereby declared and in all courts and places shall be held and treated as in violation of this Constitution, and utterly void and of no effect."

Adjourned to meet on call of the Chairman.

Saturday, February 10, 1866.

The Committee met pursuant to the call of its Chairman; absent Mr. Washburne.

The Committee resumed the consideration of the joint resolution proposing an amendment to the Constitution of the United States, as amended on motion of *Mr. Bingham* at the last meeting.

Mr. Stevens moved that the same be reported to the two Houses of Congress.

The question was taken by yeas and nays, and it was decided in the affirmative, yeas 9, nays 5, absent and not voting 1, as follows:

Yeas—The Chairman, Messrs. Grimes, Howard, Williams, Stevens, Morrill, Bingham, Boutwell and Blow—9.

Nays—Messrs. Harris, Johnson, Grider, Conkling and Rogers—5.

Absent and not voting—Mr. Washburne—1.

So the motion was agreed to.

Mr. Grider submitted the following resolution, the consideration of which was postponed till the next meeting of the Committee:

Resolved, That the sub-committee on the condition of Tennessee, as to loyalty, be requested to report to this Committee, with the proof taken touching that question, and that this Committee at its next meeting report to the House and Senate their conclusions and the evidence in the case.

Adjourned to meet on call of the Chairman.

Thursday, February 15, 1866.

The Committee met pursuant to call of its Chairman; absent Mr. Johnson.

Mr. Bingham, from the sub-committee on Tennessee, submitted a report in writing with accompanying papers; also the following bill:

Whereas, The people of Tennessee have presented a Constitution and asked admission into the Union, and which on due examination is found to be republican in its form of Government;

Be it enacted, by the Senate and House of Representatives of the United States of America in Congress assembled, that the State of Tennessee shall be one, and is hereby declared to be one of the United States of America, on an equal footing with the other states in all respects whatever.

Sec. 2. And be it further enacted that until the Representatives in Congress shall be apportioned according to an actual enumeration of the inhabitants of the United States, the State of Tennessee shall be entitled to eight representatives in Congress.

After discussion, the further consideration of the same was postponed until the next meeting.

Adjourned to 11 A. M. on Saturday next.

Washington, February 17, 1866.

The Committee met pursuant to adjournment; absent Mr. Johnson.

The Committee resumed the consideration of the bill in relation to Tennessee, as set forth in the journal of the last meeting of the Committee.

Mr. Grimes moved to amend the preamble by inserting the word "Constitution" after the word "which."

The amendment was agreed to.

Mr. Stevens moved to amend the second section so that it would read as follows:

"Sec. 2. And be it further enacted that until the next congressional election the State of Tennessee shall be entitled to eight representatives."

The question was taken by yeas and nays, and it was decided in the affirmative, yeas 9, nays 4, absent and not voting 2, as follows:

Ayes—The Chairman, Messrs. Grimes, Howard, Stevens, Washburne, Morrill, Bingham, Conkling and Boutwell—9.

Nays—Messrs. Williams, Grider, Blow and Rogers—4.

Absent and not voting—Messrs. Harris and Johnson—2.

So the amendment was agreed to.

Mr. Williams moved to strike out the second section as amended.

The motion was agreed to.

Mr. Harris moved the following as a substitute for the bill as amended:

Resolved by the Senate and House of Representatives of the United States of America in Congress assembled; That the United States do hereby recognize the government of the State of Tennessee, inaugurated under a constitution adopted by a convention of the people of that State, on the 8th day of January, 1865, and ratified by a vote of the people at an election held on the 22d day of February, 1865, as the legitimate government of said state, under which said state is entitled to the guarantee and all other rights of a state government under the Constitution of the United States.

Mr. Stevens moved to amend the preamble of the bill reported from the sub-committee by striking out the words " and asked admission into the Union."

Mr. Johnson here appeared in the committee room.

Mr. Bingham offered the following as a substitute for the bill of the sub-committee:

Whereas, The people of Tennessee did, on the 22d day of February, in the year of our Lord, 1865, adopt by a large popular vote an amended constitution of government, republican in form, and not inconsistent with the Costitution and laws of the United States; therefore,

Be it resolved, By the Senate and House of Representatives of the United States of America in Congress assembled, That the constitutional relations between Tennessee and the Government of the United States are hereby restored.

After discussion, *Mr. Bingham* submitted the following modification of his substitute:

Whereas, The people of Tennessee did, on the 22nd day of February, in the year of our Lord, 1865, adopt by a large popular vote an amended constitution of government, republican in form, and not inconsistent with the Constitution and laws of the United States,

And whereas, The people of Tennessee are in a condition for restoration to the Union as a state, and have presented said constitutional government to Congress, and asked to be restored to their constitutional relations to the Government of the United States, therefore,

Be it resolved, by the Senate and House of Representatives of the United States of America, in Congress assembled, That the constitutional relations between Tennessee and the Government of the United States are hereby restored, and the said state of Tennessee is declared to be a state in the Union on the same footing with the other states of the Union.

Mr. Harris withdrew his substitute.

The question was then taken by yeas and nays, upon adopting the substitute of *Mr. Bingham* for the joint resolution reported from the sub-committee on Tennessee, as the basis of action for the joint committee, and it was decided in the affirmative, yeas 9, nays 4, absent or not voting 2, as follows:

Yeas—The Chairman, Messrs. Grimes, Harris, Johnson, Williams, Washburne, Morrill, Bingham and Blow—9.

Nays—Messrs. Howard, Stevens, Grider and Rogers—4.

Absent or not voting—Messrs. Conkling and Boutwell—2.

So the substitute was adopted as the basis of action of the Committee.

Mr. Rogers moved the following:

Resolved, by the Senate and House of Representatives of the United States of America in Congress assembled, That the State of Tennessee is one of the states of and in this Union, with all the rights and privileges of the other states, and is entitled to her full representation in the Congress of the United States.

The same was rejected.

Mr. Williams moved that the whole subject of Tennessee be referred to a select committee of three members, to be appointed by the Chairman, and with instructions to report thereon to the joint committee at the next meeting.

The question was taken by yeas and nays, and it was decided in the affirmative, yeas 8, nays 7, as follows:

Yeas—The Chairman, Messrs. Howard, Williams, Stevens, Washburne, Morrill, Conkling and Boutwell—8.

Nays—Messrs. Grimes, Harris, Johnson, Grider, Bingham, Blow and Rogers—7.

So the motion was agreed to.

The Chairman appointed the following members as the select committee just ordered:

Messrs. Williams, Conkling and Boutwell.

Adjourned till 10½ o'clock A. M. on Monday next.

Monday, February 19, 1866.

The Committee met pursuant to adjournment; absent *Mr. Johnson.*

Mr. Conkling, from the select committee on Tennessee, appointed at the last meeting of the Committee, made a verbal report, and submitted the following as a substitute for the proposition of Mr. Bingham which was referred to the select committee:

Resolved, by the Senate and House of Representatives of the United States of America in Congress assembled, that the functions and relations of Tennessee as a member of the Union, are hereby declared to be established, and that Senators and Representatives therefrom, their several elections, qualifications and returns being regular and sufficient, shall be entitled to admission.

And be it further resolved that the foregoing declaration is made upon the following fundamental conditions and guarantees:

First. The state of Tennessee shall never assume or pay any debt or obligation contracted or incurred in aid of the late rebellion, nor shall said state ever repudiate any debt or obligation contracted or incurred in aid of the Federal government against said rebellion; and said state shall be forever bound in like manner as the other states within this Union for the debt of the United States.

Second. The said state shall forever maintain in its constitution the provision therein contained disavowing the doctrine of secession.

Third. The said state shall, for not less than five years

from the ratification of this resolution as hereinafter provided, exclude from the elective franchise, and from offices of honor, trust or profit, all those who adhered to and voluntarily gave aid or comfort to the late rebellion.

And be it further resolved, that the ratification of the foregoing conditions by a majority of the qualified electors of said state, in such manner as the legislature thereof may prescribe, shall be deemed an acceptance of this resolution; and upon a proclamation of such ratification by the President of the United States, the same shall become operative.

Mr. Bingham moved to strike out the third condition.

Mr. Boutwell moved to amend the second resolution by adding to it the following:

Fourth. The said state shall make no distinction in the exercise of the elective franchise on account of race or color.

Pending the consideration of which,

The Chairman moved to amend the first condition of the second resolution by striking out all after the words "in aid of the late rebellion."

After discussion,

The Committee adjourned till 10½ o'clock A. M. tomorrow.

Tuesday, February 20, 1866.

The Committee met pursuant to adjournment; absent *Mr. Johnson*.

The Committee resumed the consideration of the joint resolution in relation to Tennessee.

The pending question was upon the motion of the *Chair-*

man to amend the first condition of the second resolution, so that the same should read as follows:

"The State of Tennessee shall never assume or pay any debt or obligation contracted or incurred in aid of the late rebellion."

The question was taken by yeas and nays, and it was decided in the affirmative, yeas 8, nays 4, absent or not voting 3, as follows:

Yeas—The Chairman, Messrs. Harris, Howard, Washburne, Morrill, Grider, Bingham and Rogers—8.

Nays—Messrs. Williams, Stevens, Conkling and Boutwell—4.

Absent or not voting—Messrs. Grimes, Johnson and Blow—3.

So the amendment was agreed to.

The question then recurred upon the motion of *Mr. Boutwell* to still farther amend the first resolution by adding the following condition:

" Fourth. Said state shall make no distinction in the exercise of the elective franchise on account of race or color."

The question was taken by yeas and nays, and it was decided in the negative, yeas 5, nays 6, absent or not voting 4, as follows:

Yeas—Messrs. Howard, Stevens, Washburne, Morrill and Boutwell—5.

Nays—Messrs. Harris, Williams, Grider, Bingham, Conkling and Rogers—6.

Absent or not voting—The Chairman, Messrs. Grimes, Johnson and Blow—4.

So the amendment was not agreed to.

Mr. Bingham moved the following as a substitute:

"*Whereas*, The people of Tennessee have presented a constitution to Congress, which constitution on due examination is found to be republican in its form of government, and the people are found to be in a condition to exercise the functions of a state, and can only exercise the same by the consent of the law-making power of the United States; Therefore,

Be it enacted, by the Senate and House of Representatives of the United States of America in Congress assembled, That the state of Tennessee is hereby declared to be one of the United States of America, on an equal footing with the other states in all respects whatever."

Pending the consideration of which,

Mr. Stevens said his opinion as to the expediency and propriety of this action on the part of the joint committee had been materially changed since yesterday.

The first duty of the committee was to declare the power of Congress over this subject of reconstruction. He therefore moved to postpone all other business for the purpose of enabling him to offer the following concurrent resolution, which he should ask immediate action upon:

"Concurrent resolution concerning the insurrectionary states,

Be it resolved, by the House of Representatives, the Senate concurring, that in order to close agitation upon a question which seems likely to disturb the action of the government, as well as to quiet the uncertainty which is agitating the minds of the people of the eleven states which have been declared to be in insurrection, no senator or representative shall be admitted into either branch of Congress from any of said states until Congress shall have declared such state entitled to such representation."

After discussion, the question was taken by yeas and nays upon the motion to postpone, and it was decided in the affirmative, yeas 10, nays 4, absent 1, as follows:

Yeas—The Chairman, Messrs. Grimes, Harris, Howard, Williams, Stevens, Washburne, Morrill, Conkling and Boutwell—10.

Nays—Messrs. Grider, Bingham, Blow and Rogers—4.

Absent—Mr. Johnson—1.

So the motion was agreed to.

Mr. Stevens submitted the foregoing concurrent resolution, and moved it be adopted and reported forthwith to the House of Representatives.

The question was taken by yeas and nays, and it was decided in the affirmative, yeas 12, nays 2, absent 1, as follows:

Yeas—The Chairman, Messrs. Grimes, Harris, Howard, Williams, Stevens, Washburne, Morrill, Bingham, Conkling, Boutwell and Blow—12.

Nays—Messrs. Grider and Rogers—2.

Absent—Mr. Johnson—1.

So the resolution was adopted.

Adjourned to meet on call of the Chairman.

Saturday, March 3, 1866.

The Committee met pursuant to call of the Chairman; Absent, Messrs. Grimes, Howard and Blow.

The following resolution of the Senate was received and recorded:

"*February* 20th, 1866.

" On motion by *Mr. Wilson:*

" *Resolved,* That the Joint Committee on Reconstruction be directed to inquire into and report how far the states lately in rebellion, or any of them, have complied with the terms proposed by the President as conditions precedent to their resumption of practical relations with the United States; which terms and conditions were as follows, viz.:

" 1st. That the several state constitutions should be amended by the insertion of a provision abolishing slavery.

" 2nd. That the several state conventions should declare null and void the ordinances of secession and the laws and decrees of the Confederacy.

" 3rd. That the several state legislatures should ratify the amendment to the Federal Constitution abolishing slavery.

" 4th. That the rebel debt, state and confederate, should be repudiated.

" 5th. That civil rights should be secured by laws applicable alike to whites and blacks."

The Committee resumed the consideration of the joint resolution concerning Tennessee.

The pending question was upon the motion of *Mr. Bingham* to substitute for the basis of the action of the Committee that which was offered by him at the last meeting of the Committee.

Mr. Bingham modified the preamble of his substitute by inserting after the words " the functions of a state," the words "within this Union;" so that the same would read "and the people are found to be in a condition to exercise the functions of a state within this Union," etc.

After discussion,

The question was taken upon the motion to substitute, and it was decided in the affirmative, yeas 7, nays 5, absent or not voting 3, as follows:

Yeas—Messrs. Harris, Johnson, Stevens, Washburne, Grider, Bingham and Rogers—7.

Nays—The Chairman, Messrs. Williams, Morrill, Conkling and Boutwell—5.

Absent or not voting—Messrs. Grimes, Howard and Blow—3.

So the motion to substitute was agreed to.

Mr. Johnson moved to amend the substitute by striking out of the preamble the last clause as follows:

"And can only exercise the same by the consent of the law-making power of the United States."

After discussion,

The question was taken by yeas and nays, and it was decided in the negative, yeas 4, nays 7, absent or not voting 4, as follows:

Yeas—Messrs. Harris, Johnson, Grider and Rogers—4.

Nays—The Chairman, Messrs. Williams, Stevens, Washburne, Morrill, Bingham and Boutwell—7.

Absent or not voting—Messrs. Grimes, Howard, Conkling and Blow—4.

So the motion to strike out was not agreed to.

Mr. Blow entered the committee room about this time.

The Chairman stated that he had just received a note from Mr. Grimes, stating that he was absent on account of indisposition, and requesting the Chairman to cast his vote for him on all questions before the Committee.

The question was upon adopting the preamble and bill substituted for the joint resolution of the select committee, on motion of *Mr. Bingham.*

During the discussion thereon,

The Chairman read a preamble and resolution in relation to Tennessee, which he had drawn up, but stated that he would not offer it for the action of the Committee.

Mr. Bingham said he would, with the consent of the Committee, modify his preamble, in accordance with what the *Chairman* had read, and also change the form of the bill so as to make it a joint resolution.

Leave was granted and the preamble and bill of *Mr. Bingham* were modified as follows:

"*Whereas,* The people of Tennessee have made known to the Congress of the United States their desire that the constitutional relations heretofore existing between them and the United States may be fully established, and did, on the 22d day of February, 1865, by a large popular vote, adopt and ratify a constitution of government, republican in form and not inconsistent with the Constitution and laws of the United States, and a state government has been organized under the provisions thereof, which said provisions and the laws passed in pursuance thereof proclaim and denote loyalty to the Union;

And whereas, The people of Tennessee are found to be

in a condition to exercise the functions of a state within this Union; and can only exercise the same by the consent of the law-making power of the United States; therefore, be it

Resolved, by the Senate and House of Representatives of the United States of America in Congress assembled, That the State of Tennessee is hereby declared to be one of the United States of America, on an equal footing with the other states in all respects whatever."

The question was upon adopting the preamble and joint resolution as modified.

Mr. Harris and *Mr. Conkling* called for a division of the question.

The question was first taken by yeas and nays, upon agreeing to the joint resolution, and it was decided in the affirmative, yeas 8, nays 4, absent or not voting 3, as follows:

Yeas—Messrs. Harris, Johnson, Williams, Stevens, Grider, Bingham, Blow and Rogers—8.

Nays—The Chairman, Messrs. Washburne, Morrill and Boutwell—4.

Absent or not voting—Messrs. Grimes, Howard and Conkling—3.

So the joint resolution was agreed to.

The question was then taken by yeas and nays, upon agreeing to the preamble, and it was decided in the affirmative, yeas 7, nays 5, absent or not voting 3, as follows:

Yeas—The Chairman, Messrs. Johnson, Williams, Washburne, Grider, Bingham and Blow—7.

Nays—Messrs. Harris, Stevens, Morrill, Boutwell and Rogers—5.

Absent or not voting—Messrs. Grimes, Howard and Conkling—3.

So the preamble was agreed to.

Pending the calls of the yeas and nays upon agreeing to the preamble and resolution,

The Chairman asked to have the votes of *Mr. Grimes* recorded, in accordance with his request in a note to the Chairman.

Mr. Rogers objected, and the votes were recorded and the results announced as above.

Mr. Bingham moved that the preamble and joint resolution together with the memorial, accompanying papers and testimony relating to Tennessee, be reported to the House of Representatives.

Mr. Conkling moved to amend the motion of *Mr. Bingham* by adding that all the testimony taken by sub-committees in relation to the states which have been declared to be in insurrection, which may be ready for publication, be also reported to Congress and its printing recommended.

After discussion,

The question was taken upon the amendment of *Mr. Conkling*, and upon a division there were ayes 4, noes 6.

So the amendment was not agreed to.

The motion of *Mr. Bingham* was then agreed to.

Mr. Conkling and *Mr. Rogers* severally asked and obtained leave to submit minority reports.

Mr. Washburne moved that the several sub-committees

be instructed to prepare and arrange for publication the testimony taken by them, and that the same be reported to Congress and its printing recommended.

The question was taken by yeas and nays, and it was decided in the affirmative, yeas 9, nays 3, absent or not voting 3, as follows:

Yeas—The Chairman, Messrs. Harris, Williams, Stevens, Washburne, Bingham, Conkling, Boutwell and Blow —9.

Nays—Messrs. Johnson, Grider and Rogers—3.

Absent or not voting—Messrs. Grimes, Howard and Morrill—3.

So the motion was agreed to.

Adjourned to meet on call of the Chairman.

Washington, March 5, 1866.

The Committee met pursuant to the call of its Chairman; absent Messrs. Howard and Blow.

Mr. Bingham moved to reconsider the vote by which the Committee agreed to the joint resolution in relation to Tennessee, and directed the same to be reported to the House of Representatives.

The motion to reconsider was agreed to.

Mr. Bingham moved to amend the joint resolution by striking out at the close the words " in all respects whatever," and adding to the resolution the following: " upon the express condition that the people of Tennessee will maintain and enforce in good faith their existing constitution and laws excluding those who have been engaged in rebellion against the United States from the exercise of the elective franchise for the respective periods of time therein provided for, and shall also exclude for like period of time the same persons from eligibility to office."

Mr. Stevens moved to amend the amendment by addition, as follows: " which condition shall be ratified by the legislature of Tennessee, or the people thereof as the legislature may direct before this act shall take effect."

The question was taken by yeas and nays, upon the amendment to the amendment, and it was decided in the affirmative, yeas 8, nays 5, absent or not voting 2, as follows:

Yeas—The Chairman, Messrs. Grimes, Williams, Stevens, Washburne, Morrill, Conkling and Boutwell—8.

Nays—Messrs. Harris, Johnson, Grider, Bingham and Rogers—5.

Absent or not voting—Messrs. Howard and Blow—2.

So the amendment to the amendment was agreed to.

The question was then taken, by yeas and nays, upon the amendment as amended, and it was decided in the affirmative, yeas 10, nays 3, absent or not voting 2, as follows:

Yeas—The Chairman, Messrs. Grimes, Harris, Williams, Stevens, Washburne, Morrill, Bingham, Conkling and Boutwell—10.

Nays—Messrs. Johnson, Grider and Rogers—3.

Absent and not voting—Messrs. Howard and Blow—2.

So the amendment as amended was agreed to.

Mr. Conkling moved to further amend the joint resolution by inserting before the part adopted on motion of *Mr. Stevens* the following:

"and the state of Tennessee shall never assume or pay any debt or obligation contracted or incurred in aid of the late rebellion; nor shall said state ever in any manner claim from the United States or make any allowance of compensation for slaves emancipated or liberated in any way whatever."

The question was taken by yeas and nays, and it was decided in the affirmative, yeas 10, nays 3, absent or not voting 2, as follows:

Yeas—The Chairman, Messrs. Grimes, Harris, Williams, Stevens, Washburne, Morrill, Bingham, Conkling and Boutwell—10.

Nays—Messrs. Johnson, Grider and Rogers—3.

Absent and not voting—Messrs. Howard and Blow—2.

So the amendment was agreed to.

Mr. Stevens moved to further amend the preamble and joint resolution by transferring the enacting clause from just before the joint resolution to the beginning of the preamble.

The question was taken by yeas and nays, and it was decided in the affirmative, yeas 10, nays 3, absent 2, as follows:

Yeas—The Chairman, Messrs. Grimes, Harris, Williams, Stevens, Washburne, Morrill, Bingham, Conkling and Boutwell—10.

Nays—Messrs. Johnson, Grider and Rogers—3.

Absent or not voting—Messrs. Howard and Blow—2.

So the motion of Mr. Stevens was agreed to.

Mr. Harris moved to strike out the following words:

"and can only exercise the same by the consent of the law-making power of the United States."

The question was taken by yeas and nays, and it was decided in the negative, yeas 5, nays 8, absent and not voting 2, as follows:

Yeas—The Chairman, Messrs. Harris, Johnson, Grider and Rogers—5.

Nays—Messrs. Grimes, Williams, Stevens, Washburne, Morrill, Bingham, Conkling and Boutwell—8.

Absent and not voting—Messrs. Howard and Blow—2.

The question was then taken by yeas and nays, upon agreeing to the joint resolution as amended, and directing the same to be reported to the House of Representatives, and it was decided in the affirmative, yeas 8, nays 5, absent and not voting 2, as follows:

Yeas—The Chairman, Messrs. Grimes, Harris, Williams, Stevens, Morrill, Bingham and Conkling—8.

Nays—Messrs. Johnson, Washburne, Grider, Boutwell and Rogers—5.

Absent or not voting—Messrs. Howard and Blow—2.

So the joint resolution was adopted and ordered to be reported to the House of Representatives.

Adjourned to meet on call of the Chairman.

Washington, April 16, 1866.

The Committee met pursuant to the call of the Chairman; absent, Messrs. Fessenden, Harris, Grider, Conkling, Boutwell and Blow.

Mr. Morrill stated that he called on Mr. Fessenden yesterday, and found him confined to his bed by illness, and under the care of a physician.

Mr. Stevens (Chairman of the House portion of the Committee) took the chair and called the Committee to order.

The object of the meeting was stated to be to hear *Mr. Stewart,* Senator from the State of Nevada, explain the purpose and effect of the joint resolution, introduced by him in the Senate of the United States, on the 12th inst., being entitled " Joint Resolution (S. R. 62) proposing an amendment to the Constitution of the United States; also setting forth certain conditions upon which the states, the people of which have been lately in insurrection against the United States, shall be restored to their representation in Congress."

Mr. Stewart proceeded to address the Committee at length in support and advocacy of his resolution.

After he had concluded,

On motion of *Mr. Grimes,*

The Committee adjourned to 11 A. M. on Saturday next.

Washington, April 21, 1866.

The Committee met pursuant to adjournment; absent, The Chairman, and Messrs. Harris and Conkling.

Mr. Stevens moved that Mr. Johnson take the chair in absence of the Chairman.

The motion was agreed to.

Mr. Grimes stated that Mr. Fessenden was recovering and would probably be out next week.

On motion of *Mr. Stevens* it was .

Resolved, That in the opinion of this Committee it is expedient that the taking of testimony by the several sub-committees be concluded next week.

Mr. Stevens said he had a plan of reconstruction, one not of his own framing, but which he should support, and which he submitted to the Committee for consideration.

It was read as follows:

A joint resolution proposing an amendment to the Constitution, and to provide for the restoration to the states lately in insurrection of their full political rights.

Whereas, It is expedient that the States lately in insurrection should, at the earliest day consistent with the future peace and safety of the Union, be restored to full participation in all political rights; therefore,

Be it resolved, by the Senate and House of Representatives of the United States of America in Congress assembled (two-thirds of both Houses concurring), that the following Article be proposed to the Legislatures of the several states as an amendment to the Constitution of the United States, which, when ratified, by three-fourths of said legislatures, shall be valid as part of the Constitution, namely:

Article—

Section 1. No discrimination shall be made by any state, nor by the United States, as to the civil rights of persons because of race, color, or previous condition of servitude.

Sec. 2. From and after the fourth day of July, in the year one thousand eight hundred and seventy-six, no discrimination shall be made by any state, nor by the United

States, as to the enjoyment by classes of persons of the right of suffrage, because of race, color, or previous condition of servitude.

Sec. 3. Until the fourth day of July, one thousand eight hundred and seventy-six, no class of persons, as to the right of any of whom to suffrage discrimination shall be made by any state, because of race, color, or previous condition of servitude, shall be included in the basis of representation.

Sec. 4. Debts incurred in aid of insurrection or of war against the Union, and claims of compensation for loss of involuntary service or labor, shall not be paid by any state nor by the United States.

Sec. 5. Congress shall have power to enforce by appropriate legislation, the provisions of this article.

And be it further resolved, That whenever the above recited amendment shall have become part of the Constitution, and any state lately in insurrection shall have ratified the same, and shall have modified its constitution and laws in conformity with the first section thereof, the Senators and Representatives from such state, if found duly elected and qualified, shall, after having taken the usual oath of office, be admitted as such:

Provided, That no person who, having been an officer in the army or navy of the United States, or having been a member of the Thirty-sixth Congress, or of the Cabinet in the year one thousand eight hundred and sixty, took part in the late insurrection, shall be eligible to either branch of the national legislature until after the fourth day of July, one thousand eight hundred and seventy-six.

Mr. Stevens said he had submitted the proposed amendment to the Constitution with the proposed legislation by Congress, to the Committee for action together; but it would be necessary to submit the two propositions separately to Congress for its action.

The Committee then proceeded to consider the same.

The question was upon agreeing to the proposed first section of the amendment.

Mr. Bingham moved to amend the same by adding the following: "nor shall any state deny to any person within its jurisdiction the equal protection of the laws, nor take private property for public use without just compensation."

After discussion thereon

The question was taken, and it was decided in the negative, yeas 5, nays 7, absent 3, as follows:

Yeas—Messrs. Johnson, Stevens, Bingham, Blow and Rogers—5.

Nays—Messrs. Grimes, Howard, Williams, Washburne, Morrill, Grider and Boutwell—7.

Absent—Messrs. Fessenden, Harris and Conkling—3.

So the amendment was not agreed to.

The question was taken upon adopting the first section, and it was decided in the affirmative, yeas 10, nays 2, absent 3, as follows:

Yeas—Messrs. Grimes, Howard, Johnson, Williams, Stevens, Washburne, Morrill, Bingham, Boutwell and Blow—10.

Nays—Messrs. Grider and Rogers—2.

Absent—Messrs. Fessenden, Harris and Conkling—3.

The first section was accordingly adopted.

The question was upon adopting the second section.

After discussion thereon

The question was taken, and it was decided in the affirmative, yeas 8, nays 4, absent 3, as follows:

Yeas—Messrs. Grimes, Harris, Williams, Stevens, Washburne, Morrill, Bingham and Blow—8.

Nays—Messrs. Johnson, Grider, Boutwell and Rogers—4.

Absent—Messrs. Fessenden, Harris and Conkling—3.

So the second section was adopted.

The question was then taken upon adopting the third section, and it was decided in the affirmative, yeas 9, nays 3, absent 3, as follows:

Yeas—Messrs. Grimes, Howard, Williams, Stevens, Washburne, Morrill, Bingham, Boutwell and Blow—9.

Nays—Messrs. Johnson, Grider and Rogers—3.

Absent—Messrs. Fessenden, Harris and Conkling—3.

So the third section was adopted.

The question was upon adopting the fourth section.

Mr. Rogers moved to amend by striking out the words, " by any state nor," so that the clause would read—" shall not be paid by the United States."

The question was taken, and it was decided in the negative, yeas 3, nays 9, absent 3, as follows:

Yeas—Messrs. Johnson, Grider and Rogers—3.

Nays—Messrs. Grimes, Howard, Williams, Stevens, Washburne, Morrill, Bingham, Boutwell and Blow—9.

Absent—Messrs. Fessenden, Harris and Conkling—3.

So the amendment was not agreed to.

Mr. Stevens moved to amend the section by inserting after the word " debts " the words " or obligations already incurred, or which may hereafter be," so that it would read —" Debts or obligations already incurred, or which may hereafter be incurred in aid of insurrection," etc.

The amendment was agreed to.

The question was taken upon the section as amended, and it was decided in the affirmative, yeas 10, nays 2, absent 3, as follows:

Yeas—Messrs. Grimes, Howard, Johnson, Williams, Stevens, Washburne, Morrill, Bingham, Boutwell and Blow—10.

Nays—Messrs. Grider and Rogers—2.

Absent—Messrs. Fessenden, Harris and Conkling—3.

So the fourth section as amended was adopted.

Mr. Bingham moved to insert as section five the following:

" Sec. 5. No state shall make or enforce any law which shall abridge the privileges or immunities of citizens of the United States; nor shall any state deprive any person of life, liberty or property without due process of law, nor deny to any person within its jurisdiction the equal protection of the laws."

After discussion thereon

The question was taken, and it was decided in the affirmative, yeas 10, nays 2, absent 3, as follows:

Yeas—Messrs. Grimes, Howard, Johnson, Williams, Stevens, Washburne, Morrill, Bingham, Boutwell and Blow —10.

Nays—Messrs. Grider and Rogers—2.

Absent—Messrs. Fessenden, Harris and Conkling—3.

So the section proposed by *Mr. Bingham* was adopted.

The sixth section was read, giving Congress power to enforce the provisions of the article.

The question was taken upon adopting the section, and it was decided in the affirmative, yeas 10, nays 2, absent 3, as follows:

Yeas—Messrs. Grimes, Howard, Johnson, Williams, Stevens, Washburne, Morrill, Bingham, Boutwell and Blow—10.

Nays—Messrs. Grider and Rogers—2.

Absent—Messrs. Fessenden, Harris and Conkling—3.

So the sixth section was adopted.

The Committee proceeded to consider the accompanying joint resolution.

Mr. Morrill submitted the following additional resolution:

"*And be it further resolved,* That when any state lately in insurrection shall have adopted Article — of amendment to the Constitution as proposed —, any part of the direct tax under the act of August 5, 1861, which may remain due and unpaid in such state, may be assumed and paid by such state; and the payment thereof, upon proper assurances from such state to be given to the Secretary of the Treasury of the United States, may be postponed for a period not exceeding ten years."

Pending which

Mr. Bingham moved to amend the resolution submitted

by *Mr. Stevens* by striking out after the enacting clause the following words:

" That whenever the above recited amendment shall have become part of the Constitution, and any state lately in insurrection shall have ratified the same, and shall have modified its constitution and laws in conformity with the first section thereof "—

And inserting in lieu thereof the following:

" That whenever, after the first day of February, 1867, any state lately in insurrection shall have adopted this article of amendment, and shall have conformed its constitution thereto and to the constitution and laws of the United States, such state shall be entitled to representation in the Congress of the United States, and "

Mr. Conkling at this period of the session entered the Committee room, and stated that he had been unable to come earlier.

After some discussion upon the amendment proposed by *Mr. Bingham*,

On motion of *Mr. Grimes* it was

Ordered, That when the Committee adjourn to-day it be to meet at 10 A. M. on Monday next.

After further discussion,

On motion of *Mr. Conkling,*

The Committee adjourned.

Washington, April 23, 1866.

The Committee met pursuant to adjournment (Mr. Johnson in the chair). Absent, Messrs. Fessenden, Harris and Grider.

The Committee resumed the consideration of the joint resolution pending at the adjournment on Saturday.

Mr. Stevens said he desired to withdraw the joint resolution submitted by him on Saturday, so far as the same related to the admission of the states lately in insurrection, for the purpose of submitting a bill in its place—leaving the proposed amendment to the Constitution to stand by itself, as it had been adopted by the Committee.

Mr. Howard moved that *Mr. Stevens* have the leave asked.

The motion was agreed to, and the joint resolution was accordingly withdrawn.

Mr. Stevens submitted the following bill for the consideration of the Committee.

A Bill to provide for the restoration to the states lately in insurrection of their full political rights.

Whereas, It is expedient that the states lately in insurrection should, at the earliest day consistent with the future peace and safety of the Union, be restored to full participation in all political rights;

And, whereas, the Congress did, by joint resolution, propose for ratification to the legislatures of the several states, as an amendment to the Constitution of the United States, an article in the following words, to wit:

" Article.

" Section 1. No discrimination shall be made by any State nor by the United States as to the civil rights of persons because of race, color or previous condition of servitude.

" Sec. 2. From and after the fourth day of July in the

year 1876 no discrimination shall be made by any state nor by the United States, as to the enjoyment, by classes of persons, of the right of suffrage, because of race, color or previous condition of servitude.

"Sec. 3. Until the fourth day of July, 1876, no class of persons, as to the right of any of whom to suffrage discrimination shall be made by any state, because of race, color or previous condition of servitude, shall be included in the basis of representation.

"Sec. 4. Debts or obligations already incurred or which may hereafter be incurred in aid of insurrection or of war against the Union, and claims for compensation for loss of involuntary service or labor, shall not be paid by any state nor by the United States.

"Sec. 5. No state shall make or enforce any law which shall abridge the privileges or immunities of citizens of the United States; nor shall any state deprive any person of life, liberty, or property without due process of law; nor deny to any person within its jurisdiction the equal protection of the laws.

"Sec. 6. The Congress shall have power to enforce by appropriate legislation the provisions of this article."

Now, therefore,

Be it enacted, by the Senate and House of Representatives of the United States of America in Congress assembled, That whenever the above recited amendment shall have become part of the Constitution, and any state lately in insurrection shall have ratified the same, and shall have modified its constitution and laws in conformity with the first section thereof, the Senators and Representatives from such state, if found duly elected and qualified, shall, after having taken the usual oath of office, be admitted into Congress as such; *Provided,* That until after the fourth day of July, 1876, no person shall be eligible to either branch of the National Legislature who is included in any of the following classes, namely:

First. Persons who, having been officers of the army or navy of the United States, or having been members of the 36th Congress, or having held in the year 1860 seats in the Cabinet, or judicial offices under the United States, did afterwards take part in the late insurrection.

Second. Persons who have been civil or diplomatic officers of the so-called confederate government, or officers of the army or navy of said government above the rank of colonel in the army and of lieutenant in the navy.

Third. Persons in regard to whom it shall appear that they have treated officers or soldiers or sailors of the army or navy of the United States, of whatever race, or color, captured during the late civil war, otherwise than lawfully as prisoners of war.

Fourth. Persons in regard to whom it shall appear that they are disloyal.

Mr. Bingham moved to amend by striking out all after the enacting clause down to and including the word " Provided," and inserting the following:

" That whenever the above recited amendment shall have been ratified in good faith by the legislature of Tennessee, and said state shall have conformed her laws thereto, said state shall be entitled to representation in Congress, and upon the ratification in good faith by the other states lately in insurrection of the foregoing article of amendment said states shall after the first day of February, 1867, be entitled to representation in Congress, subject to the following condition, that said states so ratifying said amendment shall conform their constitutions and laws thereto; Provided, however."

The question was taken upon the amendment, and it was decided in the negative, yeas 4, nays 8, absent 3, as follows:

Yeas—Messrs. Johnson, Bingham, Blow and Rogers—4.

Nays—Messrs. Grimes, Howard, Williams, Stevens, Washburne, Morrill, Conkling and Boutwell—8.

Absent—Messrs. Fessenden, Harris and Grider—3.

So the amendment was rejected.

Mr. Stevens moved to amend the second clause of exceptions by striking out the words " civil or."

The amendment was agreed to.

Mr. Stevens moved to further amend the same clause by striking out the word " lieutenant " and inserting the word " master."

The amendment was agreed to.

Mr. Williams moved to strike out the fourth clause as follows:

" Fourth. Persons in regard to whom it shall appear that they are disloyal."

After discussion,

The question was taken, and it was decided in the affirmative, yeas 12, nays 0, absent 3, as follows:

Yeas—Messrs. Grimes, Howard, Johnson, Williams, Stevens, Washburne, Morrill, Bingham, Conkling, Boutwell, Blow and Rogers—12.

Nays—0.

Absent—Messrs. Fessenden, Harris and Grider—3.

So the motion to strike out was agreed to.

Mr. Boutwell moved to strike out all after the words " in any of the following classes, namely," and to insert in lieu thereof the following:

First. The President and Vice-President of the Confederate States of America so-called,—the heads of departments and the members of both houses of the Congress thereof.

Second. Those who in other countries have acted as agents of the Confederate States of America, so-called.

Third. Heads of departments in the government of the United States, Judges of the Courts of the United States, officers of the army and navy of the United States, and members of either house of the Congress of the United States, who aided the late rebellion.

Fourth. Those who acted as officers of the Confederate States of America so-called, above the grade of colonel in the army or master in the navy, and any one who as governor of either of said so-called Confederate States gave aid or comfort to the rebellion.

Fifth. Those who have treated officers or soldiers or sailors of the army or navy of the United States, captured during the late war, otherwise than lawfully as prisoners of war."

After discussion,

The question was taken, and it was decided in the affirmative, yeas 8, nays 4, absent 3, as follows:

Yeas—Messrs. Grimes, Howard, Williams, Stevens, Washburne, Morrill, Conkling and Boutwell—8.

Nays—Messrs. Johnson, Bingham, Blow and Rogers—4.

Absent—Messrs. Fessenden, Harris and Grider—3.

So the amendment was agreed to.

Mr. Boutwell moved to further amend by striking out after the words " Provided, That," the words " until after the fourth day of July, 1876."

After discussion,

The question was taken, and it was decided in the affirmative, yeas 7, nays 5, absent 3, as follows:

Yeas—Messrs. Grimes, Howard, Stevens, Washburne, Conkling, Boutwell and Rogers—7.

Nays—Messrs. Johnson, Williams, Morrill, Bingham and Blow—5.

Absent—Messrs. Fessenden, Harris and Grider—3.

So the amendment was agreed to.

Mr. Morrill moved the following as an additional section:

" Sec. 2. And be it further enacted, That when any state lately in insurrection shall have ratified the foregoing proposed amendment to the Constitution, any part of the direct tax under the act of August 5, 1861, which may remain due and unpaid in such state, may be assumed and paid by such state; and the payment thereof, upon proper assurances from such state, to be given to the Secretary of the Treasury of the United States, may be postponed for a period not exceeding ten years from and after the passage of this act."

After discussion,

The question was taken, and it was decided in the affirmative, yeas 11, nays 1, absent 3, as follows:

Yeas—Messrs. Grimes, Howard, Johnson, Williams, Stevens, Washburne, Morrill, Bingham, Conkling, Boutwell and Blow—11.

Nay—Mr. Rogers—1.

Absent—Messrs. Fessenden, Harris and Grider—3.

So the additional section was adopted.

Mr. Washburne moved that the chairmen of the Senate and House portions of the joint committee (Messrs. Fessenden and Stevens) be instructed to report the joint resolution and bill agreed upon by the Committee to their respective houses; and that they ask permission to submit reports upon the same at some future time.

Mr. Grimes moved to amend the motion of *Mr. Washburne,* by striking out the last clause and inserting in lieu thereof the following:

"And that they be instructed to prepare reports to accompany the same."

Mr. Rogers asked leave for the minority of the Committee to prepare and submit their views in the shape of reports.

Pending which,

Mr. Conkling moved that when the Committee adjourn to-day, it be to meet on Wednesday next at 10½ o'clock A. M.

The question was taken, and it was decided in the affirmative, yeas 8, nays 4, absent 3, as follows:

Yeas—Messrs. Grimes, Howard, Johnson, Williams, Morrill, Conkling, Boutwell and Blow—8.

Nays—Messrs. Stevens, Washburne, Bingham and Rogers—4.

Absent—Messrs. Fessenden, Harris and Grider—3.

So the motion was agreed to.

Mr. Conkling moved that the Committee now adjourn.

The question was taken, and it was decided in the affirmative, yeas 8, nays 4, absent 3, as follows:

Yeas—Messrs. Grimes, Howard, Johnson, Williams, Morril, Conkling, Boutwell and Blow—8.

Nays—Messrs. Stevens, Washburne, Bingham and Rogers—4.

Absent—Messrs. Fessenden, Harris and Grider—3.

So the motion was agreed to, and the Committee accordingly adjourned.

Washington, April 25, 1866.

The Committee met pursuant to adjournment (Mr. Johnson in the chair); absent, Messrs. Fessenden and Washburne.

The question pending at the adjournment of the last meeting was the motion of *Mr. Washburne* instructing the chairmen of the Senate and House portions of the joint committee to report to their respective houses the joint resolution and bill agreed upon by the committee at its last meeting, and to ask leave to submit written reports at some future time to accompany the same.

To this motion *Mr. Grimes* had moved an amendment, viz.: to strike out the last clause and to insert an instruction to prepare reports to accompany the joint resolution and bill when reported.

Mr. Grimes withdrew his amendment.

The question recurred upon the motion of *Mr. Washburne.*

Pending which,

Mr. Conkling moved to amend the bill by striking out the word "usual" before the words "oath of office," and inserting in lieu thereof the word "required."

The amendment was agreed to.

Mr. Bingham moved further to amend the bill by striking out the word "oath" and inserting the word "oaths."

The amendment was agreed to.

Mr. Williams moved to amend the joint resolution by striking out the fifth section of the proposed amendment to the Constitution, as follows:

"Section 5. No state shall make or enforce any law which shall abridge the privileges or immunities of citizens of the United States; nor shall any state deprive any person of life, liberty, or property without due process of law; nor deny to any person within its jurisdiction the equal protection of the laws."

After discussion,

The question was taken, and it was decided in the affirmative, yeas 7, nays 5, absent or not voting 3, as follows:

Yeas—Messrs. Harris, Howard, Johnson, Williams, Grider, Conkling and Boutwell—7.

Nays—Messrs. Stevens, Morrill, Bingham, Rogers and Blow—5.

Absent or not voting—Messrs. Fessenden, Grimes and Washburne—3.

So the amendment was agreed to.

The question recurred upon the motion of *Mr. Washburne* to report the joint resolution and bill agreed upon to the two houses, etc.

After discussion,

The question was taken, and it was decided in the affirmative, yeas 7, nays 6, absent 2, as follows:

Yeas—Messrs. Grimes, Harris, Howard, Williams, Stevens, Morrill and Bingham—7.

Nays—Messrs. Johnson, Grider, Conkling, Boutwell, Blow and Rogers—6.

Absent—Messrs. Fessenden and Washburne—2.

So the motion was agreed to.

Mr. Bingham submitted for adoption by the Committee as a separate article of amendment to the Constitution, the section which had been stricken out of the one adopted by the Committee.

After discussion,

The question was taken, and it was decided in the negative, yeas 4, nays 8, absent or not voting 3, as follows:

Yeas—Messrs. Johnson, Bingham, Grider and Rogers—4.

Nays—Messrs. Grimes, Howard, Williams, Stevens, Morrill, Conkling, Boutwell and Blow—8.

Absent or not voting—Messrs. Fessenden, Harris and Washburne—3.

So the proposition of *Mr. Bingham* was not agreed to.

Mr. Grider gave notice that at the proper time he should submit for the consideration and action of the Committee the following resolution:

Resolved, That, in the opinion of this Committee, the people of Tennessee having elected according to law loyal men as Senators and Representatives, they should be admitted to seats in the present Congress, upon taking the usual oath of office.

Mr. Williams moved to reconsider the vote by which the Committee directed the joint resolution and bill adopted by the Committee to be reported to the two houses of Congress.

After discussion,

The question was taken, and it was decided in the affirmative, yeas 10, nays 2, absent 3, as follows:

Yeas—Messrs. Grimes, Harris, Johnson, Williams, Grider, Bingham, Conkling, Boutwell, Blow and Rogers—10.

Nays—Messrs. Howard and Stevens—2.

Absent—Messrs. Fessenden, Washburne and Morrill—3.

So the motion to reconsider was agreed to.

And then, on motion of *Mr. Grimes,*

The Committee adjourned till Saturday next, at 10½ o'clock A. M.

Washington, April 28, 1866.

The Committee met pursuant to adjournment; all the members present.

The Chairman said that the vote of the Committee ordering the joint resolution and bill agreed upon to be reported to the two houses having been reconsidered at the last meeting, the Committee would resume the consideration of the same, and they would be regarded as still open to amendment.

Mr. Stevens moved to strike out all of Section two of the proposed amendment to the Constitution of the United States as follows:

" Sec. 2. From and after the fourth day of July, in the year 1876, no discrimination shall be made by any State, nor by the United States, as to the enjoyment by classes of persons of the right of suffrage, because of race, color, or previous condition of servitude."

And the following at the beginning of section three:

" Until the fourth day of July, 1876."

So that the third section would then read,

" No class of persons, as to the right of whom to suffrage discrimination shall be made by any State because of race, color or previous condition of servitude, shall be included in the basis of representation."

After discussion,

The question was taken, and it was decided in the affirmative, yeas 12, nays 2, not voting 1, as follows:

Yeas—Messrs. Grimes, Harris, Johnson, Williams, Stevens, Morrill, Grider, Bingham, Conkling, Boutwell, Blow and Rogers—12.

Nays—Messrs. Howard and Washburne—2.

Not voting—The Chairman—1.

So the motion to strike out was agreed to.

Mr. *Williams* moved to strike out what had been section three, and to insert in lieu thereof the following:

" Representatives shall be apportioned among the several states which may be included within this Union according to their respective numbers, counting the whole number of persons in each State excluding Indians not taxed. But whenever in any State the elective franchise shall be denied to any portion of its male citizens, not less than twenty-one years of age, or in any way abridged, except for participation in rebellion or other crime, the basis of representation in such State shall be reduced in the proportion which the number of such male citizens shall bear to the whole number of male citizens not less than twenty-one years of age."

After discussion,

The question was taken, and it was decided in the affirmative, yeas 12, nays 3, as follows:

Yeas—The Chairman, Messrs. Grimes, Harris, Johnson, Williams, Morrill, Grider, Bingham, Conkling, Boutwell, Blow and Rogers—12.

Nays—Messrs. Howard, Stevens and Washburne—3.

So the motion of *Mr. Williams* was agreed to.

The Committee proceeded to consider the following section:

" Sec. 4. Debts or obligations already incurred or which may hereafter be incurred in aid of insurrection or of war against the Union, and claims for compensation for loss of involuntary service or labor, shall not be paid by any State, nor by the United States."

Mr. Rogers moved to amend by striking out the words "by any State, nor."

The question was taken, and it was decided in the negative, yeas 3, nays 12, as follows:

Yeas—Messrs. Johnson, Grider and Rogers—3.

Nays—The Chairman, Messrs. Grimes, Harris, Howard, Williams, Stevens, Washburne, Morrill, Bingham, Conkling, Boutwell and Blow—12.

So the amendment was rejected.

Mr. Bingham moved to change the phraseology of the section, so that it should read,

"Neither the United States nor any State shall assume or pay any debt or obligation already incurred, or which may hereafter be incurred, in aid of insurrection, or of war against the United States, or any claim for compensation for loss of involuntary service or labor."

The motion was agreed to.

Mr. Boutwell moved to insert the following as an additional section:

"Sec. —. The President and Vice-President of the late Confederate States of America so-called; the heads of departments thereof; those who in other countries acted as agents of the Confederate States of America so-called; those who, having been heads of departments of the United States, or officers of the army or navy of the United States, or members of either house of the 36th Congress of the United States, afterwards aided in the late rebellion; and any one who as governor of either of the so-called Confederate States gave aid or comfort to the late rebellion, are declared to be forever ineligible to any office under the United States."

Mr. *Stevens* moved to amend the section proposed by *Mr. Boutwell* by inserting after the clause relating to confederate agents in foreign countries the following:

" officers of the army or navy of the Confederate States of America so-called, above the rank of colonel in the army, or master in the navy."

After discussion,

The question was taken, and it was decided in the negative, yeas 3, nays 12, as follows:

Yeas—Messrs. Stevens, Washburne and Conkling—3.

Nays—The Chairman, Messrs. Grimes, Harris, Howard, Johnson, Williams, Morrill, Grider, Bingham, Boutwell, Blow and Rogers—12.

So the amendment of *Mr. Stevens* was not agreed to.

The question was then taken upon the section proposed by *Mr. Boutwell,* and it was decided in the negative, yeas 6, nays 8, not voting 1, as follows:

Yeas—Messrs. Harris, Stevens, Washburne, Morrill, Conkling and Boutwell—6.

Nays—The Chairman, Messrs. Howard, Johnson, Williams, Grider, Bingham, Blow and Rogers—8.

Not voting—Mr. Grimes—1.

So the section was not agreed to.

Mr. Harris moved to insert the following as an additional section to follow the section in relation to representation:

" Sec. —. Until the fourth day of July, in the year 1870, all persons who voluntarily adhered to the late insurrection, giving it aid and comfort, shall be excluded from the right to vote for Representatives in Congress and for electors for President and Vice-President of the United States."

After discussion,

The question was taken, and it was decided in the negative, yeas 7, nays 8, as follows:

Yeas—Messrs. Harris, Howard, Stevens, Washburne, Morrill, Conkling and Boutwell—7.

Nays—The Chairman, Messrs. Grimes, Johnson, Williams, Grider, Bingham, Blow and Rogers—8.

So the section proposed by *Mr. Harris* was not agreed to. Subsequently, after discussion,

Mr. Grimes moved to reconsider the vote by which the section proposed by *Mr. Harris* was rejected.

The question was taken, and it was decided in the affirmative, yeas 8, nays 5, not voting 2, as follows:

Yeas—The Chairman, Messrs. Grimes, Harris, Howard, Stevens, Morrill, Conkling and Boutwell—8.

Nays—Messrs. Johnson, Grider, Bingham, Blow and Rogers—5.

Not voting—Messrs. Williams and Washburne—2.

So the motion to reconsider was agreed to.

Mr. Williams said that upon this section he was paired with *Mr. Washburne* who had temporarily left the committee room.

The question recurred upon agreeing to the section proposed by *Mr. Harris*.

The question was taken, and it was decided in the affirmative, yeas 7, nays 6, not voting 2, as follows:

Yeas—Messrs. Grimes, Harris, Howard, Stevens, Morrill, Conkling and Boutwell—7.

Nays—The Chairman, Messrs. Johnson, Grider, Bingham, Blow and Rogers—6.

Not voting—Messrs. Williams and Washburne—2.

So the section was adopted.

The section granting power to Congress to enforce the provisions of the article was adopted.

Mr. Bingham moved to strike out the first section of the proposed amendment to the Constitution, which was as follows:

"Section 1. No discrimination shall be made by any State, or by the United States, as to the civil rights of persons, because of race, color or previous condition of servitude."

and to insert in lieu thereof the following:

"Sec. 1. No State shall make or enforce any law which shall abridge the privileges or immunities of citizens of the United States; nor shall any State deprive any person of life, liberty, or property, without due process of law, nor deny to any person within its jurisdiction the equal protection of the laws."

After discussion,

The question was taken, and it was decided in the affirmative, yeas 10, nays 3, not voting 2, as follows:

Yeas—Messrs. Johnson, Williams, Stevens, Washburne, Grider, Bingham, Conkling, Boutwell, Blow and Rogers—10.

Nays—Messrs. Grimes, Howard and Morrill—3.

Not voting—The Chairman and Mr. Harris—2.

So the motion of *Mr. Bingham* was agreed to.

The Committee then proceeded to the consideration of the bill to provide for restoring to the states lately in insurrection their full political rights.

Mr. Boutwell moved that that portion relating to certain persons to be excluded from office be considered as a separate bill.

The motion was agreed to.

The preamble was modified, in so far as it recites the proposed amendment to the Constitution, to correspond with the action of the Committee this morning.

The Committee proceeded to consider the following section:

"*Be it enacted, etc.,* That whenever the above recited amendment shall have become part of the Constitution of the United States, and any State lately in insurrection shall have ratified the same and shall have modified its constitution and laws in conformity with the first section thereof, the senators and representatives from such state, if found duly elected and qualified, shall, after having taken the required oaths of office, be admitted into Congress as such."

After discussion,

The Chairman moved to strike out the word "shall" and insert the word " may " before the words " after having taken," etc.

The motion was agreed to.

Mr. Boutwell moved to amend the section by striking out all after the word " that " and inserting the following:

" whenever the above recited amendment shall have become a part of the Constitution of the United States and whenever either Tennessee or Arkansas shall have ratified the same, and shall have so modified its constitution and laws as to make them conform thereto, and shall have provided a system of equal suffrage for all loyal male citizens within its jurisdiction who are not less than twenty-one years of age, the Senators and Representatives from such state, if found duly elected and qualified, shall, after having taken the required oaths of office, be admitted into Congress as such; provided, that nothing contained in this act shall be so construed as to disfranchise any loyal person now entitled to vote."

Mr. Bingham moved to amend the amendment by striking out all the first part to and including the words " the same," and inserting " whenever either Tennessee or Arkansas shall have ratified the above recited amendment."

After discussion,

The question was taken upon the amendment to the amendment, and it was decided in the negative, yeas 4, nays 7, not voting 4, as follows:

Yeas—Messrs. Johnson, Williams, Bingham and Blow—4.

Nays—The Chairman, Messrs. Grimes, Howard, Stevens, Morrill, Grider and Rogers—7.

Not voting—Messrs. Harris, Washburne, Conkling and Boutwell—4.

So the amendment to the amendment was not agreed to.

The question was then taken upon the amendment of *Mr.*

Boutwell, and it was decided in the negative, yeas 2, nays 9, not voting 4, as follows:

Yeas—Messrs. Johnson and Boutwell—2.

Nays—The Chairman, Messrs. Grimes, Howard, Williams, Stevens, Grider, Bingham, Blow and Rogers—9.

Not voting—Messrs. Harris, Washburne, Morrill and Conkling—4.

So the amendment was not agreed to.

Mr. Conkling moved to amend the first section of the bill under consideration by striking out the words " with the first section thereof," and inserting the word " therewith " in lieu thereof.

The amendment was agreed to.

Mr. Williams moved to amend by striking out all after the words " That whenever," and inserting the following:

" any one of the states lately in rebellion shall ratify the above recited amendment as required by the Constitution of the United States, the Senators and Representatives of such state shall, after the 4th day of March, 1867, if found duly elected and qualified and after taking the required oaths of office, be admitted into Congress as such; Provided that Senators and Representatives from Tennessee and Arkansas, elected and qualified as aforesaid, shall be admitted into Congress as soon as said states respectively shall ratify said amendment as aforesaid."

After discussion,

The question was taken, and it was decided in the negative, yeas 4, nays 9, not voting 2, as follows:

Yeas—Messrs. Johnson, Williams, Bingham and Blow —4.

Nays—The Chairman, Messrs. Grimes, Howard, Stevens, Morrill, Grider, Conkling, Boutwell and Rogers—9.

Not voting—Messrs. Harris and Washburne—2.

So the amendment was not agreed to.

The first section as amended was then agreed to.

The second section in relation to the direct tax was agreed to.

The Committee then proceeded to consider the bill declaring certain persons ineligible to office.

The first part was as follows:

"*Be it enacted, etc.*, That no person shall be eligible to either branch of the National Legislature who is included in any of the following classes, namely,"

Mr. Conkling moved to amend by striking out the words " either branch of the National Legislature," and inserting the words " any office under the government of the United States."

The amendment was agreed to.

The next clause was as follows:

" First. The President and Vice-President of the Confederate States of America so-called, the heads of departments and members of both houses of Congress thereof."

The Chairman moved to amend by striking out the words " and members of both houses of Congress."

The question was taken, and it was decided in the affirmative, yeas 10, nays 5, as follows:

Yeas—The Chairman, Messrs. Grimes, Johnson, Williams, Morrill, Grider, Bingham, Boutwell, Blow and Rogers—10.

Nays—Messrs. Harris, Howard, Stevens, Washburne and Conkling—5.

So the amendment was agreed to.

The next clause was as follows:

" Second. Those who in other countries acted as agents of the Confederate States of America so-called."

Mr. Howard moved to strike it out.

The question was taken, and it was decided in the negative, yeas 3, nays 12, as follows:

Yeas—Messrs. Howard, Grider and Rogers—3.

Nays—The Chairman, Messrs. Grimes, Harris, Johnson, Williams, Stevens, Washburne, Morrill, Bingham, Conkling, Boutwell and Blow—12.

So the motion to strike out was not agreed to.

The next clause was as follows:

" Third. Heads of departments in the Government of the United States, officers of the army and navy of the United States, Judges of the Courts of the United States, and members of either house of the 36th Congress of the United States who aided the late rebellion."

Mr. Grimes moved to amend by inserting before the word " Judges," the words " and all persons educated at the naval or military academy of the United States."

The amendment was agreed to.

The next clause was as follows:

" Fourth. Those who acted as officers of the Confederate States of America so-called, above the grade of colonel in the army or master in the navy; and any one who as governor of either of the so-called Confederate States gave aid or comfort to the rebellion."

Mr. Grimes moved to amend by striking out the words " Those who acted as officers of the Confederate States of America so-called, above the grade of colonel in the army or master in the navy, and."

After discussion,

The question was taken, and it was decided in the negative, yeas 4, nays 11, as follows:

Yeas—Messrs. Grimes, Johnson, Grider and Rogers—4.

Nays—The Chairman, Messrs. Harris, Howard, Williams, Stevens, Washburne, Morrill, Bingham, Conkling, Boutwell and Blow—11.

So the amendment was not agreed to.

The next clause was agreed to as follows:

" Fifth. Those who treated officers or soldiers or sailors of the army or navy of the United States, captured during the late war, otherwise than lawfully as prisoners of war."

Mr. Grider submitted the following resolutions:

Resolved, That, in the opinion of this Committee, the people of Tennessee having elected according to law loyal men as Senators and Representatives, they should be admitted to seats in the present Congress upon taking the usual oath of office.

Resolved, further, That each of the states not now represented should be allowed representation upon the same terms.

Mr. Grimes moved to amend the first resolution by adding thereto the following:

" Provided they comply with the terms agreed upon by the Committee this session."

The question was taken, and it was decided in the affirmative, yeas 9, nays 4, not voting 2, as follows:

Yeas—The Chairman, Messrs. Grimes, Harris, Howard, Williams, Stevens, Morrill, Bingham and Conkling—9.

Nays—Messrs. Johnson, Grider, Blow and Rogers—4.

Not voting—Messrs. Washburne and Boutwell—2.

So the amendment was agreed to.

Mr. Stevens moved to lay the resolutions on the table.

The question was taken, and it was decided in the negative, yeas 5, nays 7, not voting 3, as follows:

Yeas—Messrs. Howard, Williams, Stevens, Morrill and Bingham—5.

Nays—Messrs. Grimes, Harris, Johnson, Grider, Conkling, Blow and Rogers—7.

Not voting—The Chairman, Messrs. Washburne and Boutwell—3.

So the motion to lay on the table was not agreed to.

The question recurred upon agreeing to the resolution as amended.

The question was taken, and it was decided in the negative, yeas 2, nays 10, not voting 3, as follows:

Yeas—Messrs. Grimes and Johnson—2.

Nays—Messrs. Harris, Howard, Williams, Stevens, Morrill, Grider, Bingham, Conkling, Blow and Rogers—10.

Not voting—The Chairman, Messrs. Washburne and Boutwell—3.

So the resolutions were not adopted.

Mr. Stevens moved that the joint resolution and bills adopted by the Committee to-day be reported on Monday next to the two houses of Congress, and that leave be asked to submit at some future time reports to accompany the same.

Mr. Boutwell asked that a separate vote be taken upon the joint resolution and bills; which was ordered.

The first question was upon reporting the joint resolution proposing an amendment to the Constitution of the United States.

The question was taken, and it was decided in the affirmative, yeas 12, nays 3, as follows:

Yeas—The Chairman, Messrs. Grimes, Harris, Howard, Williams, Stevens, Washburne, Morrill, Bingham, Conkling, Boutwell and Blow—12.

Nays—Messrs. Johnson, Grider and Rogers—3.

So the motion to report the joint resolution was agreed to.

The next question was upon reporting the bill to provide for restoring to the States lately in insurrection their full political rights.

The question was taken, and it was decided in the affirmative, yeas 12, nays 3, as follows:

Yeas—The Chairman, Messrs. Grimes, Harris, Howard, Williams, Stevens, Washburne, Morrill, Bingham, Conkling, Boutwell and Blow—12.

Nays—Messrs. Johnson, Grider and Rogers—3.

So the motion was agreed to.

The next question was upon reporting the bill declaring certain persons ineligible to office under the government of the United States.

The question was taken, and it was decided in the affirmative, yeas 12, nays 3, as follows:

Yeas—The Chairman, Messrs. Grimes, Harris, Howard, Williams, Stevens, Washburne, Morrill, Bingham, Conkling, Boutwell and Blow—12.

Nays—Messrs. Johnson, Grider and Rogers—3.

So the motion was agreed to.

On motion of *Mr. Rogers,* it was

Ordered, That the minority of the Committee have leave to submit minority reports.

On motion of *Mr. Grimes,* it was

Ordered, That the injunction of secrecy be removed, so far as relates to the results of the action of the Committee at this session.

On motion of *Mr. Boutwell,* it was

Ordered, That the stenographer of this Committee be authorized to furnish to the agent of the associated press, and the correspondents of such newspapers as may apply to him, copies of the joint resolution and bills adopted by the Committee to-day, after the same shall have been submitted to and approved by the Chairman.

The joint resolution and bills adopted are as follows:

A joint resolution proposing an amendment to the Constitution of the United States.

Be it resolved, by the Senate and House of Representatives of the United States of America in Congress assembled (two-thirds of both Houses concurring), That the following article be proposed to the Legislatures of the several States as an amendment to the Constitution of the United States, which, when ratified by three-fourths of said

Legislatures, shall be valid as part of the Constitution, namely:

Article —

Sec. 1. No state shall make or enforce any law which shall abridge the privileges or immunities of citizens of the United States; nor shall any State deprive any person of life, liberty, or property without due process of law; nor deny to any person within its jurisdiction the equal protection of the laws.

Sec. 2. Representatives shall be apportioned among the several States which may be included within this Union according to their respective numbers, counting the whole number of persons in each State, excluding Indians not taxed. But whenever in any State the elective franchise shall be denied to any portion of its male citizens not less than twenty-one years of age, or in any way abridged, except for participation in rebellion or other crime, the basis of representation in such State shall be reduced in the proportion which the number of male citizens shall bear to the whole number of such male citizens not less than twenty-one years of age.

Sec. 3. Until the 4th day of July, in the year 1870, all persons who voluntarily adhered to the late insurrection, giving it aid and comfort, shall be excluded from the right to vote for Representatives in Congress and for electors for President and Vice-President of the United States.

Sec. 4. Neither the United States nor any State shall assume or pay any debt or obligation already incurred, or which may hereafter be incurred, in aid of insurrection or of war against the United States, or any claim for compensation for loss of involuntary service or labor.

Sec. 5. The Congress shall have power to enforce by appropriate legislation the provisions of this article.

A bill to provide for restoring to the States lately in insurrection their full political rights.

Whereas, It is expedient that the States lately in insurrection should at the earliest day consistent with the future peace and safety of the Union, be restored to full participation in all political rights; and whereas the Congress did, by joint resolution, propose for ratification to the Legislatures of the several States, as an amendment to the Constitution of the United States, an article in the following words, to wit:

" Article—

" Sec. 1. No State shall make or enforce any law which shall abridge the privileges or immunities of citizens of the United States; nor shall any State deprive any person of life, liberty, or property without due process of law; nor deny to any person within its jurisdiction the equal protection of the laws.

" Sec. 2. Representatives shall be apportioned among the several States which may be included within this Union, according to their respective numbers, counting the whole number of persons in each State, excluding Indians not taxed. But whenever, in any State, the elective franchise shall be denied to any portion of its male citizens not less than twenty-one years of age, or in any way abridged except for participation in rebellion or other crime, the basis of representation in such State shall be reduced in the proportion which the number of such male citizens shall bear to the whole number of male citizens not less than twenty-one years of age.

"Sec. 3. Until the 4th day of July, in the year 1870, all persons who voluntarily adhered to the late insurrection, giving it aid and comfort, shall be excluded from the right to vote for Representatives in Congress, and for electors for President and Vice-President of the United States.

"Sec. 4. Neither the United States nor any State shall assume or pay any debt or obligation already incurred, or which may hereafter be incurred, in aid of insurrection or of war against the United States, or any claim for compensation for loss of involuntary service or labor.

"Sec. 5. The Congress shall have power to enforce by appropriate legislation the provisions of this article."

Now, therefore,

Be it enacted, by the Senate and House of Representatives of the United States of America in Congress assembled, That whenever the above recited amendment shall have become part of the Constitution of the United States, and any State lately in insurrection shall have ratified the same, and shall have modified its constitution and laws in conformity therewith, the Senators and Representatives from such State, if found duly elected and qualified, may, after having taken the required oaths of office, be admitted into Congress as such.

Sec. 2. And be it further enacted, That when any State

lately in insurrection shall have ratified the foregoing amendment to the Constitution, any part of the direct tax under the act of August 5, 1861, which may remain due and unpaid in such State may be assumed and paid by such State; and the payment thereof, upon proper assurances from such State to be given to the Secretary of the Treasury of the United States, may be postponed for a period not exceeding ten years from and after the passage of this act.

A Bill declaring certain persons ineligible to office under the Government of the United States.

Be it enacted, by the Senate and House of Representatives of the United States of America in Congress assembled, That no person shall be eligible to any office under the Government of the United States who is included in any of the following classes, namely:

1. The President and Vice-President of the Confederate States of America, so-called, and the heads of departments thereof.

2. Those who in other countries acted as agents of the Confederate States of America, so-called.

3. Heads of Departments of the United States, officers of the Army and Navy of the United States, and all persons educated at the Military or Naval Academy of the United States, judges of the courts of the United States, and members of either House of the Thirty-Sixth Congress of the United States who gave aid or comfort to the late rebellion.

4. Those who acted as officers of the Confederate States

of America, so-called, above the grade of colonel in the army or master in the navy, and any one who, as Governor of either of the so-called Confederate States, gave aid or comfort to the rebellion.

5. Those who have treated officers or soldiers or sailors of the Army or Navy of the United States, captured during the late war, otherwise than lawfully as prisoners of war.

And then on motion of *Mr. Grimes,*

The Committee adjourned to meet upon the call of its Chairman.

Washington, June 6, 1866.

The Committee met pursuant to the call of its Chairman; absent, Messrs. Washburne, Blow, Rogers, Johnson, Grider and Conkling.

The Chairman stated that he had called the Committee together for the purpose of laying before them a report he had prepared to accompany the measures which at the last meeting the Committee directed to be reported to the two houses of Congress.

The report was read and adopted.

On motion of *Mr. Howard,*

The Chairmen of the Senate and House portions of the Joint Committee were instructed to submit the report just adopted to their respective houses.

Adjourned to meet on call of the Chairman.

    Attest

      (Sgd.) WM. BLAIR LORD, *Clerk.*

SECOND SESSION.

IN THE HOUSE OF REPRESENTATIVES,

December 4th, 1866.

Resolved (the Senate concurring), That the Joint Committee of Fifteen on Reconstruction, appointed during the last session of Congress, shall be reappointed under the same rules and regulations as then existed, and that all the documents and resolutions which were referred then be now considered as referred to them anew.

Attest

EDWD. MCPHERSON, *Clerk.*

IN THE SENATE OF THE UNITED STATES,

December 5, 1866.

Resolved, That the Senate concur in the foregoing resolution of the House of Representatives, relative to the reappointment of the Joint Committee of Fifteen on Reconstruction.

Attest

J. W. FORNEY, *Secretary.*
by W. J. MCDONALD, *Chief Clerk.*

OFFICE HOUSE OF REPRESENTATIVES U. S.,

February 15th, 1867.

I certify that the foregoing is a true copy of the original now on file in this office.

Attest

EDWD. MCPHERSON, *Clerk.*

Members on the part of the Senate.

Mr. William P. Fessenden of Maine.
" James W. Grimes, " Iowa.
" Ira Harris, " New York.
" Jacob M. Howard, " Michigan.
" Reverdy Johnson, " Maryland.
and " George H. Williams, " Oregon.

Members on the part of the House of Rep's.

Mr. Thaddeus Stevens, of Penn'a.
" John F. Farnsworth, " Illinois, vice Mr. Washburne excused.
" Justin S. Morrill, " Vermont.
" Elijah Hise, " Kentucky, vice Mr. Grider deceased.
" John A. Bingham, " Ohio.
" Roscoe Conkling, " New York.
" George S. Boutwell, " Mass.
" Henry T. Blow, " Missouri.
and " Andrew J. Rogers, " New Jersey.

Washington, Feb. 2, 1867.

The Committee met on call of the Chairman at Senate Committee Room on the Pacific Railroad. Present, Mr. Fessenden (Chairman) and the entire Committee.

On motion of *Mr. Stevens,* House Bill (Substitute for House Bill No. 543) was read, when,

On motion of *Mr. Bingham,* the original Bill was also read. After reference had been made to both bills, *Mr. Stevens* submitted the following resolution:

" That the States lately in Rebellion shall be reconstructed upon the principle of granting them enabling Acts to form their State Constitutions," which, after some discussion, was modified by him on leave as follows:

"That the States lately in Rebellion shall be reconstructed upon the principle, " *providing by Act of Congress that they may form State Constitutions and Governments.*"

The discussion upon this motion was continued by Messrs. Stevens, Howard, Bingham, Conkling, Johnson, Williams, Farnsworth and Boutwell, during which time, *Mr. Bingham* asked leave to amend the original House Bill No. 543 as follows, add after word " therewith " the following, " And shall have secured impartial suffrage to the male citizens of the U. S. of full age resident therein," the section amended reading as follows:

" *Be it enacted,* by the Senate and House of Representatives of the United States of America in Congress assembled, That whenever the above recited amendment shall have become part of the Constitution of the United States, and any State lately in insurrection shall have ratified the same, and shall have modified its constitution and laws in conformity therewith, and shall have secured impartial suffrage to the male citizens of the United States, of full age resident therein, the senators and representatives from such State, if found duly elected and qualified, may, after having taken the required oaths of office, be admitted into Congress as such.

Pending discussion of *Mr. Stevens'* Resolution, it being near 12 o'clock,

On motion of *Mr. Howard,* the Committee adjourned to meet on Wednesday morning next at 10 o'clock.

Wednesday, Feb. 6, 1867.

The Committee met pursuant to adjournment. Present, The Chairman, Messrs. Grimes, Harris, Howard, Johnson, Williams, Stevens, Farnsworth, Morrill, Bingham, Conkling, Boutwell and Blow.

Absent, Messrs. Hise and Rogers.

On motion of the *Chairman,* Geo. A. Mark was appointed as clerk to the Committee.

On motion of the *Chairman,* it was agreed that the proceedings of the Committee should be considered as secret and confidential.

Mr. Conkling moved that the further consideration of pending resolution be postponed, and Senate Bill 564 be taken up.

The motion was agreed to.

After reading of S. B. 564 [1] by the Chairman, Mr. Conkling presented the same with amendments.

The Committee then proceeded to the consideration of the preamble, and the several sections of the bill.

Mr. Conkling moved to amend the preamble, by inserting after the word " Congress," in the fourth line, " and without the sanction of the people."

The amendment was agreed to.

[[1] This was the number of a bill which became the Reconstruction Act of March 2, 1867. For the language of the bill as introduced, see *infra,* ch. viii.—B. B. Kendrick.]

It was also agreed to strike out in the fifth line the words " and therefore are of no constitutional validity."

Mr. Farnsworth moved to insert after the word "whereas" the words " said pretended governments," striking out down to the word, " afford," in the seventh line, so that it would read, " and whereas said pretended governments afford, etc."

The question was taken by yeas and nays, and it was decided in the affirmative, yeas 8, nays 5, absent 2.

Yeas—The Chairman, Messrs. Grimes, Harris, Johnson, Farnsworth, Morrill, Bingham and Blow—8.

Nays—Messrs. Howard, Williams, Stevens, Conkling and Boutwell—5.

Absent—Messrs. Rogers and Hise—2.

So the amendment was agreed to.

Mr. Johnson moved to further amend, by striking out in the eigth line the words, " but countenance and encourage lawlessness and crime."

The amendment was not agreed to.

In the eleventh line it was agreed to amend by striking out the word " formed," and inserting the word "established."

Mr. Bingham offered the following as a substitute for the preamble, viz.:

" *Whereas,* It is necessary that peace and good order should be enforced in the several states of Virginia, North Carolina, South Carolina, Georgia, Mississippi, Alabama, Louisiana, Florida, Texas and Arkansas, lately in rebellion, until said states shall be fully restored to their constitutional relations to the Government of the United States."

The question was taken by yeas and nays, and it was decided in the negative, yeas 4, nays 9, absent 2.

Yeas—Messrs. Grimes, Johnson, Bingham and Blow—4.

Nays—The Chairman, Messrs. Harris, Howard, Williams, Stevens, Farnsworth, Morrill, Conkling and Boutwell—9.

Absent—Messrs. Rogers and Hise—2.

So the substitute of *Mr. Bingham* was not agreed to.

The Committee next proceeded to the consideration of the first section, amended by *Mr. Conkling,* so that after the enacting clause, it should read as follows:

" That said so-called states shall be divided into military districts and made subject to the military authority of the United States as hereinafter prescribed, and for that purpose Virginia shall constitute the first district; North Carolina and South Carolina the second district; Georgia, Alabama and Florida the third district; Mississippi and Arkansas the fourth district; Texas and Louisiana the fifth district."

Mr. Bingham moved to amend the section as amended by substituting after the enacting clause the following:

" That said states be divided into five military districts as follows," etc.

The question was taken by yeas and nays, and it was decided in the negative, yeas 2, nays 9, absent or not voting 4.

Yeas—Messrs. Johnson and Bingham—2.

Nays—The Chairman, Messrs. Harris, Howard, Stevens, Farnsworth, Morrill, Conkling, Boutwell and Blow —9.

Absent or not voting—Messrs. Grimes, Williams, Rogers and Hise—4.

So the amendment of *Mr. Bingham* was not agreed to.

Mr. Bingham moved to amend by striking out in the third line the word, " so-called."

The amendment was not agreed to.

The question then recurred upon the adoption of the section as amended by *Mr. Conkling,*

And the section was adopted.

The amendments to the second section submitted by *Mr. Conkling* were agreed to and the section read as follows:

" Sec. 2. And be it further enacted, That it shall be the duty of the General of the army, under the authority of the President, to assign to the command of each of said districts an officer of the regular army, not below the rank of brigadier-general, and to detail a sufficient military force to enable such officer to perform his duties and enforce his authority within the district to which he is assigned."

The third section was then taken up, and after discussion,

Mr. Harris moved to amend by striking out in the sixth line the word " local " and insert the word " civil."

The amendment was agreed to.

Mr. Bingham moved to amend by striking out in the second and third lines the words, " peaceable and law-abiding."

The amendment was agreed to.

Mr. Bingham moved further to amend by inserting in line nine, after the word " tribunals," the words " in the mode prescribed by existing laws for courts-martial."

The amendment was not agreed to.

Mr. *Bingham* moved to amend by inserting after the word " all," in the eleventh line, the word " local."

The amendment was not agreed to.

And the section as amended was then adopted.

The amendments to section four submitted by *Mr. Conkling* were agreed to, and the section read as follows:

" Sec. 4. And be it further enacted, That courts and judicial officers of the United States shall not issue writs of habeas corpus in behalf of persons in military custody, unless some commissioned officer on duty in the district wherein the person is detained shall indorse upon said petition a statement certifying, upon honor, that he has knowledge, or information, as to the cause and circumstance of the alleged detention, and that he believes the same to be wrongful; and further that he believes that the indorsed petition is preferred in good faith, and in furtherance of justice, and not to hinder or delay the punishment of crime. All persons put under military arrest by virtue of this act shall be tried without unnecessary delay, and no cruel or unusual punishment shall be inflicted."

And the section as amended was adopted.

The amendments to Section five, as proposed by *Mr. Conkling* were agreed to, and it then read as follows:

" Sec. 5. And be it further enacted, That no sentence of any military commission or tribunal hereby authorized, affecting the life or liberty of any person, shall be executed until it is approved by the officer in command of the district, and the laws and regulations for the government of the army shall not be affected by this act, except in so far as they conflict with its provisions."

And the section was adopted as amended.

Mr. *Howard* moved to further amend the second section, by striking out in the second and third lines, the words, " under the authority of the President."

After discussion, the amendment of Mr. *Howard* was agreed to.

Mr. *Harris* moved that the Chairmen of the Senate and House portions of the Committee report the bill to their respective bodies.

The motion was not agreed to.

It was then moved that Mr. *Stevens* report the bill as amended to the House.

The motion was agreed to.

Mr. *Bingham* moved to report back to the House the bill previously reported.

The motion was not agreed to.

After discussion, the Committee adjourned to meet on Saturday next at 10 o'clock.

Saturday, February 9, 1867.

The Committee met pursuant to adjournment.

Present, The Chairman, Messrs. Williams, Bingham, Boutwell and Blow.

A quorum not being present, the Committee adjourned to meet on call of the Chairman.

GEORGE A. MARK, *Clerk.*

PART II

THE HISTORY OF THE JOINT COMMITTEE ON RECONSTRUCTION

CHAPTER I

Origin of the Committee

So long as the Civil War continued, the interest of people and politicians in the North was directed almost entirely toward the movements of the Union armies in their contests with those of the Confederacy. But it was realized by the thoughtful that the question of restoring the seceded states to their places in the Union must be met so soon as the authority of the United States should again be recognized throughout their territory. Certain members of Congress, under the leadership of Representative Henry Winter Davis, of Maryland, and Senator Benjamin Wade, of Ohio, succeeded in 1864 in passing a bill, in which the conditions whereby the rebellious states might be readmitted, were defined. Lincoln, however, refused to commit himself to any general plan of reconstruction, but thought it best to act separately on each state according to the conditions existing in it. In the case of Louisiana [1] he had caused to be established a government based on the suffrage of the loyal voters, who constituted but little more than ten per cent of the voting population of 1860. Though he recognized this government as legal and in proper relation to the executive department of the United States Government, it was not so recognized by the legislative department, and some of the more radical Congressmen referred to it derisively as the President's "ten per cent" government.

[1] Likewise Arkansas. The military government in Tennessee and the Peirpoint government in Virginia were of a different character.

Just what the attitude of the country toward President Lincoln's attempts at reconstruction in Louisiana and elsewhere was, it is difficult to say. Certainly the protest of Wade and Davis against Lincoln's pocket veto of their bill met with no marked public response, but the fact must not be lost sight of that neither Wade nor Davis had any great amount of popular following, while Lincoln was becoming already something of a popular idol. Therefore, the indorsement of his policy and his unanimous renomination by the Union party in 1864 does not imply that his reconstruction policy was approved, or that the Wade-Davis bill was opposed either by the politicians or by the rank and file of the Republican electorate. Hence, during the war, no theory of reconstruction was enacted into law, and of so little consequence was Lincoln's actual reconstruction in a few of the states, that the whole discussion of the question remained, until the death of Lincoln, of little importance.[1]

As the end of Lincoln's administration marked the close of the war, so the beginning of Johnson's ushered in reconstruction. The ideas of the two men regarding the status of the seceded states were identical. Hence, within a few weeks after becoming President, Johnson began to carry forward the work of reconstruction along the lines laid down by his predecessor. He recognized as regular those state organizations that had been established during the war, and appointed provisional governors in the states where no such organizations existed. At the direction of the President, each of these provisional governors called a convention for the purpose of creating a permanent government in harmony with that of the United States. To the

---

[1] Rhodes, *History of the United States*, vol. iv, pp. 484-486; Dunning, *Essays on Civil War and Reconstruction*, pp. 67-70, 76-78.

conventions which assembled, Johnson cannot be said to have given definite instructions, but he did let it be understood that the executive department of the Federal Government, while leaving the franchise in the hands of the whites, desired that at least three conditions be complied with, viz., the ratification of the thirteenth amendment abolishing slavery, the repudiation of the war debts, and a declaration that the ordinances of secession were null and void from the beginning.

During the summer and fall of 1865, most of these conventions succeeded in creating new state governments, state officers were elected, and in some cases senators and representatives to Congress were chosen. Thus, by the time Congress met on December 4, 1865, the process of restoration was from the standpoint of the executive well-nigh complete.[1] There is little doubt that the majority of the people in the North were in sympathy with the President's plan of restoration. Party conventions, Democratic and Union, in nearly every state endorsed it.[2] Few if any newspapers opposed it, though a certain element of the press, like the New York *Tribune, Harper's Weekly* and the *Nation*, advocated making negro suffrage a fourth condition precedent to readmission of the seceded states.[3]

---

[1] For discussion of Johnson's policy of reconstruction and the process of its accomplishment, see Dunning, *Reconstruction, Political and Economic*, chap. iii; also *Essays*, pp. 78-84, 103, 104; Rhodes, vol. v, chap. xxx.

[2] Rhodes, vol. v, pp. 533, 534.

[3] The early success of the President's policy proved to be one element at least in its later weakness. Its hearty approval by the Democrats was sufficient to cause many Republicans to view it with suspicion. Henry J. Raymond, editor of the Republican New York *Times*, declared that the majority of Union Congressmen would have supported the President had the Democrats opposed him. See Blaine, *Twenty Years of Congress*, vol. ii.

But there was opposition to the President's policy, and it came from a source where it was most likely to cause trouble —the radical members of Congress. Several reasons, explanatory of this opposition, may be stated. Of prime importance among these were party considerations. Every Republican politician believed that the Democrats in the South, upon the restoration of their states, would renew their ancient party affiliations with their friends in the North. He also believed that since negroes in the South were not allowed to vote, all the southern Congressmen would belong to the Democratic party. He therefore demanded that either the negroes be given the franchise, thereby dividing the southern delegation and securing the election of a fair number of Republicans; or failing that, that the negroes be excluded from the basis of representation.[1] A second reason for Congressional opposition is to be found in the prevalence of the feeling that the legislative branch of the government should resume that superiority which during the war it had lost to the executive.[2] Third, among most Congressmen there was a sincere or pretended affection for the negroes in the South, and it was believed that unless something else be done for their security, they would be reduced to a condition bordering on slavery. Fourth, there was a determination on the part of some of the more statesmanlike members of Congress, that the Federal Government should now be strengthened by

[1] See speech by Thaddeus Stevens, December 18, 1865, *Globe*, 1st session, 39th Congress, pp. 72-75.

[2] See *Globe*, 1st session, 39th Congress, p. 27, for Senator Fessenden's speech on this question. Among other things he said: "In all countries, in a time of extreme peril, extreme and somewhat questionable measures are inevitable, but in time of peace, when we live under a written constitution it is our duty to come back as fast as possible; to forget if necessary any precedent which might, if made in times like these, have occasioned very serious difficulty and trouble."

putting in its keeping the power to enforce throughout the Union the bill of rights.[1] Fifth, it cannot be denied that some of the opposition to the President's liberal policy was due to hatred of the South. There was a class of public men who were captious, exacting, and implacable, not so much from devotion to any principle as from original bent. There was no end to the requirements they would have imposed. They dealt with the whole business in the mood of a Shylock and seem to have desired principally to " feed fat the ancient grudge." [2]

For these reasons, as the time for the meeting of Congress approached, it became more and more evident that the radicals [3] would not adopt the policy of the President; but there was considerable doubt as to whether they would be able to carry with them, in their opposition to Johnson, a majority of the members of Congress. At this time, December 4, 1865, the President was still popular, and the ordinary politicians, who, then as always, were interested principally in holding their positions and retaining the confidence of their constituents, hardly would have dared to oppose a policy which most of them had previously endorsed, had it not been for the astute leadership of Thaddeus Stevens. To bring into line against the policy of the President those Republican Congressmen who, tacitly at least, had promised to support it, was the task of no ordinary politician. The story of how Stevens forced the majority party in the lower House to commit themselves against the policy of the President, is the story of the origin of the joint committee on reconstruction.

[1] See *infra*, ch. iii.

[2] *New York Times*, December 11, 1865.

[3] The term *radical* as here employed, signifies a person who desired the reconstruction of the southern states in such a manner, and by such methods, as would perpetuate the Republican party in control of the national government.

For at least two years he had strenuously advocated treating the southern states as conquered provinces, and favored a sweeping and universal confiscation of rebel lands, with which he would have paid the national debt, established a pension fund, and given a small farm to each adult freedman.[1] He advocated this in and out of Congress, and at the same time held that whenever the states in rebellion were admitted again to the Union, they must come in under organic acts of Congress after a period of probation, during which time they were to be kept under military or territorial government. Readmission as states must be by special permission of Congress under whatever restrictions that body might provide. He went to Washington several days in advance of the opening of Congress, determined either to force acceptance of his views upon the President, or failing in that, as he doubtless anticipated, to secure their adoption by Congress in spite of the President. On the Wednesday previous to the opening of the session, Stevens had a long interview with Johnson, and there took bold ground in opposition to the views of the latter.[2] He

[1] The fullest explanation by Stevens of his plan of confiscation was made in a speech at Lancaster, Pennsylvania, September 6, 1865. See New York *Herald,* December 13, 1865. For Stevens' speech outlining his "conquered province" theory of reconstruction, see *Globe,* 1st sess., 39th cong., pp. 72-75. See also Woodburn, *Life of Thaddeus Stevens,* pp. 343-346, 521-535. A brief analysis of Stevens' ideas on reconstruction is given *infra,* ch. ii, p. 155.

[2] For my account of Stevens' maneuvers just previous to the opening of Congress, I have relied on the Washington correspondence of the New York papers, December 1 to December 4, 1865; and especially on a carefully prepared letter from the Washington correspondent, Hiram Caulkins, for the New York *Herald* of December 11, 1865. Caulkins was able to follow more accurately than any other newspaper man the course of events in Washington; and the *Herald,* unlike most other newspapers of the day, was not a party organ, and was thus able to give the facts in a more straightforward and unbiased manner than most of the other papers, which had party interests to serve and colored the news accordingly.

opposed the idea of pardoning the late rebels, and told the President that the rank and file of the Union party in Pennsylvania was not in sympathy with his (Johnson's) policy of reconstruction. Stevens then frankly stated that unless the executive policy were materially altered, the President need not expect any support from the majority of the Union members of Congress. Johnson gave no indications of yielding but appealed for harmony, which appeal Stevens did not heed.

On Friday, December 1st, Stevens and some twenty-five or thirty of the most extreme radicals in Congress held a caucus for the purpose of coming to some mutual understanding and thereby concentrating their strength. Stevens related the substance of his conversation with Johnson, and said that he was fully convinced that the latter was wedded to his own plan of reconstruction, and that if they expected to accomplish any of their own purposes, they must do so in spite of the President and not hesitate, if need be, to break entirely with him. During this meeting the Senate was thoroughly canvassed, and Stevens and his friends came to the conclusion that a majority of the members of that body were inclined to be conservative. Fears were manifested that the Senate would admit properly qualified members from the southern states. Such action on the part of the upper house, of course, would defeat Stevens' program; and to prevent it, he and the others concluded that a joint committee must be secured, to whom everything relating to the southern delegations and the treatment of the rebel states, should be referred. Therefore the resolution appointing this committee ought to have some provision that would prevent one house from admitting southern representatives until the other had come to the same decision. In this way it was thought that the Senate could be restrained from admitting southern senators until a majority of that body could be converted to radicalism. Some doubt was expressed as to whether such a resolution could be railroaded through the Senate, to which Stevens replied that it was the only mode whereby they could accomplish their great object—delay. In order to assure the passage of their resolution through the upper house, it would be necessary for the Union party in the lower house to present an undivided front. In this case their party associates in the Senate would be inclined to support it. Accordingly, this plan was adopted, and Stevens was requested to present the resolution to the party caucus which was to be held the next evening. This group of radicals planned to manipulate matters in such a way that the conservatives would not suspect their design, but be led into committing themselves to it.[1]

It is perfectly clear from what has been said, that this coterie of radicals at the meeting on December 1st, was determined to commit their party against Johnson's policy. They realized that the great majority in their party, especially in the Senate, did not desire at that time a break with the President. They therefore planned a resolution that on its face would look innocent enough, and that even the conservatives would unsuspectingly support; but which was really the first step on the road toward committing the Union party against the Presidential theory of reconstruction. They trusted that time and circumstances might reveal what the next step should be.

At the regular meeting of the Republican caucus on Saturday evening, December 2, 1865, all the radicals were present. J. S. Morrill, an extreme radical from Vermont, was elected chairman of the caucus. On motion, a com-

---

[1] New York *World*, December 2 and 4; New York *Herald*, December 2 and 11, 1865.

mittee of seven was appointed to consider what should be done with regard to the southern representatives. Stevens was made chairman of the committee, but some of the other members were conservatives, notably, Henry J. Raymond, of New York. Stevens, of course, offered his resolution,[1] and Raymond, though an astute politician, failed entirely to grasp its real significance, and allowed it to be reported unanimously, and adopted without a dissenting vote.[2] He therefore lost the only real opportunity he ever had of administering a severe blow, if not a defeat, to the Stevens coterie. After a week or so, Raymond saw his great mistake, and bitterly denounced the whole scheme of delay,[3] but it was too late; the Union party in the House of Representatives had unanimously committed itself in caucus to the program of the radicals. When party politicians once commit themselves in caucus, they seldom abandon their position. Thus Stevens not only carried his point, but the radical program was put through with the supporters of the President advocating it.

In the history of our national legislature, next in importance to the First Congress, whose task was the organization of the government under the Constitution, stands the Thirty-ninth, which met on December 4, 1865. Its problem was to reorganize the government after a destructive Civil War that had altered fundamentally our institutions. Public interest in its assembling was keen, owing to the uncertainty as to what disposition would be made of the question of southern representation. Although it was generally understood that southern members would not be allowed to take their seats at once, still there was sufficient doubt to

[1] For the text of the resolution, see *supra*, p. 37.

[2] New York *World*, December 3, 4, 1865; New York *Times*, December 4, 1865.

[3] *Globe*, 1st sess., 39th cong.

cause the galleries to be filled with people who eagerly awaited the action of the House.[1]

At the opening of each new Congress it is the duty of the clerk of the House to preside over that body until a speaker is elected. Before the House proceeds to the election of that official the clerk, who at this time was Edward McPherson, calls the roll. McPherson was a native of Pennsylvania, and owed his position to the favor of Thaddeus Stevens. Under ordinary circumstances the clerk puts on the roll the names of all persons whose credentials are in regular form, leaving to the House the decision as to whether they had, in all cases, been legally obtained. Stevens, however, had seen to it that McPherson had omitted the names of all the members-elect from the " conquered provinces."[2] Though James Brooks, a Democratic member from New York, protested against this action of Clerk McPherson, his protest was of no avail.[3] It was also in vain that Horace Maynard, a member elect from Tennessee, and a man whose loyalty was unquestioned, asked for recognition.[4] After Schuyler Colfax had been elected speaker and the organization of the House perfected, Thaddeus Stevens asked unanimous consent to introduce the following resolution:[5]

Be it resolved, by the Senate and House of Representatives in Congress assembled: That a joint committee of fifteen members shall be appointed, nine of whom shall be members of the House, and six members of the Senate, who shall inquire into the condition of the states which formed the so-called Confederate States of America, and report whether they, or any

---

[1] New York *World*, December 8, 1865.
[2] Rhodes, vol. v, p. 544.
[3] *Globe*, 1st sess., 39th cong., pp. 4-6.
[4] *Ibid.*
[5] See *supra*, p. 37.

of them, are entitled to be represented in either House of Congress, with leave to report at any time, by bill or otherwise; and until such report shall have been made, and finally acted on by Congress, no member shall be received into either House from any of the so-called Confederate States: and all papers relating to the representation of said states shall be referred to the said committee without debate.

Not securing unanimous consent, Stevens moved a suspension of the rules, which was carried, and under the operation of the previous question debate was shut off and the resolution passed. In all of these test votes, Stevens was sustained by the entire Union party, every member of which, thus knowingly or unknowingly, committed himself against the policy of the President.[1]

Before proceeding to a consideration of the Senate's action on this resolution, it should be noted that in form the resolution was a joint, rather than a concurrent one. This distinction is important, for in order that a resolution of the former kind become effective, the President's signature is necessary; whereas one of the latter sort does not require executive approval. Stevens, of course, was fully conscious of this and seems purposely to have presented his resolution in such a form as to require the President's signature. Stevens was willing to force the issue with Johnson immediately. Had the resolution passed the Senate in the same form as in the House, Johnson must either have signed it, and thereby abandoned his own policy and consented to work with Congress; or, what was more likely, he must have vetoed the resolution, and at once brought on the breach between the executive and legislative departments of the government.[2] It was probably a fortunate

[1] *Globe*, 1st sess., 39th cong., pp. 5 *et seq.*
[2] *Cf.* editorial in New York *World*, December 7, 1865.

thing for Stevens and his scheme of reconstruction that his plans miscarried, and that the issue with the President was postponed to be forced later on a different question.[1] It was the more conservative Senate that saved him and his fellow radicals in the House from committing this political blunder.

In the Senate were four groups of political opinion. First, there were the extreme radicals, led by such men as Sumner of Massachusetts, Wade of Ohio, and Howe of Wisconsin, who gladly would have joined the radicals in the House in at once forcing the issue with the President.[2] Second, conservative Republicans, under the leadership of such men as Fessenden of Maine, Grimes of Iowa, and Trumbull of Illinois, who, while not believing that the President had gone far enough in his policy of restoration, yet were unwilling that any break should be made with him, and hoped, by making mutual concessions, and maintaining an attitude of mutual respect, to work in harmony with him, and thus keep the Union party intact. Third, there were what may be called the administration Republicans, consisting of such men as Doolittle of Wisconsin, Cowan of Pennsylvania, and Dixon of Connecticut, who, believing in the justice and sufficiency of the President's policy, and having pledged themselves to its support, were willing to do all that lay within their power to champion his cause in Congress. Fourth, there were the Democrats, the most prominent being Johnson of Maryland, Guthrie of Kentucky, and Hendricks of Indiana, who tended gradually to support more and more cordially the policy of the President and thus coalesce with the preceding group.

[1] See *infra*, ch. iv.

[2] *Cf.* conversations between Sumner and Welles in *Diary of Gideon Welles*, vol. ii, pp. 397, 405, 415, 416.

When the resolution came before the upper house on December 5, unanimous consent was not given for its consideration. In the Senate the previous question has no existence, so under the rules of that body the resolution was postponed.[1] The next day it came up in regular order, but as the three factions of the Republican party had come to no agreement as to its disposition, Senator Fessenden suggested that it be again postponed. Though Senator Sumner contended that the matter required immediate attention, Fessenden's suggestion prevailed.[2]

On December 11, the Republican members of the Senate held a caucus,[3] and by a vote of 16 to 14 changed the resolution to the same form in which it next day passed the Senate, namely:[4]

Resolved by the House of Representatives, (the Senate concurring) that a joint committee of fifteen members shall be appointed, nine of whom shall be members of the House, and six members of the Senate, who shall inquire into the condition of the states which formed the so-called Confederate States of America, and report whether they, or any of them, are entitled to be represented in either House of Congress, with leave to report at any time, by bill or otherwise.

It will be noted that the resolution as passed by the Senate differed from the original House resolution in three particulars. First, the House resolution was joint, while the Senate's was concurrent in form, and hence did not need the President's approval. Second, by the terms of the former resolution, the House pledged itself to receive no members from the southern states until the committee had

---

[1] *Globe*, 1st sess., 39th cong., p. 7.
[2] *Ibid.*, p. 12.
[3] New York *World*, December 12, 1865.
[4] *Globe*, 1st sess., 39th cong., pp. 29, 30. See *supra*, p. 38.

reported. The Senate would not so bind itself. Third, the House agreed to surrender to this joint committee those prerogatives given it by the Constitution of judging of the election, returns and qualifications of its own members. The Senate was unwilling so to curtail its own powers. Before discussing further the significance of these differences, it will be well to obtain some idea of existing political opinion as expressed in the Senate debate on the resolution, and in the comments on it by the press.

Senator Howard,[1] of Michigan, voicing the opinion of the fourteen radical members who favored the resolution as it came from the House, declared that the country expected that Congress would pledge itself not to admit any of the rebel states until after the committee had reported. He continued:

Sir, what is the present position and status of the rebel states? In my judgment they are simply conquered communities, subjugated by the arms of the United States—communities in which the right of self-government does not now exist. We hold them, as we know well, as the world knows today, not by their own free will and consent, as members of the Union, but solely by virtue of our superior military power. I object to the amendment [i. e. the change from the House form to the Senate form of the resolution] for the reason that it leaves the implication—and the implication will be drawn and clearly understood by the public—that one or the other house of Congress may, whenever it sees fit, readmit senators or representatives from a rebel state without the concurrence of the other house; and I hold it to be utterly incompetent for the Senate or the House to admit members from the rebel states without the mutual consent of each other.[2]

---

[1] For brief sketch of Senator Howard, who later became a member of the joint committee, see *infra*, ch. ii.

[2] *Globe,* 1st sess., 39th cong., p. 24.

The attitude of the administration Republicans was shown in a speech by Senator Doolittle, of Wisconsin, in which the whole idea of a joint committee was opposed. He declared that the judiciary committee could properly attend to the matter so far as the Senate was concerned. As a choice between two evils, however, he preferred the Senate form of the resolution. The most interesting point in Doolittle's speech is, that it shows that the President's friends, and no doubt the President himself, recognized that Thaddeus Stevens' resolution and the method used in passing it, meant an attack upon the administration. He further declared:

Stevens is bitterly and uncompromisingly hostile to the policy of the present administration on the subject of reconstruction. He goes with him who goes the farthest, holding that even the state of Tennessee is an alien state at war with the United States; and in the convention at Baltimore he objected to the nomination of Andrew Johnson because he was an alien enemy.[1]

Doolittle therefore felt that since every one understood the source of this resolution and its animus, the Senate should not lend itself to the furthering of Stevens' schemes.[2]

As representative of the conservative Republicans, the opinions of Senator Fessenden[3] are worth noting. He said:

I trust that there are not in the Senate any persons who desire to consider themselves the exclusive friends of the President. That I am ready and disposed to support the executive to the best of my ability is evidenced by the fact that I have long

[1] *Globe,* 1st sess., 39th cong., p. 26.
[2] *Ibid.*
[3] For a short biographical account of Fessenden, who was made chairman of the committee, see *infra,* ch. ii.

acted with him; but though I have supported him in time of war in measures for which I could find no strict constitutional warrant, I consider that the time has now come when Congress must revert to it original position.[1]

The passage of the resolution creating the joint committee of fifteen on reconstruction, was watched with eager interest by the public. What the process of reconstruction would be in Congress and the attitude to be taken by that body toward the policy of the President, was a matter of hardly less interest than the progress of the war had been. The creation of this committee, if the press may be regarded as a true reflection of public opinion, was viewed as a good or an evil act according as one did or did not regard the conditions placed upon the seceded states by the President as sufficient guarantees of their future loyalty. For, the passage of the concurrent resolution by Congress was judged to be an indication that it intended demanding further conditions precedent to the admission of representatives and senators from the late Confederate States.

Democratic feelings, as expressed in the *New York World,* were bitter against what was called the radical attempt to thwart President Johnson's plan of restoration. The *World* declared:

They [the radicals] did not wait till the opening of Congress today, to give that plan the honor of a decent burial under the clerk's table, but put the party bow-string around it, and pitched it at midnight out of the window of a partisan caucus. The resolution adopted unanimously by 124 Republican members in their caucus, shows with what promptitude Thaddeus Stevens strangled the infant "Restoration," stamped upon it with his brutal heel, and proclaimed his plan for keeping the Union disunited.[2]

[1] *Globe*, 1st sess., 39th cong., p. 27. *Cf.* also *supra*, p. 36, note 2.
[2] New York *World*, December 4, 1865.

Continuing next day the same line of comment, the *World* maintained that the action taken by the Republican majority in the House was a declaration that the Civil War had not been brought to an end by the cessation of armed resistance to the Federal authority.

A Congressional majority had renounced the object of the war, avowed at its beginning—the restoration of the Union under the Constitution—and now maintained that the states which went out, now came back as an American Poland or Ireland, to be ruled by the capricious will of accidental majorities, to be held by the strong arm, to be coerced and moulded, both socially and politically, into such a form as the theories of Republican politicians and the passions of a radical multitude should suggest.

It is not maintained by the Republicans that the South will again take up arms, for every one knows that its power for war is broken. But there is a state of peace, of which it has been truly said that it is more disastrous than war itself, and such is the peace which the radical majority in Congress have now proclaimed. Let no man deceive himself. The peace we have believed in, hoped for, struggled for, the peace we have so fondly dreamed was won, recedes from us afresh into a darkening vista of sectional passions, tenfold embittered, into a tenfold heated furnace of sectional wrong, triumphantly inflicted, and sectional tyranny to be remorselessly enforced. The reunited nation is to enter upon its new career with all its wounds torn open afresh. And this beneath the banner of a so-called philanthropy—this at the behest of a party of great moral ideas.[1]

The *New York Tribune* had supported President Johnson in his policy of reconstruction, but at the same time had felt that the conditions which he had imposed on the southern

---

[1] New York *World*, December 5, 1865.

states might very well be supplemented by Congress. It was especially desirous that the southern states should be required to grant at least some qualified form of negro suffrage, and while it admitted that the President was perhaps not legally authorized to impose negro suffrage upon those states, it believed that Congress was thoroughly competent to make such an imposition. It therefore favored the appointment of the committee and thought that there was nothing about it hostile to the President. It would simply formulate some measures of reconstruction, supplementary, and not in opposition, to those conditions which the executive had insisted upon—measures which the President and all loyal members of the Union party could support.[1]

The *New York Times,* which since the organization of the Republican party had been a consistent supporter of it, now found itself in a peculiar situation. Its editor, Henry J. Raymond, was a member of Congress and belonged to the political firm of Weed, Seward, and Raymond. He therefore was under obligation to support an administration in which his partner, Seward, was reputed to be the controlling factor. Moreover, Raymond was chairman of the national executive committee of the Union party, and as such, naturally dreaded a split in his organization. Therefore, when Congress met the *Times* professed to see nothing in the appointment of the joint committee that might cause a breach between Congress and the President. That Stevens succeeded in hoodwinking Raymond by causing him to believe that the appointment of a joint committee was not intended as a thrust at the administration, seems to be proved by the following editorial in the *Times* of December 5th:

[1] New York *Tribune,* December 5, 1865, *et ante.*

Since the great question before Congress is whether the rebel states are entitled to representation or not, a committee to investigate that question is necessary in order that the matter come before Congress in an orderly manner. When their report comes in, the subject will be properly before both houses; and the main question involved can then be discussed and decided upon its intrinsic merits, without being complicated or embarrassed by questions of regularity of the elections or returns in the case of individual members. Without any such provisions as this, the question would be debated upon the presentation of each new certificate, and we should have a perpetually recurring wrangle instead of a decorous and formal discussion.

By the time the resolution passed the Senate, Raymond was undeceived. But it was too late; the radicals in the House had succeeded in committing practically all the Republicans against the President's policy. In spite of his position and his ability, Raymond was unable to build up in the House any considerable following among the members of the Union party, who would co-operate with him in supporting the administration.

The more or less independent New York dailies—the *Post*, the *Herald*, the *Sun*, and the *Commercial-Advertiser*—were anxious that the question of reconstruction should be settled at as early a date as possible. They were perhaps representative of New York commercial interests, and believed that business would not resume its normal channels until the uncertainty as to the political future of the South should be removed. They therefore opposed the appointment of a joint committee, fearing that it would act altogether in a spirit of partisanship and cause unnecessary delay in settling the question of reconstruction.[1] The

---

[1] New York *Evening Post*, December 13, 1865.

Herald was especially fearful lest the appointment of the committee would create a lack of confidence in business both in the South and in the commercial parts of the North. Such a lack of confidence, of course, would hinder the economic development in the South and to that extent limit New York's commercial prosperity. It was especially alarmed that Thaddeus Stevens should use the committee as an engine for carrying out his scheme of confiscation of southern lands.[1] Such wholesale confiscation would neither increase the substantial wealth of the country, nor accomplish its main purpose of paying off the national debt. Both ends could be much easier reached by following President Johnson's policy which, by establishing local harmony, law, and order, looked to the development of the vast industrial resources of the South. The increase in wealth which would follow such a course would rapidly strengthen the national treasury.

It is now possible to make a few general statements in regard to the political situation of the country during December, 1865. As has been seen, the President proposed to allow the rebel states to resume their relations with the Government of the United States with the sole proviso that they recognize and abide by the results of the war. In his opinion the war had only two results, *viz.*, a guarantee of the perpetuity of the Union, and the destruction of the institution of slavery. These were the only objects for which the war had ever at any time been professedly waged, and Johnson believed that a war could have no political results different from the objects for which it had been waged.

The radical members of Congress, under the leadership of Thaddeus Stevens, realized that this was Johnson's opinion. Their own opinion was different. They believed that

[1] New York *Herald,* December 5 and 14.

additional conditions should be imposed upon the South. As to what these conditions should be, they were by no means agreed; but they *were* agreed that the wager of battle should be thrown down to the President at once, for him to accept or surrender his position. As has been seen, the radicals by shrewd maneuvring were able to commit practically all the members of the Union party in the House to their cause. In the Senate only about one-half the members of that party were willing to commit themselves unreservedly against the policy of the President. By explaining the significance of the differences between the House and Senate form of the resolution for raising a joint committee on reconstruction, the attitude of the conservative Republicans will become clear. Had the conservatives been unreservedly in favor of the President's policy, they would have completely destroyed the resolution by refusing to pass it in any form. Had they been willing to join the radicals in opposition to that policy, they would have passed the resolution without amendment. Their amendment of the House resolution simply meant that they, holding the balance of power between the Democrats and administration Republicans on the one hand and the radical Republicans on the other, would retain for the Senate its right to admit at any time it might see fit the senators from the rebel states and thus thwart any schemes of the radicals with which they might not agree. It meant, moreover, that at any time their relations with the President should reach the breaking point by his refusing to concede anything to their wishes, they could go over to the radicals in opposition to the executive.

The stake, therefore, in the political game between Andrew Johnson and Thaddeus Stevens was possession of the ten or a dozen conservative Republicans in the Senate. The President, by discerning the nature of the contest, and by making a few slight concessions to those whom he would win, might have returned victor; Stevens was destined to be victorious because he understood the game better than Johnson, and was more ready than he to make temporary concessions in order to obtain his principal objects.

This characteristic of Stevens is shown by the fact that he was willing to accept the Senate substitute for his original resolution. He stated, however, that when it should be in order, he would move a resolution applicable to the House alone, which in substance would embody that part of his original resolution stricken out by the Senate.[1] This he did on December 14,[2] and the House, as usual, accepted his will.

[1] *Globe*, p. 46.   [2] *Ibid.*, p. 60.

CHAPTER II

Personnel of the Committee [1]

The nine members on the part of the House were appointed on December 14,[2] but it was not until December 21, that the president *pro tempore* announced the six Senate members. Much light on the work of the committee may be derived from the personal and political history of these fifteen men.

THADDEUS STEVENS

Thaddeus Stevens was born in Danville, Vermont, April 4, 1792. His parents were of Massachusetts origin and had come to Vermont when that state was very thinly populated.[3] Society in Vermont during the youth of Stevens was naturally democratic, and he grew up under conditions that fostered hatred of aristocracy. Stevens' early education was obtained in the town of Peacham, to which his mother moved in order to take advantage of the superior school facilities that existed there. In 1811, young Stevens entered Dartmouth College, from which he graduated in 1814. After teaching school in Peacham for a year Stevens moved to York, Pa., to take a position as instructor in an academy there. While teaching in York, Stevens studied law, and at the end of a year was admitted to the bar. He began his law career at Gettysburg, where he gradually built up a lucrative practice.

---

[1] For part of the journal relating to this chapter, see *supra*, p. 38.
[2] *Globe*, p. 57.
[3] Woodburn, *Life of Thaddeus Stevens*, pp. 1-9.

It was not until 1833, when Stevens was over forty years of age, that he entered actively into political life. He was by nature one of those politicians who seizes upon some one idea and exploits it so consistently as to win for himself a reputation. That idea is generally based on dissatisfaction with some existing institution, and if public opinion happens to become so thoroughly wrought up as to cause the destruction of that institution, the one-idea man or reformer is likely to come into great popular favor. In all his career Stevens seldom appeared in any other rôle than that of an advocate for the destruction of some established order which was tending to meet with general disapproval. When he first entered the Pennsylvania legislature, it was as a member of that party which had for its purpose the extermination of the Masonic Fraternity. Of Stevens' attempt to ride into political fame on the anti-Masonic hobby horse, it is not necessary to give a detailed account. His power to denounce something which he did not like, however, is fairly well illustrated in the following excerpt from a speech that he delivered on the subject of Freemasonry in 1835:

Wherever the Genius of Liberty has set a people free, the first object of their solicitude should be the destruction of Freemasonry and all other secret societies. Where tyrants rule they are fit engines of despotism, but under free republican government secret societies are dangerous, and are not to be tolerated. The oaths of Freemasons are inconsistent with pure morals, true religion, and the permanent existence of liberty. Two things are indispensable to the continuance of national liberty—the independence of the public press and the impartial administration of justice. The tyranny of Masonry destroys both. This prostituted harlot has entered the courts of justice and seduced the venerable judges into her foul embrace. They, too, seek to extricate their brothers, whether right or wrong. . . . Has this institution outgrown the law, become stronger than the civil power or the will of a sovereign people? Has this baseborn issue of a foreign sire become so powerful, that even the Young Lion of American Liberty cannot crush him? Is this bloody god too strong for us to overcome? Then let us tremble at his power, fall down, bow ourselves in the dust before him and supplicate his favor. For my single self I would rather be the victim of his fury that the slave of his favor.[1]

After the death of the anti-Masonic party, for a long time Stevens was unable to find any issue in politics radical enough to support a man of his decided opinions. He did useful service in defending and strengthening his state's newly created and feeble public school system; and played an important part in the so-called "Buckshot War," a political contest between the Whigs and Democrats over the state election of 1838, resulting, so far as Stevens was concerned, in his retirement from active political life for a number of years.

After his first retirement from politics, Stevens resumed his law practice at Gettysburg, but in 1842 moved to Lancaster, which was his home for the rest of his life. He had fallen heavily into debt during the time he had been a member of the Pennsylvania legislature, so he now gave the major portion of his time to his law practice, and succeeded in paying off his debts.[2]

Stevens had always been an anti-slavery man, but he had not taken up the slavery question as a political issue during his early career in public life. He was always a consistent friend of the negro race, and gave free much of his time

[1] "Free Masonry Unmasked," 1835. *Pamphlet of the Historical Society of Pennsylvania*, cited in Woodburn, p. 21.

[2] Woodburn, chap. iii and iv.

and legal talents to prevent runaways being carried back into slavery. In 1838, while he was a member of the convention that drew up a new constitution for Pennsylvania, he refused to sign the document because it limited the elective franchise to the white race.[1]

In 1848, Stevens was elected from the Lancaster district to the 31st Congress as a Whig, but because of that party's failure to come out boldly in support of the Wilmot Proviso, Stevens generally acted with the Free-Soilers, though he continued for the present his party relations with the Whigs. He was one of the few northern men who at this time was not afraid to stand up boldly and declare his convictions about slavery and its extension. From this time on until slavery was destroyed, it was the one question upon which Stevens relied for his political ammunition. As one of his opponents from the South expressed it, " Since anti-Masonry will no longer serve for a hobby-horse, the gentleman must preach against the horrors and despotism of slavery."[1]

During this Congress Stevens made several speeches on the slavery question and denounced that institution in no uncertain terms, of which the following excerpt is typical:

In this government the free white citizens are the rulers,— the sovereigns, as we delight to call them. All others are subjects. In this government the subject has no rights, social, political or personal. He has no voice in the laws which govern him. He can hold no property. His very wife and children are not his. His labor is another's. He and all that pertains to him are the absolute property of his rulers. He is governed, bought, sold, punished, executed, by laws to which he never gave his assent, and by rulers whom he never chose.

[1] Statement made by Representative Kelly, of Pennsylvania, in 39th Cong. *Globe*, p. 283.
[2] Quoted in Woodburn, p. 101.

He is not a serf merely, with half the rights of men, like the subjects of despotic Russia; but a naked slave, stripped of every right which God and nature gave him, and which the high spirit of our revolution declared inalienable—which he himself could not surrender, and which man could not take from him. Is he not then the subject of despotic sway?

But we are told that it is none of our business; that southern slavery is a matter between the slave-holder and his own conscience. I trust it may be so decided by impartial history and the unerring Judge; that we may not be branded with that great stigma and that grievous burden may not weigh upon our souls. But could we hope for that justification, if now, when we have the power to prevent it, we should permit this evil to spread over thousands of square leagues now free and settle upon unborn millions? Sir, for myself, I should look upon any northern man, enlightened by a northern education, who would, directly or indirectly, by omission or commission, by basely voting or cowardly skulking, permit it to spread over one rood of God's free earth, as a traitor to liberty and a recreant to God!

Stevens denounced the two pro-slavery measures of the Compromise of 1850—organizing the territories without the Wilmot Proviso, and the new fugitive slave law—and voted consistently against them. He was reëlected to Congress in 1850, but since the Compromise of 1850 had settled temporarily the slavery question, he had but little occasion to speak upon his favorite theme. He actively advocated the policy of protection, as a true son of Pennsylvania always did in those and later days, but as his real power lay in a zealous attack upon slavery, he found public life tiresome in that period of calm which succeeded the turmoil of 1850. At the expiration of the 32d Congress he again retired to private life at the age of 61—an age when with most men retirement would have been permanent. With Stevens it was merely a recess, for his fame as a political leader was yet to be won.

As with Lincoln, it was the repeal of the Missouri Compromise in 1854 that brought Stevens again into active political life. In 1855, he was one of the organizers in Pennsylvania of the new Republican party, which had for its purpose resistance to the further extension of slavery in the territories. He was a delegate to the first Republican national convention in 1856, and for the nomination for President supported Justice McLean—the anti-slavery member of the Supreme Court who rendered a dissenting opinion in the famous Dred Scott case. In 1858, Stevens was again elected to Congress from the Lancaster district, and served continuously in the House from the meeting of the 36th Congress in December of 1859 to his death in 1868.

In the 36th Congress Stevens took a prominent part in the debates, and by the time of its expiration in 1861 he was regarded as one of the leading members of the lower house. In the first session of that Congress, he used his great powers of satire and irony in prodding on the "fire-eaters" from the South, into making extreme statements and expressing sentiments of disunion. It seems clear that at this time he understood the temper of the southerners, knew they were in earnest, and really desired that they carry out their numerous threats of secession, though he professed to believe that all their threats were mere gasconade. He said he did not blame the southerners for their language of intimidation, for using "this threat of rending God's creation from turret to foundation. All this is right in them, for they have tried it fifty times, and fifty times they have found weak and recreant tremblers in the North who have been affected by it and who have acted from those intimidations. They are right, and I give them credit for repeating with grave countenances that which they have so often found to be effective when operating upon timid men."[1] In his ability to cause opponents to make reckless assertions which would redound to the discredit of their cause, Stevens was a past grand master. He later used the same tactics in his fight with Andrew Johnson over the question of reconstruction. In the long contest over organizing the House, Stevens used all his talent to keep northern representatives from being frightened by southern menaces, which he dubbed " idle rantings and barren thunders."

During the second session of the 36th Congress, after Lincoln had been elected and while the cotton states were seceding, Stevens employed all his powers against any of the proposed compromises. He spoke of the House committee of thirty-three—one from each state—as a " committee on incubation," and believed the time for compromise and conciliation had passed. He, like a great many other Republicans of his time, had used the platform of that party in 1856 and 1860 which declared only against the further extension of slavery, merely as a stepping-stone toward working up sentiment for its complete abolition. Had the South tamely submitted in 1861 and allowed the Republicans to carry out their policy of prohibiting slavery in the territories, in the District of Columbia, and the other public places belonging to the United States, there is no doubt that in a short time, perhaps by 1864 or 1868, they would have begun an attack upon slavery in the states themselves. In this case, however, it would doubtless have taken two or three generations to have accomplished its total abolition. Stevens was one of the few men who, at the beginning of the war, believed it would result in the abolition of slavery.[2] He hated the South, and while he believed that section would put up a good fight, and thought the war

---

[1] Woodburn, p. 135. [2] *Ibid.*, pp. 171, 172.

would last for at least two years, he never had any serious doubts as to the final results. Therefore, he favored the government's taking a decisive attitude at once, and really courted war. He declared that the whole blame for the war rested with the southerners, that the challenge was theirs, and for his part, he was unwilling to make any humiliating concessions to appease them. Soon after the war commenced, Stevens began to demand the immediate emancipation of the slaves as a war measure. He never admitted that it was not the purpose of the North in waging the war, to interfere with the "domestic institutions" of the southern states. He was one of the four representatives, who, in July of 1861, voted against the Crittenden resolutions which defined the object of the war as being solely the preservation of the Union.[1] On August 2, 1861, a week after the passage of the Crittenden resolutions, he said: "God forbid that I should ever agree that the slaves should be returned again to their masters and that you should rivet again the chains which you have once broken."[2] Stevens was a strong critic of Lincoln's "border state policy" and bitterly denounced the President for overruling military emancipation by Generals Fremont and Hunter in 1861 and 1862. He regretted the influence of border-state men on the President, and did all he could to have Blair ousted from the Cabinet.

Stevens not only believed that the negroes should be freed, but thought they should be armed and employed in the United States army. Just before Lincoln announced his preliminary emancipation proclamation, Stevens said: "I no longer agree that this administration is pursuing a wise policy. Its policy should be to free the slaves, enlist and drill them, and set them to shooting their mas-

---

[1] Woodburn, pp. 171, 172.   [2] *Ibid.*, pp. 173, 174.

ters if they do not submit." After Lincoln issued the emancipation proclamation, Stevens began to support the administration much more heartily and voted for the renomination of Lincoln in 1864.

It is Stevens' attitude on reconstruction that principally interests us here. As early as August in 1861, he had taken the ground that the people of the Confederate states were public belligerent enemies, and that the nation in its efforts to overcome them was bound only by the laws of war and the law of nations. The Constitution was abrogated with respect to the hostile Confederate States that had rejected and repudiated it. Stevens adhered strictly to this principle throughout the war.[1] He elaborated this principle from time to time during the progress of the struggle as different questions came up affecting the constitutional relations of the seceded states to the United States. When the war was over, he was not disposed to regard them as states in the Union, but as "conquered provinces." In a speech[2] delivered in Congress on December 18, 1865, he summarized his opinions on reconstruction and therein laid down the essential reasons why Congress, under his leadership, refused to adopt the reconstruction policy of President Johnson. The Confederate States for four years were belligerents, acknowledged so by Europe and the United States. Mr. Justice Grier, following Vattel, in the decision in the *Prize Cases*,[3] held that the rebel states were belligerents and the contest they waged was a war, it not being necessary that both the parties be foreign nations. " A war may exist where one of the belligerents claims sovereign rights as

---

[1] Woodburn, pp. 212 *et seq.*
[2] *Globe*, 1st sess., 39th cong., pp. 72-75.
[3] 2 Black, 666.

against the other."[1] The idea that the states could not and did not make war, and that the war was one of individuals, was ridiculous. Individuals cannot make war, and to say that the states did not make war because the Constitution forbids it, was as foolish as to say that A did not kill B because he could not have done so as the law forbids it. Moreover, all the rebel states themselves maintained they were out of the Union; their laws, the Confederate government, the speeches of their members of Congress, and the answers of their government to propositions of peace, went upon the ground that no terms would be considered, except upon the prior acknowledgment of the entire and permanent independence of the Confederacy. After this, to say that the United States has no right to treat them as a conquered belligerent, severed from the Union in fact, was not argument but mockery. The only question to be considered was, whether it was to the interest of the North so to treat them.

But suppose, as some contend, they are not out of the Union, but in it, in a state of "suspended animation." In either case, Congress has control of the matter. If they are conquered provinces, Congress has power over them under the clause of the Constitution which declares, "New states may be admitted into the Union." If they are states in the Union out of their proper relation with it, Congress,—i. e. the Senate, the House, and the President in his legislative capacity,—has control under the clause of the Constitution that requires the National Government "to guarantee to every state a republican form of government." A joint committee of both houses is justified, for Congress as a whole must create states and declare when they are entitled to be represented. The clause in the Constitution enforcing upon each house the duty of judging the elections, returns, and qualifications of its own

---

[1] 2 Black, 666.

members, has no bearing on the question until Congress as a whole has acted on their right to be represented. Then each house must judge whether the members presenting themselves from a recognized state, possess the requisite qualifications, and whether the elections and returns are according to law. The houses separately can judge of nothing else.

The first duty of Congress then was to declare the condition of these states and fix a government for them. This government should not be military but territorial;[1] for in territories Congress may fix the qualifications for voters. Voters should include all males over twenty-one years of age without regard to race or color, who had not given aid or comfort to the rebellion. Under certain conditions and within certain restrictions the rebels might be allowed to participate in the government. In the territorial legislatures, they would mingle with those to whom Congress would extend the franchise (*i. e.*, the negroes), and there learn the principles of freedom and democracy, and eat the fruit of foul rebellion. Let them remain in the position of territories until the loyal states had amended the Constitution as they might see fit. Among other amendments, Congress should propose to the states one for apportioning representatives according to voters and not population,[2] and

---

[1] Stevens consistently favored a territorial form of government for the rebel states; this in spite of the fact that he supported the Reconstruction act of March 2, 1867, which established military governments. He had previously introduced two bills providing for territorial governments which he was unable to have passed. See *infra*, ch. vii and viii.

[2] If the negroes should be allowed to vote as Stevens proposed, it is difficult to see the reason for any change in apportioning representation. He did not explain it himself, but he perhaps feared, what has come to pass, that as soon as the southern states were in full fellowship again, they would set about disfranchising the negroes in one way or another. He did not propose an amendment forbidding the states the right to deny the franchise on account of race or color, as he did not believe it would be ratified by the northern states. See *infra*, ch. vi.

another giving the national government the right to levy export duties, so that cotton might be properly taxed. These amendments should not be submitted to the present so-called governments in the southern states, as they were merely governments under duress. Finally, Congress should at once declare its power over the whole subject of reconstruction.[1]

Stevens also maintained that the negroes should be given equal civil rights, and that something in a material way should be done for them. He had explained previously what these material benefits should be, and did not at this time give a detailed account of his plan for confiscating southern lands. Such confiscation, however, was an important part of his plan for reconstructing the South, and though it was the one thing that he did not succeed in accomplishing, so long as he lived he cherished it and never gave up hope that it might be carried out.

Stevens' fullest exposition of his plan of confiscation was made in a speech at Lancaster, Pa., in September, 1865.[2] He figured that there were in the rebel states four hundred sixty-five million acres of land. Of this three hundred ninety-four million acres were owned by 70,000 persons, each of whom possessed more than two hundred acres. He argued that these three hundred ninety-four million acres ought to be confiscated by the government. To each adult freedman should be given forty acres, which approximately would dispose of about forty million acres. The remaining three hundred fifty-four million acres he would divide into suitable farms, and sell to the highest bidder. Including the

[1] The above is a brief analysis of Stevens' speech of December 18, 1865, *Globe*, pp. 72-75.

[2] This speech was printed in full in the New York *Herald* on December 13, 1865. A fuller discussion and a partial defense of Stevens' policy of confiscation will be found in Woodburn, ch. xx.

city property it should bring an average price of ten dollars an acre, making a total of three billion five hundred forty million dollars. Of this money he would invest three hundred millions in six per cent bonds, the income of which should go towards the payment of pensions to deserving veterans and the widows and orphans of soldiers and sailors who had been killed in the war. Two hundred million dollars should be appropriated to reimburse loyal men in both North and South whose property had been destroyed or damaged during the war. With the remaining three billion forty million dollars he would pay the national debt. Stevens argued that since all this property which was to be confiscated was owned by 70,000 persons, the vast majority of the people in the South would not be affected by this policy. These 70,000 were the arch-traitors, and since they had caused an unjust war they should be made to suffer its consequences.

Such was the reconstruction policy of the man who, at the opening of the 39th Congress, undertook the task of overthrowing the policy of the President and having his own substituted therefor. What of the man himself? At this time Stevens was seventy-three years old, but as a correspondent for the *Independent* [1] described him, in spite of his age and feebleness, " his spirit is not bated, his sarcasm cuts as keenly as ever, his wit flashes as brightly, and his great intellect seems in no wise dimmed. His face in outline approaches the Indian type. The square perceptive brow, the deeply set eyes, the high cheek bones, the broad jaw and saturnine mouth are most marked. The face in repose is stern, but not savage. Thaddeus Stevens' inevitable sarcasm and wit seem purely intellectual gifts."

---

[1] *The Independent*, June 14, 1866; *Letters from a Woman in Washington*.

John Sherman, while discussing Johnson's speech of February 22,[1] and trying to palliate it, said of Thaddeus Stevens: "We must not forget that he [Stevens] has shown violent and bitter feeling at various times, and that he wields great influence and in such a way as to exasperate even a patient man. I know him well—a man of great intellect, with a controlling will, and possessing the dangerous power of great sarcasm, which he wields against friend and foe, cutting like a Damascus blade."[2] Another observer said of him: "Thaddeus Stevens has the courage of his opinions. He sees plainly that the end we must seek is sure rather than swift reconstruction, and he states clearly the steps which he thinks essential to that end."[3] To the Washington correspondent of the *Nation,* he was the "inexorable Thaddeus Stevens who holds the business of the House in the hollow of his hand." As his biographer, Mr. McCall, says: "Before that day (December 4, 1865), Stevens had been the leader of the House of Representatives. Henceforth he was to be its dictator, and the leader of his party throughout the country."[4]

Radical was the man, and radical his policy, that the Republican members of the House of Representatives faithfully followed from the beginning of the struggle over reconstruction until the President was completely vanquished. The principal source, no doubt, of Stevens' great influence was his ability as a debater and his effective use of the party whip. But to understand why he became the "dictator" of his party in the lower house, it should be remembered that this was an era essentially revolutionary, when radical

---

[1] See *infra,* ch. iv.
[2] *Globe,* 1st sess., 39th cong., appendix, p. 129.
[3] *Harper's Weekly,* January 6, 1866.
[4] *Thaddeus Stevens* (American Statesman), p. 259.

principles enunciated to-day, existing yesterday only in the minds of extreme men, would be adopted to-morrow.

Nearly every new measure which the government had adopted during the course of the war had been advocated in advance by Stevens. For instance, at the beginning of secession he had opposed making any further compromise with the slave power. In January of 1861, this was considered radical, while in January of 1866, there was no member of the Republican party who did not glory in the fact that no compromise had been made. When, in the fall of 1861, Stevens demanded that the slaves be emancipated as a war measure, most of the members of his party held back, and yet a year later this was done. When Stevens first advocated arming the slaves there were few who agreed with him, but long before the close of the war, thousands of negroes were to be found in the army of the United States.

Is it any wonder, then, that when so many radical measures had been adopted, and their adoption proved popular, that he who was the great *Radical* of them all, should be looked upon as the natural leader of the Republican party? So it was that for better or for worse, for weal or for woe, the politicians of that party, at the opening of 1866, were willing to follow Thaddeus Stevens almost anywhere he might lead, and this, in spite of executive disapproval and loss of patronage.

WILLIAM PITT FESSENDEN

The chairman of the committee on the part of the Senate was William Pitt Fessenden, who thus, in accordance with precedent, became chairman of the whole committee. At the time of his appointment to this important position he was already well known as a statesman, having served continuously as a senator from Maine since 1854, except for the short time that he acted as Secretary of the Treasury in the closing months of Lincoln's first administration.

Fessenden was born October 16, 1806, at Fryeburg, Maine. Truly may it be said that he was dedicated to politics from the beginning, for at his christening no less a person than Daniel Webster attended as godfather. At the age of twelve he entered Bowdoin College, from which he was graduated in 1823. He then took up the study of law, and in 1827 was admitted to the bar. Two years later he moved to Portland, which continued to be his home for the rest of his life. In 1831 he was elected to the Maine legislature as an anti-Jackson representative, and on the formation of the Whig party he became identified with it. Fessenden remained in the legislature for only one year, but during that time acquired a reputation as a clear and logical thinker as well as an eloquent speaker. In 1837, when Daniel Webster was making plans to capture the Whig nomination for President in 1840, he invited his godson to accompany him on a political tour through the western states. This invitation Fessenden accepted, and the experience doubtless proved valuable for him in his subsequent political career. In 1840, Fessenden was nominated by the Whigs to represent the Portland district in Congress, and although Portland was usually Democratic, Fessenden's own popularity and the Whig tidal wave that carried in Harrison and Tyler, combined to bring about his election. He served only one term in Congress, and long before the close of the first session he found congressional life so utterly " detestable " that he determined not to become a candidate for re-election. Because of the defection of Tyler and the consequent shattering of the Whig program, he wrote: " As a member of the Whig party I feel absolutely degraded. I am ashamed of our leaders, and could not have deemed it possible that men honored with the confidence of the people, and who have talked patriotism so loudly, would be governed by motives so contemptible. I am cured, I hope, forever of all fondness for public life, and could I do so without forfeiting obligations to others, would gladly resign." [1]

It was during the time that Fessenden was a member of the House of Representatives, that John Quincy Adams was attempting to break down the " gag " rule in regard to petitions against slavery. Though Fessenden considered that Adams sometimes talked too violently and unwisely, he determined to support the old man on principle, for he said:

The insolence of these southern boys is intolerable, and the subserviency of their northern hirelings should cast them back into their native insignificance. I am every day growing more of the opinion that we must abandon all differences at home, except that between the northern and southern parties. I fear that a few years more will see the North and South entirely at issue, and for one, if the North is to be eternally sacrificed for the benefit of slave labor, I am willing to see that day come, terrible as it will be.[2]

Though Fessenden was not an abolitionist, this short experience in Congress enabled him to perceive that slavery was the pernicious institution over which all important political contests were to be waged. At the adjournment of Congress on March 4, 1843, he retired from political life, firmly convinced that slavery should be confined within its existing limits.

From this retirement he was not called forth until 1854.

---

[1] Fessenden, *Life of William Pitt Fessenden*, vol. i, pp. 22, 23. Unless otherwise stated, this work is my source of information for all strictly biographical material relating to Fessenden.

[2] *Ibid.*

At the very time that the Nebraska bill was reported by Stephen A. Douglas, the Maine legislature was balloting to fill a vacancy in the United States Senate. The Whigs, who nominated Fessenden, were in a minority in the legislature, but among the Democrats there were many anti-slavery men who would not support the regular Democratic nominee, and after several futile ballots the anti-slavery Democrats combined with the Whigs and elected Fessenden. He arrived in Washington just in time to take part in the debate on the Kansas-Nebraska bill. His maiden speech announced the arrival of a "new champion," as Sumner expressed it, in the fight against the extension of slavery.[1]

With the dissolution of the Whig party, Fessenden, as a matter of course, became identified with the Republicans, and took an active part in the campaigns of 1856 and 1860. When the southern states began to secede, Fessenden, like Thaddeus Stevens, was opposed to making any concessions to the slave power in order to prevent disunion. Unlike Stevens, however, he does not seem to have appreciated the seriousness of the situation, as he continued to believe until the secession of South Carolina that the whole thing was a "kind of flourish."[2] Even as late as December 22, 1860, he wrote: "Any man with half an eye can see what all this means. It [secession] was begun for the purpose of frightening us into an abandonment of our position, thus strengthening the South and disgracing the Republicans."

Moreover, it is doubtful whether Fessenden expected the government to use force in preserving its integrity, for in the same letter he wrote: "If the Union can only be saved by acknowledging the power of a minority to coerce the majority through fear of disruption, I am ready to part companywith the slave states."[3] A few weeks later, how-

---

[1] Fessenden, *op. cit.*, vol. i, p. 33.
[2] *Ibid.*, p. 118.   [3] *Ibid.*, p. 119.

ever, after the Gulf states had seceded, he began to realize that the South was in earnest, and also came to believe that war was probable.[1]

When the war was begun, Fessenden was made chairman of the Senate finance committee, and served in that capacity until July, 1864, when, upon the resignation of S. P. Chase as Secretary of the Treasury, Lincoln appointed him to fill the vacancy. Like almost everybody else in his own time, as well as before and since, Fessenden knew very little about the question of finance, but differed from most of the financial quidnuncs of all ages in that he was honest enough to confess his own ignorance.[2] Upon the expiration of Lincoln's first term, Fessenden resigned his place in the Cabinet and again took his seat in the Senate, where he served until his death in 1869.

During the war Fessenden had considered the discussion concerning reconstruction premature. He was not favorably disposed toward the Wade-Davis scheme, and as for the President's attempt in Louisiana and Arkansas, he was of the opinion that it would have been better to have waited until the majority of the people in those states had returned to their allegiance. He therefore voted against the admission of the senators from Arkansas in the spring of 1864, and at the same time expressed the opinion that the question of what constitutes a state to be represented in Congress, should properly be settled by Congress and could not be settled by any other authority.[3]

Fessenden believed that Johnson had made a great mistake in attempting to restore the rebel states without con-

---

[1] Fessenden, *op. cit.*, p. 125.

[2] *Globe*, February 12, 1862, p. 756; cited in Woodburn, *Life of Thaddeus Stevens*, p. 248.

[3] Fessenden, *Life of Fessenden*, vol. ii, pp. 10 and 11.

sulting Congress, but when that body met in December of 1865, he was not among those who desired a breach with the President, for he thought that a quarrel might be fatal to the party and disastrous to the country.[1] He was firmly convinced that additional guarantees should be demanded from the rebel states, and he was unwilling to accept what the President had done as a finality, but was almost equally unwilling to allow the process of reconstruction to be controlled by the radicals, as he thought it would be in case the breach were made. He therefore desired, and at first hoped, that the President would work in harmony with the conservative Republicans, to the end that moderate though sound measures of reconstruction might be enacted. The following extracts from personal letters that he wrote, soon after being made chairman of the committee, will give some idea of the dilemma in which Fessenden felt himself to be; and some of his hopes and fears for the future may be seen.

The committee on reconstruction has a severe and onerous duty to perform, which must for some weeks occupy a great share of my time and attention. It is a difficult subject to deal with for it has become much complicated by the steps already taken. Yet I think I see the way through it if Congress stands firm, as I think it will. We are embarrassed by men of extreme opinions who think all ways but their own are necessarily bad ways, and by others who cannot wait till the proper time, through fear lest their own names may not be sufficiently known in connection with the work to be done. The committee has a large majority of thorough men who are resolved that ample security shall attend any restoration of the insurgent states, come what will, while they desire, if possible, to avoid a division between Congress and the executive, which could only result in unmixed evil. My belief is still that the President is as anxious as we are on that point; and if meddle-

---

[1] Fessenden, *op. cit.*, p. 13.

some people will leave him in peace, I think he would try hard to establish matters on a firm and safe basis. He manifests no desire to interfere with the proper prerogatives of Congress, and appears willing to yield much to its opinions.[1]

Writing on the same day—December 24, 1865—he said:

I am placed at the head of the committee on reconstruction, and this, besides its delicacy will be a position involving very great labor and requiring great care and circumspection. I could not decline it any more than I could decline the Treasury. Mr. Sumner was very anxious for the place, but, standing as he does before the country, and committed to the most ultra views, even his friends declined to support him, and almost to a man fixed upon me. Luckily, I had marked out my line, and everybody understands where I am. I think I can see my way through, and if Sumner and Stevens and a few other such men do not embroil us with the President, matters can be satisfactorily arranged—satisfactorily, I mean, to the great bulk of Union men throughout the states.[2]

Then again on January 14, 1866, he writes in the same strain:

It is very unlucky for me that I have been forced to take hold of this reconstruction business. As I anticipated, the work of the finance committee will give me no trouble. This, however, engrosses me, and with all other matters makes the burden heavy. In addition to all other difficulties, the work of keeping the peace between the President and those who wish to quarrel with him, aided as they are by those who wish him to quarrel with us, is a most difficult undertaking. The fools are not all dead, you know. I hope we shall be able to put things upon a sound basis. That *must* be done, quarrel or no quarrel, but I hope to avoid the necessity.[3]

[1] Fessenden, *op. cit.*, p. 18.
[2] *Ibid.*, p. 20. [3] *Ibid.*, p. 21.

Thus the position of Fessenden, who was typical of the conservative Republican senators, is clear. He was anxious to avoid a breach with the President, and had Johnson been the least bit compromising or tactful, there is no doubt that the process of reconstruction would not have fallen, as it eventually did, into the hands of the extreme radicals. As it was, when Johnson placed himself in opposition to proposals designed to protect the civil rights of the negroes, and showed himself out of sympathy with measures which tended to strengthen the authority of the National Government, and especially when he began to resent any suggestion that there was anything more to be done in the matter of reconstruction, and that a Congress in which the southern states were not represented, could not with propriety legislate for those states,[1] Fessenden lost all patience with him and no longer had any hope for coöperation between the President and the conservatives.

It has been said that Fessenden, during the first session of the 39th Congress, was able to hold the Republican members of the committee to a comparatively moderate policy of reconstruction; and that to him was chiefly due the credit for perfecting the fourteenth amendment.[2] As a matter of fact, the record does not bear out this assertion, for the radicals were deterred from proposing anything more extreme than the fourteenth amendment, not by Fessenden and the moderates, but by the fear that they would not be sustained by the people. Fessenden's own attitude toward reconstruction, and his part in it, will be discussed somewhat in succeeding chapters, but it may be well to point out here what he preferred. Fessenden always believed that

---

[1] Johnson made this point in his veto of the Freedmen's Bureau bill, February 20. See *infra*, ch. iv.

[2] Rhodes, vol. v, p. 599.

the people of wealth and intelligence in the southern states would eventually rule them, and he had none of that faith which so obsessed his " furious radical friends " as to cause them to believe that they could secure the votes of all those states through the aid of the negroes.[1] It will be seen in the succeeding chapter[2] that he supported a resolution providing that any distinction made in civil or political privileges on account of race or color should be inoperative and void. He would then, after offering them this simple proposition, have continued the southern states under military control, and let them remain outside the Union until they chose to accept it.[3] After making such a clear avowal of a principle which meant the giving of the suffrage to the negroes on an equal basis with the whites, one would be inclined to think that Fessenden should be classed among the radicals. Such, however, is not the case, for negro suffrage in itself was not wrong, as some writers have seemed to think, and the calamity which accompanied it was due to the fact that the Reconstruction acts of 1867 took the machinery of government out of the hands of the men who had formerly controlled it, and put it into the hands of unscrupulous persons who depended upon the credulity and ignorance of the negroes for political support.[4] This was a vastly different thing from what Fessenden proposed. He

---

[1] See letter of Fessenden to F. H. Morse; Fessenden, *Life of Fessenden*, vol. ii, p. 306. In August, 1869, just a few weeks before his death, Fessenden wrote to his friend Senator Grimes: "The election in Tennessee, the result of which you will know before this reaches you, is, in my judgment, but an indication of what we must expect in most of the rebel states at the next Presidential elections [that is, 1872]. The result there, as in Virginia, is no more than any man of ordinary sagacity must have foreseen. I both foresaw and foretold it."

[2] See *infra*, ch. iii.

[3] Fessenden, *Life of Fessenden*, vol. ii, pp. 23, 24.

[4] *Cf.* Rhodes, vol. vi, ch. i.

would have said to the governing classes in the South: "You must extend to the negroes civil and political rights on an equality with yourselves; you may make any property or educational qualifications for voting so long as these qualifications operate equally on whites and blacks alike; and until you ratify an amendment to the Federal Constitution providing for equal civil and political rights and change your state constitutions and laws in conformity therewith, you must remain unrepresented in Congress, and subject to the military jurisdiction of the United States Government."[1] There was no party politics in this, for Fessenden did not expect that any considerable number of Republican representatives would be returned to Congress from the South under his proposed amendment. But he did not think that the southern states would accept his proposal before the election of 1868, which would therefore result in a Republican victory. That they would accept it, sooner or later, however, he was firmly convinced.[2] Of course this amendment proposed by Fessenden was not accepted by his associates, not, however, because of its radicalism, but because it was not a good party measure. Fessenden was a statesman; his associates were mere politicians.

Fessenden supported the fourteenth amendment and was very much disappointed when, in the second session of the 39th Congress, the radicals would not let it stand as a permanent basis of reconstruction, and were unwilling to wait until the southern states ratified it, as Fessenden thought eventually they would do. Writing of this matter in the fall of 1868, Fessenden said: " I got my name of conservative by advising against the Reconstruction act. It seemed to me, that when we had proposed the fourteenth amend-

---

[1] Fessenden, *Life of Fessenden*, vol. ii, pp. 23, 24, 306.
[2] *Ibid.*

ment, the rebel states had rejected it, and we had provided military protection for our friends, enough was done by Congress towards reconstruction, and we had better leave the matter where it was until the people of those states asked for admission in proper form." [1] Fessenden, though he advised against the Reconstruction acts, did not vote against them, as to have done so would have caused the radicals to read him out of the party. In fact they tried to do so as it was,[2] because from this time on he opposed most of their plans in their war on Andrew Johnson. For instance, he thought a continuous session of Congress unnecessary;[3] he refused to vote against confirming every non-Republican nominated by the President for public office; he defended Secretary of the Treasury McCulloch at a time when to speak kindly of any Cabinet member except Stanton was considered treachery to the "cause;" he did not vote for the Tenure of Office bill or for the resolution declaring the act of the President in removing Stanton, illegal.[4] This was a trying year for Fessenden, and though outwardly he maintained cordial relations with his radical colleagues, yet privately he denounced them and their schemes in no uncertain terms. So weary was he of it all, that he would have resigned his position in the Senate, could he have done so with honor.[5] " I am becoming disgusted with public life," he wrote to one of his friends. " Treachery on the one hand and folly on the other have almost disheartened me.

---

[1] Fessenden, *op. cit.*, p. 306. See *ibid.*, p. 65.

[2] See *ibid.*, pp. 135 *et seq.*, for attacks by Chandler and Sumner upon Fessenden because of his " conservatism." These and other men attempted to destroy Fessenden as they had destroyed Cowan, Doolittle and Dixon, by forcing him into the party of the President.

[3] *Ibid.*, p. 127.

[4] *Ibid.*, pp. 154, 155.

[5] *Ibid.*

We are doing some very foolish things in Congress, and others still more foolish are attempted. The truth is, we are disgusting all sensible people very fast. The effort to impeach the President will fail as the whole thing is mere madness."[1]

In the eyes of his radical colleagues, Fessenden was guilty of the sum of all infamy when he, acting with six conservative associates, voted for the acquittal of Andrew Johnson, and thus prevented his removal from office.[2] For this he was roundly denounced.[2] Fessenden, however, voted in accordance with what he considered the strict discharge of his duty. Soon after the impeachment trial was over, he wrote to his son: "The satisfaction of knowing that I have acted from the purest motives, and a devotion to the honor and best good of my country, regardless of my own personal interest and comfort, cannot be taken away from me. The whole thing, however, has made me sick at heart. I have seen in the Senate so much of meanness, such utter want of conscientiousness, such base cowardice, even among men calling themselves Christians, that I almost despair of the future, and when I look around me and see what the people are, how easily misled, how willing to be both unjust and ungenerous, I am surprised that anybody should be willing to render them an honest service."[3]

There was much talk to the effect that the National Republican convention, which met in the interval between the first and second vote in the Senate, would read Fessenden and the other six Republicans who voted for the acquittal of Johnson, out of the party. It did nothing of the sort, however, but for a while Fessenden was in doubt as to whether

---

[1] Fessenden, *op. cit.*, p. 129.

[2] *Ibid.*, p. 207, *et seq.*

[3] *Ibid.*, p. 222.

he desired to stay in a party which had treated him so ill. The reaction in public opinion which followed the impeachment trial, led many Republicans to believe that the "seven" had saved the party from utter ruin. A large number of Republicans, some of whom had formerly advocated the conviction of the President, wrote Fessenden and congratulated him upon the stand he had taken.[1] This, together with the more satisfactory stand taken by the Republicans on the money question in the presidential campaign of 1868, caused Fessenden to conclude actively to support the candidate of that party.[2] He considered that the Democratic doctrine of paying the bonds of the United States in greenbacks was dishonest, and was the essence of repudiation.[3] Moreover, while he was not in sympathy with reconstruction as carried on by the radicals, he did not believe that what had been done should be undone as the Democrats proposed. He therefore entered the campaign, and rendered such valuable service to the Republicans, that by the time Congress met in December, he had succeeded in reinstating himself in the good graces of the party. It was even suggested that Fessenden might be appointed Secretary of the Treasury by Grant, but however excellent such an appointment might have been, it was not made on account of his poor health. Fessenden was never again active in politics, and his career was ended by death in September, 1869.

Before closing the account of Fessenden something should be said of the personality of the man who, though comparatively neglected by the historians of the Civil War and Reconstruction period, was nevertheless, one of the three or four ablest and most farsighted statesmen of his

---

[1] Fessenden, *op. cit.*, pp. 227 *et seq.*
[2] *Ibid.*, ch. xi.
[3] *Ibid.*, pp. 300, 308.

time. For instance, Charles Sumner, whose service in the Senate was contemporaneous with Fessenden, is very much better known, though a comparison of the two men shows Fessenden to be very much the superior in practical common sense, and quite the equal of Sumner in point of intellect. Both men were idealists, but Sumner was never willing to yield one iota of his ideal for the sake of accomplishing a practical piece of legislation, even though it should tend in the general direction of the end which he desired to accomplish. When thoroughly exasperated with Sumner's obstinacy, Fessenden exclaimed: "My constituents did not send me here to philosophize. They sent me here to act, to find out, if I could, what is best, and to do it, and they are not so short-sighted as to resolve that if they cannot do what they would, therefore they will do nothing."[1] Theodore Tilton, an extreme radical, and somewhat unfriendly towards Fessenden, said of him: "I believe that on the whole Fessenden has more continuous influence in the Senate than belongs to any other senator. He is the best debater in the body—a complete parliamentarian—a recognized authority on many and various subjects of legislation and an incorruptible man. If he were less conservative and more bold, he would approach my ideal of an American legislator."[2] Everybody who knew Fessenden, testified to his ability as a debater, to his intellectual acumen, and to his far-seeing statesmanship, as well as to his honesty, straightforwardness, and high character. Himself of absolute sincerity and integrity, he was almost petulant in opposition to sentimentality and rhetoric, and had no sympathy with those politicians who attempted to win popularity by vituperating unpopular opponents. The delicate task of reorganization

[1] *Globe*, 1st sess., 39th cong., p. 707.
[2] Editorial in the *Independent*, April 12, 1866.

should have been left to men who possessed the qualities of firmness and forbearance, of prudence and conciliation, of faith and patience. Such qualities Fessenden possessed in a high degree, while to Stevens, his eminent colleague on the committee they were foreign, and as so often happens, the task was given to the man least fitted for it.

Of the remaining thirteen members of the committee only three or four exercised any perceptible influence on the course of reconstruction, and even they were of but little importance in comparison with Stevens and Fessenden. Accordingly on account of this fact, and because of lack of space, only a brief account of each can be given here.[1]

JOHN A. BINGHAM

The chief contribution of John A. Bingham to congressional reconstruction is that part of the fourteenth amendment which provides for equality of civil rights to all citizens of the United States.[2] He was born in Mercer, Pennsylvania in 1815, but early in his life his parents removed to Ohio. After spending a couple of years at Franklin College, he took up the study of law and was admitted to the bar in 1840. This was the year of the famous " log cabin, hard cider " Presidential campaign, and young Bingham took part in it as an active supporter of the Whig ticket. In 1848, he was made a delegate to the national Whig convention at Philadelphia, where he made a fruitless effort to have his party take a bold and unequivocal stand against the further extension of slavery into the territories. In 1854,

---

[1] My biographical notices of the members of the committee are here given in the order of what seems to have been the relative importance of their contributions to the reconstruction measures of the 39th Congress, and not according to the whole life work of each.

[2] See *infra,* ch. iii and ch. vi.

he was elected to Congress as a Republican, and, with the exception of one term, served continuously until 1873. Having temporarily lost his seat in Congress because of the Democratic reaction of 1862, he was appointed in 1863 by Lincoln as judge advocate in the army and later as solicitor of the court of claims. He came conspicuously before the public in 1865, when he acted as special judge advocate in the trial of the assassins of President Lincoln. From his re-entrance into the House of Representatives in 1865 to the termination of his career in that body, he was regarded as among the five or six leading Republican members. He failed of re-election in 1872, but was solaced by an appointment the next year as minister to Japan. This position he held until 1885, when he was recalled by President Cleveland. He died in 1900 at his home in Cadiz, Ohio.[1]

In his attitude on reconstruction, Bingham is to be classed with Fessenden rather than with Stevens. Like Fessenden, he wished to avoid a breach with the President, but he was unwilling to sacrifice his principles for the sake of harmony. As has been said, he particularly desired to have the civil rights of the individual put into the special keeping of the National Government, and it is not too much to say that had it not been for his untiring efforts the provision for nationalizing civil rights would not have found a place in the fourteenth amendment. In the second session of the 39th Congress, Bingham bitterly opposed and denounced the radical members of his party because of their abandonment of the fourteenth amendment as the rock of the congressional reconstruction policy. Party ties were too strong, however, for him to oppose the party decrees, so he finally

---

[1] Memorial address of Senator J. B. Foraker, Cadiz, Ohio, 1901; *Ohio Archeological and Historical Society Publications*, vol. x, pp. 331-351. Also, Appleton's *Cyclopedia of American Biography*.

voted for the Reconstruction bill. At first, he was opposed to the impeachment of Andrew Johnson, which brought down upon him the wrath of Benjamin F. Butler, and feud existed between the two for the remainder of Bingham's career in Congress. When the Senate passed the resolution declaring illegal Johnson's removal of Stanton, Bingham was no longer able to hold out against what he had formerly termed the impeachment folly, and like every other member of his party voted for impeachment. It was in special recognition of his great legal ability that in spite of his conservative tendency, he was elected as one of the board of managers for the prosecution of the President, and made one of the best legal arguments on his side of the case. Bingham was a man of intense nervous force, great intellect, powerful in argument and masterful in speech, but his personality prevented him from ever becoming a popular idol.

ROSCOE CONKLING

With the possible exception of Thaddeus Stevens, Roscoe Conkling is the best known at the present day of the members of the committee. Though he took quite an important part in reconstruction, his principal title to fame is derived from the part played by him in politics, from the inauguration of Grant as President until his resignation from the Senate in 1881, occasioned by his difference with President Garfield over New York patronage. Conkling was born at Albany, New York, in 1829, but when he was only nine years old, his father, a United States district judge, moved to Auburn. His education extended only through high school, as "his impatience to begin the battle of life was such that he declined to enter upon a collegiate course of study."[1] In 1846, he removed to Utica, studied law in

[1] Conkling, *Life and Letters of Roscoe Conkling*, p. 14. Unless otherwise stated, this biography is my authority for all the facts concerning Conkling's life.

the office of two of the best-known attorneys in that city, and in 1850, when only twenty-one years old, was admitted to the bar. At the same time he entered politics, and after serving as district attorney and mayor of Utica, he was elected in 1858 to Congress. In politics he had been a free-soil Whig and naturally by this time had become identified with the Republican party. He served in the House from 1859 to 1863, and from 1865 to 1867. In the latter year he was elected to the Senate, where he served until 1881. He was offered the position of Chief Justice by President Grant in November, 1873, in succession to Salmon P. Chase, but declined it. "I could not take the place, for I would be forever gnawing my chains," he said in explanation of his declinature. During the whole of Grant's administration, it is no exaggeration to say that Roscoe Conkling was the power behind the throne.

During the last seven years of his life (1881-88), he engaged in the practice of law in New York City, usually acting as counsel for large commercial and transportation companies.

It was during his first four years of service in the House that Conkling won a reputation as an orator, and, barring Thaddeus Stevens, who in prominence was head and shoulders above every other member, Conkling was recognized, along with Garfield, Blaine, and Bingham, as one of the ablest four men in that body. Though Conkling differed from Thaddeus Stevens in matters of finance, and voted against the legal tender bill in 1862, he was a protégé and favorite of Stevens, and during this early period of his public career, generally took his cue in matters concerning the South from that ancient radical. Thus when Conkling entered the 39th Congress in 1865, Stevens secured for him a place on the joint committee on reconstruction. Here his chief service was rendered in drawing up, defending, and expounding the political theory of that part of the fourteenth amendment which concerns the basis of representation.[1] He was also of service in perfecting the language of other bills and resolutions for amending the Constitution which emanated from his colleagues on the committee.[2] Conkling did not favor Bingham's pet proposition (section 1 of the fourteenth amendment), though in later days, when arguing great corporation cases before the Supreme Court, he was instrumental in having that tribunal take the ground that the provision of the fourteenth amendment which forbids a state to deny to any person within its jurisdiction the equal protection of the laws, can be applied to the protection of corporations in the matter of excessive taxation.[3]

When one reviews Roscoe Conkling's life as a whole, it is impossible to feel that the claim made by himself and echoed by his biographer, that he was ever the friend of the common man, the poor and the oppressed, especially the negro, was well-founded.

GEORGE S. BOUTWELL

Perhaps the coldest, most calculating and yet unreasoning fanatic on the committee was George S. Boutwell, of Massachusetts. The reason for placing him fifth in importance is not because of any great ability which he possessed, nor because he contributed anything worthy of note to the measures of reconstruction proposed by the committee, but because he was constantly urging his colleagues on to more radical actions.

Boutwell was born in Brookline, Mass., in 1818. He was almost entirely self-educated, and like men who attain success largely through their own efforts, his ten-

---

[1] See *infra*, ch. iii.
[2] See *infra*, ch. vi and viii.
[3] See *supra*, p. 29.

dency seems to have been to over-estimate his own importance. When seventeen years old, he moved to Groton, Mass., and there as clerk in the village grocery store, he learned his first lessons in practical politics.[1] Ever a practical politician, and always desirous above all things of being on the winning side, he became a Democrat because the Democratic party was predominant in his village. In 1842, he was elected to the lower house of the Massachusetts legislature and between that time and 1851, he served for seven sessions. During 1851 and 1852 he was Governor of Massachusetts. From 1852 to 1863, he held several political positions in the state or Federal governments. He assisted in the organization of the Republican party in Massachusetts, and in 1862 was elected a member of Congress, where he served until 1869. In that year he was appointed Secretary of the Treasury by President Grant and held that office for four years. His last public service of importance was rendered as a United States senator, he having been elected in 1873 to finish the four remaining years of the term of Henry Wilson, who had been elected Vice-President. From 1877 until a few years before his death in 1905 he remained in Washington as a superannuated politician, picking up such crumbs as fell from the table of his more prosperous Republican allies.

Boutwell was a professional politician, and depended upon his political offices for his livelihood, therefore, as has been said, his chief interest was to keep his party in power and himself in office. A contemporary says of him: " Boutwell is an ardent, narrow-minded partisan, without much judgment, not devoid of talents, with more industry than capacity, ambitious of notoriety, with a mind without com-

---

[1] Unless otherwise stated, the source of my information concerning Boutwell's life is his autobiography, *Reminiscences of Sixty Years in Public Affairs*.

prehension nor well trained; an extreme radical, destitute of fairness where party is involved."[1] Because he believed the surest way to continue the supremacy of the Republican party was to commit it to radicalism, Boutwell advocated the most extreme measures in dealing with the South. He desired a wholesale disfranchisement of the rebels, and an equally sweeping enfranchisement of the negroes. To Boutwell is due the credit of the authorship of the fifteenth amendment. He professed to believe that unless negro suffrage were granted, the United States Government would fall. His theory of suffrage and his idea of the necessity for negro suffrage may be seen in the following excerpt from one of his speeches on the subject:

The right to vote exists independently of all human agency in the sense of law; and the doctrine that the right of voting is a conventional right, is not sustained by reason or history. . . . I believe that negro suffrage ought to be made a condition precedent to the readmission of the southern states, and unless it is made so, a way is open leading to the destruction of this government, from which there is no escape. . . . It will fail and fall from the fact that by restoration without this all essential guarantee, we put into the hands of our enemies in the South two weapons, the blows of which we shall be powerless to parry. These weapons are: (1) The re-admitted rebels, in conjunction with their copperhead friends, will assume the Confederate debt, and force the national government to pay for the slaves. This will cause government paper and bonds to fall so low that our credit abroad will be ruined. As a result, England and France, taking advantage of our situation, will go to war with us, during which the southerners will again march out of the Union and bid the North defiance. (2) If you fail to secure the black man in his rights, he will become in a degree alien and hostile to the national government. In

[1] *Diary of Gideon Welles,* vol. iii, p. 239.

this condition he will be ready to accept the right of suffrage from the southern leaders, and transfer his allegiance from you to them. Then when the next struggle comes, and the southern leaders undertake the destruction of the government, he will be on their side, and not on ours as he was before.[1]

J. W. GRIMES

Grimes was born in Deering, New Hampshire, in 1816. In 1836 he was graduated from Dartmouth College, and in the same year moved to Burlington, Iowa. Here he practised law, served as territorial librarian, as delegate in the territorial legislature, and as a member of the state assembly after the admission of Iowa into the Union. In 1854, he was elected governor of the state by a combination of the Whigs and Freesoilers, and during his four years of office he did much towards building up the Republican party, and developing anti-slavery sentiment in his state. As a reward for his services, and as a recognition of his ability, the Republicans elected him to the United States Senate in 1859, which position he held for ten years, retiring because of ill health. He died in 1871.[2]

Grimes' chief service in the Senate during the war was rendered as chairman of the committee on naval affairs. Theodore Tilton said of him: " Senator Grimes, of Iowa, who speaks little and accomplishes much, is one of the pillars against whom weaker men lean and are propped into strength. It is hard to find anywhere a better worker in public business than Senator Grimes, though he is not a man of popular reputation."[3] At this time Grimes was acting

[1] *Globe*, 1st. sess., 39th cong., p. 309.

[2] Salter, *Life of Grimes;* Appleton's *Cyclopedia of American Biography.*

[3] *Independent,* April 12, 1866. Tilton was editor of this paper. He was a talented fanatic who kept constant watch on political affairs, and was intimate with some of the Republican members of Congress.

with the radicals, and in the opinion of Gideon Welles, he was directing their course.¹ Though he was no doubt instrumental in preventing some weak members of the party from surrendering to the President during the early stages of the quarrel with the executive, Grimes, like Fessenden, with whom he generally acted in concert, opposed the most extreme measures of his associates, and was one of the seven Republican "traitors" who voted for the acquittal of Andrew Johnson. Grimes was not the author of any of the reconstruction measures proposed by the committee, but there seems little doubt that during the first session of the 39th Congress, at least, his influence was potent. Welles² even thought that he really controlled Fessenden, and that the leadership of the latter in the Senate was only nominal, Grimes being the real leader. This, however, is doubtful, as the unanimity of the two men on public questions was more likely due to their friendship and the similarity of their ideas.

GEORGE H. WILLIAMS ³

Williams of Oregon, whom the acrimonious Welles characterizes as "a third-rate lawyer, weak and corrupt," ⁴ owes his importance to the fact of his being the author of the first Reconstruction act of 1867.⁵ He was a native of Columbia county, New York, having been born in 1823. His first important political position came in 1853 when he was appointed by Franklin Pierce to the chief justiceship of the territory of Oregon. In 1865, after that territory had

---

¹ *Diary*, vol. iii, p. 14. For the reason of Grimes' opposition to the President, see *infra*, ch. iv, p. 229.

² *Diary*, vol. ii, p. 635.

³ *National Cyclopedia of Biography*.

⁴ *Diary*, vol. iii, pp. 358, 359.

⁵ See *infra*, ch. viii.

become a state, he was elected to the United States Senate as a Republican. He was in all respects of the same type as Boutwell, being a mere time-server and office-seeker. His other contribution to legislation during his senatorial term was the Tenure of Office act, and he worked indefatigably for the conviction of Andrew Johnson. When the radicals made Grant their President, Williams became one of his chief flatterers and hangers-on, and was rewarded with a place in the Cabinet as Attorney-General, which he held from 1872 to 1875. In 1873 Grant nominated him for Chief Justice of the Supreme Court, but even the radical Senate retained sufficient respect for that high office, and his confirmation was refused.

HOWARD, MORRILL, WASHBURNE, BLOW AND HARRIS [1]

None of the other five Republican members of the committee were of any particular importance in shaping the course of reconstruction.

Jacob M. Howard, senator from Michigan, was a worthy protégé of his colleague Zachary Chandler—one of the most vulgar and reckless of the radicals—and served consistently in the vanguard of the extreme negrophiles. His chief claim to fame rests upon the important part played by him in organizing the Republican party. He drew up the platform of the first convention ever held by the Republicans, and is said to have given his party its name. Howard served in the Senate from 1862 to 1871, and never held any other very important position. He was born in 1805 and died in 1871.

Justin S. Morrill, of Vermont, born in 1810, engaged in

[1] The sources of my information for the lives of these men are Appleton's *Cyclopedia* and the *National Cyclopedia of Biography*. My opinions of them are derived from their speeches and votes in Congress and in the committee; also contemporary estimates of them.

mercantile and agricultural pursuits until 1854, when he was elected to Congress. It is quite possible that he holds the record for length of continuous service in the legislative department of the United States Government. He was a member of the lower house for twelve years, and of the upper for thirty-one years, making a continuous service in Congress of forty-three years. He was an honest and hard-working legislator, but his chief labors were directed towards maintaining a protective tariff and a sound financial system. The only part taken by him in reconstruction was to attend the meetings of the committee and cast his vote, which was regularly on the side of radicalism.

Elihu B. Washburne was, like Morrill, an honest man and though he was long in politics he does not deserve to rank as a statesman of conspicuous ability. He was born in Maine in 1816, and in 1840 he removed to Illinois, taking up his residence at Galena. Here he began the practice of law, engaged actively in politics as a Whig and in 1852 was elected to Congress, where he served continuously until 1869. He was appointed by President Grant Secretary of State as a compliment for the assistance which Washburne had rendered him personally toward gaining recognition of, and promotion for, his ability as a commander during the first two years of the war. Washburne almost immediately resigned the premiership and accepted the mission to France in its stead. He was in Paris during the terrible days of the Prussian siege and the still more horrible period succeeding, and discharged the delicate duties devolving upon him in such a manner as to win the appreciation and approval of President Grant and Secretary Fish. After serving the United States in Paris for nearly nine years, he returned to America and retired to private life in Chicago, where he died in 1887.

Washburne was deeply interested in reconstruction and was classed among the most extreme radicals but was not prominent in originating or in advocating any of the measures proposed by the committee. Upon the death of Thaddeus Stevens, he was made chairman of the committee on appropriations, and from the jealousy with which he guarded the financial interests of the government against the efforts of the "lobby" and the "log-rollers," he was the first to win the sobriquet, "Watchdog of the Treasury."

Henry T. Blow, of Missouri, and Ira Harris, of New York, were practcally nonentities. They were not by nature radicals, but neither had force of character sufficient to act independently of party. The former was a Virginian by birth, but removed to Missouri in 1830, when only thirteen years old. For a few years preceding the war he served in the state senate, and though a southerner and a Democrat, he was opposed to secession and rendered valuable service to the Union cause in Missouri by assisting in preventing that state from joining the Confederacy. For this he was rewarded by Lincoln with the appointment to the Venezuela mission. After holding this position for less than a year, he resigned, and in 1862 was elected to Congress, where he served two terms. In the committee he at first acted with the radicals, but in the second session of Congress he was a follower of Bingham, who, as has been seen, opposed Stevens in his attempt to reduce the rebel states to the position of territories. In 1869 he was appointed by Grant minister to Brazil, where he remained for two years. He died in 1875.

Harris was born in Montgomery county, New York, in 1802, graduated from Union College in 1824, and was admitted to the bar in 1828. During the thirties and forties he figured in state politics as a Whig, and served several terms as a legislator. From 1848 to 1861, he was a judge of the state supreme court, and in the latter year was elected to succeed William H. Seward in the United States Senate. He did not distinguish himself as senator, and though he acted with the radicals in all matters pertaining to reconstruction, the Republicans in the New York legislature did not re-elect him in 1867, but instead chose Roscoe Conkling, who, it was believed, would make the influence of the Empire State felt, and who could speak on behalf of its interests as Harris and his colleague Morgan had not done. After his defeat for re-election, Harris retired to private life and died in 1875.

THE DEMOCRATS [1]

The Democratic minority in the 39th Congress was very small, being hardly more than one-fourth of the membership in either house. In mental calibre and political acumen the Democrats were even more woefully weak than they were in numbers. To this general statement there were a few exceptions, the most notable being Reverdy Johnson. He was born in Annapolis, Maryland, in 1796, received his education at St. John's College, and studied law in the office of his father, who was chancellor of the state. In 1817, he moved to Baltimore and practiced law with great success. Like most lawyers of his time, he engaged in politics and became well-known in the public life of the state and nation. During the thirties he served several years in the Maryland senate, and was in the United States Senate from 1845 till 1849, but resigned in the latter year to accept the position of Attorney-General in President Taylor's Cabinet. Until 1856 he was a Whig but in that year, when his party practically ceased to exist, he entered the Democratic party and

[1] *Op. cit.*

supported the candidacy of Buchanan. In 1860, he voted for Douglas and in the following year re-entered the Senate. Like Crittenden, of Kentucky, and other Border State men, he did all in his power to avert hostilities, but when attempts at compromise proved unavailing he gave cordial support to the administration in its measures for prosecuting the war. When peace was restored, he urged the immediate restoration of the southern states to their former place in the Union. Though acting generally with the Democrats, Johnson was not primarily a party man, and in the committee preferred to use his influence and vote in mollifying the measures of his adversaries, rather than in hopeless opposition to everything proposed by them. For instance, when in March, 1867, he saw that the radicals were becoming more and more extreme in their demands for a "thorough" reconstruction, he voted for the Reconstruction bill, because he feared their next move would be to reduce the southern states to the position of territories. In 1868, upon the retirement of Charles Francis Adams as minister to the court of St. James, Johnson was appointed in his place and negotiated the Johnson-Clarendon treaty concerning the damage done to American commerce by the English-built Confederate cruisers. The treaty was not acceptable, however, to the Republican party, so it was rejected by the Senate and Johnson was recalled by President Grant in 1869. He retired to private life and died in 1876.

Henry Grider, of Kentucky, and Andrew Jackson Rogers, of New Jersey, were the two remaining Democratic members of the committee, and as such exercised no influence on its deliberations. The former, born in the same year as Reverdy Johnson, was of Whig antecedents and served in the House as a member of that party for two terms in the middle forties. Re-entering the House as a war Democrat in 1861, he served through the first session of the 39th Congress, but died before the meeting of the second session.

Rogers, born in 1828, entered Congress for the first time in 1863. He belonged to that brand of Democrats designated contemptuously as "copperheads." He opposed every measure of the Republicans that had for its purpose the alleviation of the condition of the colored race. He was violent in his hatred of that race, and because of his capacity for speaking in denunciatory terms of it, he was one of the few minority members whom the majority allowed to speak at will. They correctly estimated the value of his remarks as political capital for themselves, as convenient texts to cite, showing what might be expected to be the fate of the " wards of the nation " should a combination of copperheads and rebels again get control of the government.

CHAPTER III

Representation and Civil Rights [1]

The particular phase of the negro question which most concerned Republican politicians in 1865-6 was the problem of representation of the colored population in Congress. It will be remembered that, according to the Constitution, the slave states had been entitled to representation for three-fifths of their slaves. Under this provision the fifteen slave states had, in 1860, eighteen more representatives than they would have had if representation had been based on the white population alone.[2] Now that the slaves were free, the three-fifths rule would no longer operate, and should there be no amendment to the Constitution on the subject, all the negroes would be counted in apportioning representation. This would entitle the former slave states to about a dozen representatives in addition to what they had in 1860. That is to say, should no change be made in the Constitution, the southern states [3] would be entitled to about thirty representatives for their colored population, though not a single

---

[1] For the part of the journal relating to this chapter, see *supra*, pp. 41 to 63.

[2] These and the succeeding figures are based on a table of statistics carefully prepared by Roscoe Conkling and used by him in a debate on this question on January 22, 1866. *Globe*, 1st sess., 39th cong., pp. 356-359.

[3] This included the four states which did not secede, but since their negro population was comparatively small, they would not have been much affected. According to Conkling's figures, the fifteen former slave states would have been entitled to ninety-four representatives based on their

negro could vote in any of them. This state of affairs the Republicans determined to remedy before they would consent to admit the representatives from the rebel states. It is not surprising then to find that the first task undertaken by the committee after its organization was the readjustment of the basis of representation. It was with this subject that the committee busied itself during the first weeks of January, 1866.

Propositions to amend the Constitution so that representatives should be apportioned among the states according to their respective numbers of voters had been submitted to the House by Thaddeus Stevens and others as early as December 5, 1865.[1] Opposition to such method of apportionment was raised by the New England members; and James G. Blaine, speaking for his section,[2] declared that New England had fewer voters in proportion to her population than the states further west. This was due to two causes: first, more of her males than females emigrated to the West, and thus left her with a disproportionately large number of women; second, her suffrage was not on so broad a basis as most of the other states, as educational qualifications for voting were generally required.

On the other hand, Blaine's rival, Roscoe Conkling, defended the proposition and declared[3] that there were only two sensible methods of apportioning representation; one, according to the entire population, and the other, according to the voting population of the states. Any method not embodying one

total population, whereas they would have been entitled to only about sixty-five if based on their white population alone. According to the apportionment under the census of 1860 (when the three-fifths rule was still in operation) they were entitled to eighty-five.

[1] *Globe*, 1st sess., 39th cong., pp. 9, 10.
[2] January 8, 1866, *ibid.*, pp. 141, 142.
[3] *Globe*, 1st sess., 39th cong., p. 233.

or the other of these principles, would prove indefensible from the standpoint of political science, and could not be easily applied in practice. Moreover, he maintained that New England would not lose any representatives by an apportionment according to voters, and referred to his table of statistics in proof thereof. His argument, however, did not convince the New England men, and so persistent was their opposition to an apportionment according to voters, that both Conkling and Stevens abandoned their proposition, and after considering several suggestions, the committee finally, on January 20th, fixed upon the following resolution:[1]

Representatives and direct taxes shall be apportioned among the several states which may be included within this Union, according to their respective numbers, counting the whole number of persons in each state, excluding Indians not taxed; provided that whenever the elective franchise shall be denied or abridged in any state on account of race or color, all persons of such race or color shall be excluded from the basis of representation.

This was virtually the resolution that had been introduced in the House by Blaine on January 8th, when he objected to an apportionment according to voters. Consequently it was satisfactory to the New England members.

The resolution was reported to the House by Thaddeus Stevens on January 22nd.[2] He consumed a few minutes in explaining its meaning, and its effect on the basis of representation. He considered it very important that it be sent immediately to the state legislatures then in session, so that they would have time to act upon it before they adjourned. He therefore hoped that it would pass the House before

---

[1] See *supra*, p. 53.   [2] *Globe*, p. 351.

sunset, and proposed that only two hours, divided equally between the two sides of the House, be allowed for its debate. Even his own followers, however, were unwilling to sustain him in such precipitancy, and the debate continued for a week on the resolution, after which it was recommitted for amendment.[1] The only change made by the committee was to strike out the words, "and direct taxes," and on January 31st, it was reported back to the House. On the same day it passed the House by the requisite two-thirds majority.[2] After a long drawn out and desultory debate, frequently interrupted by other business, it was brought to a vote in the Senate on March 9th. Charles Sumner considered it a compromise of human rights and he was able to carry enough radical senators with him in opposition to it to compass its defeat.[3]

In truth the measure deserved no better fate, for it was entirely partisan. It was intended to deprive the South of as many representatives as possible without decreasing the number to which any northern state was then entitled. It will be noted that it provided that if any negro should be disfranchised on account of his color the entire negro race was to be deducted from the basis of representation. It was thus even more of a party measure than the later section 2 of the fourteenth amendment, and much more so than the proposition which apportioned representatives according to the number of voters. In spite of its partisan character, it was ably defended as being consistent with the sound political philosophy that had been evolved concerning the right of representation.[4] Conkling's speech, which is epitomized in the succeeding paragraphs, was the best de-

[1] *Globe*, p. 493. See *supra*, p. 58.
[2] *Ibid.*, pp. 535 *et seq.*
[3] *Globe*, p. 1289.
[4] Conkling, *Globe*, pp. 356-359.

fense made of the proposition from the standpoint of political theory.

It changes, he held, no principle laid down in the Constitution, as the original provision (article 1, section 2) clearly indicates that political representation does not belong to those who have no political existence. The government of a free political society belongs to its members, and does not belong to others. If others are allowed to share in its control, they do so by express concessions, not by right. It was this principle that brought the so-called "three-fifths compromise" into the national charter.

The slaves of the South were not part of that political society which formed the Constitution of the United States. Hence it followed that political power was not to be apportioned by treating them as political persons. Natural persons they were, producers they were, and the product of their labor was the proper subject of taxation. But direct taxes and representation ought to be distributed uniformly among the members of a free government. All alike should bear the burdens, all alike should share the benefits.

Here was a clear principle, palpably right, easy and certain in its application. It applied itself universally and covered the whole case with one exception. The slave alone was the anomaly and the nondescript—a man and not a man; in flesh and blood, alive; politically dead; a native, an inhabitant, a producer, but without recognized political attribute or prerogative; the representative in the system of nothing but value.

What could be done with him? The free states could not maintain that he was a person to be taxed. The slave states could not maintain that he was a person to be represented without some special provision. Both taxation and representation, however, were desirable from the respective standpoints of the two sections. Therefore they made the "three-fifths compromise," which was purely an arbitrary agreement.

This operated so long as there was anything for it to operate on. Now a new anomaly exists. The four million people who have suddenly been released from slavery, while falling within the category of " free persons," are not yet political persons. This emancipated multitude has no political status. Emancipation vitalizes only natural rights, not political rights. Enfranchisement alone carries with it political rights, and these emancipated millions are no more enfranchised now than when they were slaves. They never had political power. Their masters had a fraction of power, but since the relationship of master and slave is destroyed, this fraction of power cannot longer survive in the masters. There is only one place where it could logically go, and that is to the negroes; but since it is said they are unfit to have it, it is a power without a rightful owner, and should be resumed by the whole nation at once. If a black man counts at all now, he counts not as three-fifths of a man but as five-fifths. Four millions, therefore, and not three-fifths of four millions, are to be reckoned with now, and all these four millions are presumed to be unfit for political existence. Since the framers of the Constitution did not foresee such a contingency, and expected that emancipation would come gradually and be accompanied by education and enfranchisement, they provided for no situation whereby eleven states might claim twenty-eight representatives besides their just proportion.

Twenty-eight votes to be cast here and in the Electoral College for those held not fit to sit as jurors, not fit to testify in court, not fit to be plaintiff in a suit, not fit to approach the ballot box! Twenty-eight votes, to be controlled by those who once betrayed the government, and for those so destitute, we are assured, of intelligent instinct as not to be fit for free agency!

Shall this be? Shall four million beings count four millions, in managing the affairs of the nation, who are pronounced by their fellow beings unfit to participate in administering government in the states where they live, who are pronounced unworthy of the least and most paltry part in political affairs? Shall one hundred twenty-seven thousand white people in New York count but one vote in this House while the same number of white people in Mississippi have three votes? Shall the death of slavery add two-fifths to the entire power which slavery had when slavery was living? Shall one white man have as much share in the government as three other white men merely because he lives where blacks outnumber whites two to one?[1] Shall this inequality exist, and exist only in favor of those who without cause drenched the land with blood and covered it with mourning? Shall such be the reward of those who did the foulest and guiltiest act which crimsons the annals of recorded time? No, sir; not if I can help it.

This proposition rests upon a principle already imbedded in the Constitution, and as old as free government itself—a principle that representation does not belong to those who have not political existence, but to those that have. The object of the amendment is to enforce this truth. Every state will be left free to extend or withhold the elective franchise on such terms as it pleases, and this without losing anything in representation, if the terms are impartial as to all. If, however, there is found a race so worthless that to belong to it is alone cause of exclusion from political action, the race is not to be counted here in Congress.

In spite of Conkling's able defense of the amendment, even he acknowledged that it was primarily for party and sectional advantage, as the concluding part of his speech will show: "Though the amendment is common to all

---

[1] This was the stock argument of the Republicans in favor of the amendment. *Cf.* speeches by Blaine, Fessenden and Stevens. *Globe,* pp. 376, 702, 536.

states, and equal for all; its operation will of course be practically only in the South. No northern state will lose by it; even New York, in her great population, has so few blacks that she could exclude them all from enumeration and it would make no difference in her representation."

Some of those radicals who believed that the Declaration of Independence was to all intents and purposes a part of the Constitution, thought Congress already had the power to enfranchise the negroes. Moreover, they maintained that at the present time the state had no right to disfranchise persons on account of race or color, and therefore opposed the amendment because it acknowledged the existence of such a right.[1] Sumner, for instance, argued that since Congress had derived its authority for granting equal civil rights from the second section of the thirteenth amendment, the same provision empowered it to pass a simple resolution declaring there should be no inequality in political privileges.[2] He believed that the section referred to, together with the "guarantee clause" of the Constitution, would justify Congress in declaring by joint resolution that there shall be "no Oligarchy, Aristocracy, Caste, or Monopoly," invested with peculiar powers; but all persons shall be equal before the law, whether in the court room or at the ballot box. "And this statute, made in pursuance of the Constitution, shall be the supreme law of the land, anything in the constitution or laws of any state to the contrary notwithstanding." This resolution Sumner designated the "Great Guarantee," and declared that without it, any constitutional amendment would be utterly worthless.

To this argument Fessenden replied that the amendment neither granted nor took away a privilege from any state in the control of the suffrage.[3]

[1] Kelley, Shellabarger and Sumner, *Globe*, pp. 377, 405, 673 *et seq.*
[2] Ibid.
[3] *Globe*, pp. 702 *et seq.*

It merely punishes the abuse of a privilege which the states certainly possess and always have possessed and exercised.[1] Suffrage is not such a natural right that it must be conferred upon every free man, but is rather in the nature of a privilege. A voter is an officer as much in substance as the man who enters the jury box or as any man who holds an office. Voting is a trust imposed by law, and although suffrage should be extended as far as the public good will allow, no man can complain that he is injured when a just and reasonable law provides that something more is necessary to him than a bare existence as a free man in a community in order to exercise it. Any disability imposed, however, should be one that by thrift, education, and right-living can be overcome. Certainly color or race is not a just disability. The amendment, however, should serve as an inducement to the southern states to build school houses and churches and educate their colored people until they are fit to vote, as these states will desire the full quota of representation to which their population would ordinarily entitle them.

Before leaving the arguments of the Republicans on the amendment and taking up those of the Democrats, it should be remarked that a great number of the former, while not following the vagaries of Sumner, professed themselves to be in favor of a proposition like the later fifteenth amendment, whereby the right to vote could not be denied on account of race or color.[2] There were two reasons, however, why they could not be induced to vote for such an amendment at this time. In the first place, as they themselves pointed out, most of the northern states did not then permit negroes to vote, some having repeatedly pronounced against it; therefore, it would have been futile to ask three-fourths of the states to ratify such an amendment when only one-

---

[1] In only six states were negroes allowed to vote at that time.
[2] See, for instance, speech of Henderson, *Globe*, appendix, pp 105-124.

fourth of even the loyal states had then adopted its principle. They did not openly mention the second reason, but it was none the less potent on that account. Such an amendment as the fifteenth would not at that time have been of any political value to the Republican party. The only method whereby the radicals might have received any addition to their number through negro suffrage in the South, would have been that employed by them a year later in the Reconstruction act. Few of them, however, dared go so far at this time. Simply to have prescribed negro suffrage in such terms as those of the fifteenth amendment, and left the southern state governments, controlled as they then were by the native whites, to put in operation the machinery for its enforcement, would not have resulted in the election of any more representatives by negroes then, than are elected by them to-day.

The Democrats were quite as much opposed to having the representation in the South cut down as the Republicans were to having it increased. Hence they too were actuated most by considerations of party, but like their opponents, they brought forward arguments not of a partisan character. The principal grounds upon which they based their opposition were:

First, there is a difference between the right to vote and the right to representation. This difference the Republicans do not appear to perceive. It is the interests of the entire people of a given section that are represented by their chosen delegates in Congress; and the interests of those people are generally identical whether they all have the right to vote or not. Thus the negroes in the South draw their sustenance from the same industries as do the white people, and it is equally to their advantage that those industries be adequately represented in the national legislature. For instance, the colored agricultural laborer or small farmer in

Georgia or Mississippi would suffer just as much from the tax of three cents a pound on cotton as his white employer or landlord. In fact, since taxes of that sort are generally shifted from the employer to the employee, or the landlord to the tenant, he probably would suffer even more in proportion than his former master. Likewise high protective duties on such manufactured articles as are required in the agricultural regions of the South would bear quite as heavily on the colored population as on the white.[1]

Second, the proposition violates the doctrine sacred to Americans, that there shall be no taxation without representation. It inflicts upon the states for refusing to the colored population an unqualified right of suffrage a penalty which it does not inflict upon them for refusing the same thing to the white population. While it denies representation to the states for their negroes, they are counted when direct taxes are levied; and in that indirect way, the states are compelled to grant unqualified negro suffrage in order to obtain their rights under the present organic law.[2]

Third, since the Republicans were doing so much for human rights, the Democrats very pertinently asked why they were neglecting the rights of the women, who surely were as capable of voting as were the negroes.[3] It was therefore moved that if any person be disfranchised by a state on account of sex, that all persons of that sex be deducted from the basis of representation.[4] It is not probable

---

[1] Reverdy Johnson, *Globe*, pp. 763-770.

[2] Rogers, *Globe*, pp. 353-356.   [3] Brooks, *Globe*, pp. 379, 380.

[4] James Brooks, of New York, presented a petition signed by Mrs. E. Cady Stanton, Susan B. Anthony and others, in which they said: "We respectfully ask an amendment of the Constitution that shall prohibit the several states from disfranchising any of their citizens on the ground of sex—for justice and equality, your petitioners will ever pray." They subsequently asked that at least no new barrier be interposed against woman's right to the ballot. *Globe*, p. 380.

that the Democrats were at heart any more in favor of woman suffrage than were the Republicans, and they made this move with the sole idea of embarrassing their opponents; they were doubtless sincere, however, in declaring that they preferred woman suffrage to negro suffrage.

Fourth, if the Republicans are so desirous of readjusting representation on a basis of perfect fairness, why, asked the Democrats, do they not change the composition of the Senate? It is true that there was a time when it would have been sufficient to reply to this question with the simple statement that in the Senate the states are represented in their sovereign capacity as equals; but now, when talk of state sovereignty and state equality is scoffed at, why should the Senate be spared? New England, for instance, has twelve senators, and thereby exercises a preponderating influence; whereas, by a just reapportionment according to voting strength or population she would not be entitled to nearly so many.[1]

Fifth, the Democrats had two objections that were not directed against the merits of the amendment but against the methods employed in passing it. (1) It was being passed without consulting the very people whom it most concerned —the white people of the South. (2) The amendment should not be submitted to those partisan state legislatures in the North which had not been elected when this question was an issue; for those legislatures would act solely with a view to party advantage. The only fair method would be to submit it to state conventions whose members should be elected with reference to their attitude on this question alone. The people of the northern states were too fair-

---

[1] Buckalew, *Globe*, pp. 957 *et seq*. *Cf.* also editorial in *New York World*, January 23, 1866. New England members exercised preponderating influence at that time by holding the chairmanships of the more important Senate committees.

minded to force upon the South universal negro suffrage, as this measure was calculated to do, when they had not adopted it for themselves.[1]

The opinions of the press varied from the extreme radical position taken by the *Independent*[2] that the amendment was calculated to put the negroes back into the hands of the rebels, to that of the Democratic New York *World*,[3] which declared that its object was the permanent disfranchisement of the southern states. The Republican press as a whole did not support the measure with enthusiasm. *Harper's Weekly*[4] opposed the amendment at first on the ground that it would fail in its purpose of forcing the southern whites to grant suffrage to the negroes. Later, however, the same journal withdrew its opposition, not because it viewed the amendment with any more favor, but because it had come to understand that it was only the first of a series of measures which the committee would propose for securing the negroes in their civil and political rights. The New York *Times*,[5] voicing the sentiment of the administration Republicans, strongly opposed the resolution and declared that the first duty of Congress was to restore the Union; amendments could be considered later. Even the New York *Tribune*[6] was at first lukewarm, for it, like *Harper's Weekly*, desired that Congress should make negro suffrage one of the conditions precedent to the readmission of the southern delegations. The *Tribune*, however, being too good a party organ not to see the value of the amendment as a party measure, soon came to its de-

---

[1] Rogers, *Globe*, pp. 353-356.
[2] *Ibid.*, February 1, 1866.
[3] *Ibid.*, January 23, 1866.
[4] *Ibid.*, February 10 and 17, 1866.
[5] *Ibid.*, February 17, 1866.
[6] *Ibid.*, January 24 and 29, 1866.

fense and declared it to be intrinsically just and proper. The New York *Herald*,[1] which at that time was friendly to the administration, saw nothing unfair in the amendment, but opposed it on the ground that it would necessitate further delay in restoring the Union. Moreover, it declared that the position taken by the extreme radicals as to the power of Congress over civil and political rights, was correct; and it asked the radicals why they did not grant the negroes the right to vote by a simple legislative enactment. Replying to its own question, it said the answer was clear; the radicals dared not face the American people on the direct issue of negro suffrage. The New York *Sun*[2] saw in the amendment an attempt to force the southern people to grant unqualified negro suffrage, and feared that their love for political power would bring about such a result. This it opposed, and declared that already there were too many illiterate voters in the country; to add a million more to their number, would be an act treasonable to enlightened democratic government.

The consensus of opinion among the thinking non-political element of the Republican party was no doubt well expressed by an editorial in the *Nation*[3] on the question of apportioning representation. An epitome of this editorial may well conclude the discussion of the subject.

The amendment as reported has two advantages over the proposition to make legal voters the basis of representation. (1) It does not punish, as the other would have done, the older states for sending large drafts of their young men to the West. (2) It does not tempt the states into competing for voters, thus cheapening the suffrage. The amendment,

[1] Rogers, *Globe*, January 10 and 24, 1866.
[2] *Ibid.*, January 23, 1866.
[3] *Ibid.*, February 1, 1866.

however, does not secure any human being in any of the revolted states in the possession of his rights. It does not provide for freedom of speech, of the person, or of instruction.[1] It does nothing for the restoration of industry. It does not furnish any southerner with a single reason for laying aside his old fear or hatred for the Union or for desiring to be in feeling, as well as in fact and in law, one of its citizens. It does not remove any of the causes, whatever they may be, which now either hinder or retard the assimilation of society in both sections into one homogeneous whole. The fact that it fails to do any of these things is not necessarily a good reason for opposing it. It may have good ends without accomplishing one of these results. But these are the great ends of any process of reconstruction. Any amendment now up, or likely to come up for consideration, that does not materially help to obtain these results ought to have striking merits of some kind to entitle it to the solemn confirmation of a national vote.

The only thing the amendment will accomplish is the reduction of the southern delegation—and this is a gain only so long as there is a disposition in that part of the country to embarrass the national credit by desiring the repudiation of the debt, or so long as they exhibit any disposition to make the national government pay for the damage done them during the war. But it is likely that they will soon cease to show any such disposition, after which what position does this amendment leave us in? The South would have a few delegates less in Congress and one great cause of northern uneasiness would have been removed, but the problem of social and political inequality in the South would remain as far from solution as ever. A large portion of the southern population might still, probably would still, be permanently excluded from citizenship on grounds which we all hold to be absurd and unchristian, if not utterly repugnant to the spirit of our institutions. Caste

---

[1] One of the chief complaints of northern people, traveling or dwelling in the South, was the restraint under which they were placed in expressing their sentiments in regard to slavery and questions connected with it.

at the South might still be created and perpetuated. A feudal system, based on serfdom, would still be possible under the Constitution.

The *Nation*[1] then demanded that Congress frame an amendment that would put into the hands of the national government the safeguarding of the civil and political rights of all persons within its jurisdiction. This journal, like its radical contemporaries, was confident that the moral force of such an amendment would prove irresistible and was certain that it would be ratified by the states. That the radicals in Congress did not share the confidence of their party organs, however, is made evident by their action in regard to a resolution to amend the Constitution so as to give Congress the power to enforce equal civil rights in all the states of the Union.

At this time laws discriminating against the negroes and denying to them civil rights on an equality with white people, were being passed by the legislatures in the southern states.[2] To the North these laws seemed harsh and unjust, and on the very day that the 39th Congress met, Charles Sumner introduced some resolutions, providing among several other things for equal civil rights.[3] By a reference to the journal of the committee, it will be seen that on January 9th Fessenden proposed that in addition to an amendment modifying the basis of representation, another giving the national government the power to secure all persons in their civil rights should be passed before representatives from the insurgent states could be permitted to resume their seats in Congress.[4] On January 11th, a bill giving Congress

[1] *Ibid.*, February 1 and 8, 1866.
[2] Dunning, *Reconstruction, Political and Economic*, pp. 54-59.
[3] *Globe*, p. 2.
[4] See *supra*, p. 42.

power over the subject was reported to the Senate from the judiciary committee,[1] and though there was not much doubt that it would become law, yet some of the Republicans, either because they doubted the constitutionality of the bill or because they feared that it might be repealed by some subsequent Congress, desired to insert the guarantee of civil rights in the Constitution and thus place the subject beyond cavil or repeal.

Therefore, as soon as the committee had disposed of the resolution on the basis of representation it began to devote its attention to the formulation of a resolution amending the Constitution in regard to civil rights.[2] The task was not an easy one, as there was much diversity of sentiment on the question, even among the Republican members, and it was not until February 3rd that the committee by a vote of 7 to 6 adopted the following resolution:[3]

The Congress shall have power to make all laws which shall be necessary and proper to secure to the citizens of each state all privileges and immunities of citizens in the several states (Art. 4, Sec. 2); and to all persons in the several states equal protection in the rights of life, liberty and property (5th amendment).

It was not until the 13th, however, that Bingham reported the resolution, as adopted by the committee, to the House.[4] That body did not receive the proposition with wild enthusiasm, and even denied it the privilege of being considered as a special order. Since to have placed it on the regular calendar would have meant its indefinite post-

[1] Flack, *Adoption of the Fourteenth Amendment*, p. 19.
[2] See *supra*, pp. 46 to 62.
[3] *Ibid.*, p. 61.
[4] *Globe*, p. 813.

ponement, it was recommitted, its friends hoping to present it on a later and more propitious occasion. Nearly two weeks elapsed before such an occasion offered itself, and Bingham had the temerity to bring it again to the attention of the House.[1] After a debate lasting three days, it became evident that the resolution could not secure the two-thirds majority necessary for its passage as a proposed amendment to the Constitution. It was therefore agreed with the tacit consent of Bingham to defer its further consideration until the second Tuesday in April.[2] When the second Tuesday in April arrived, nothing was said about the proposed civil rights amendment. Indeed, it was never heard of again as a separate proposition, but a few weeks later, clothed in different language, it appeared as section 1 of the fourteenth amendment.

This difference in language is worthy of notice, as the proposition under consideration differs from the latter in that in express terms it conferred upon Congress positive power to enforce the bill of rights in the states.[3] Bingham so stated when he introduced the resolution into Congress.[4] He stood almost alone as its champion and defender, and made the only important speech advocating its adoption.

---

[1] *Globe*, p. 1033, February 26.

[2] *Globe*, p. 1095. In addition to the Democrats, a great many Republicans, including practically the entire New York delegation, were opposed to the amendment. The Republicans, when postponing it, gave as their reason a desire for further conference concerning its exact terms. As a matter of fact they considered it poor political ammunition, and feared it would have an adverse effect on the Connecticut election which then was held early in April. *Cf.* editorial in New York *World*, Mar. 3, 1866. Even in the fall campaign the Republican orators attempted to make but little political capital out of this measure. See *infra*, ch. vii.

[3] The language employed was adapted from section 2 of article iv and from the fifth amendment.

[4] *Globe*, p. 1033.

Before proceeding with the consideration of his speech, however, some notice will be taken of the principal points made against it.

The opponents of the measure believed it to be the embodiment of centralization, and thought that by it the states would be deprived of those rights which were reserved to them by the organic law.[1] It was impolitic and out of harmony with the whole theory of the Constitution, which was intended to give Congress power over matters of a general nature only, and leave to the individual states control over their own municipal concerns. It was especially uncalled for at this time, when, after five years of centralization, the tendency should all be the other way. During those five years the government had destroyed the heresy of state sovereignty; let not another heresy of the opposite kind, and still more dangerous to freedom, rise in its place.[2]

Not every immunity and privilege, granted to citizens in one state, should be forced upon any other state. This amendment if adopted would coerce all states into giving the franchise to negroes and would annul all laws on marriage, divorce, and so forth, in the several states. Under it all state legislation in codes of criminal and civil jurisprudence and procedure, affecting the individual citizen, might be over-ridden, repealed, or abolished, and the law of Congress established instead. In this respect it was an ultra departure from every principle ever dreamed of by the men who framed the Constitution.[3]

Finally the Democrats opposed it on the grounds that its language was too vague and general; that the states most to be affected by it and which would be expected to conform

---

[1] Rogers, *Globe*, appendix, pp. 133 *et seq.*
[2] Davis of New York (Rep.), *Globe*, pp. 1083 *et seq.*
[3] Hale of New York (Rep.), *Globe*, pp. 1063 *et seq.*

to it as the fundamental law of the country, had no representatives present to participate in its consideration; and that it would be submitted to state legislatures partisan in their character and not representative of the true sentiment of the people on this question.[1]

As Bingham's speech [2] in defense and advocacy of his amendment comprehends practically everything that was said in the press or on the floor of the House in favor of the resolution, an abridgment of his speech is here inserted as a summary of the points made in the debate on the affirmative side of the question.

The amendment is for the simple purpose of arming Congress, by consent of the people of the entire nation, with a weapon with which it will be able to enforce the bill of rights in every state. The friends of the measure are not seeking to take away from the various states or their citizens any rights that belong to them under the Constitution. The Constitution, however, does not reserve to any state the right to withhold from a citizen of the United States within its limits, under any pretext whatsoever, any of the privileges of a citizen of the United States; or to impose upon him, no matter from what state he may have come, any burden contrary to that provision which declares that the citizen shall be entitled in the several states to all the immunities of a citizen of the United States.

The opposition to the amendment has not come from gentlemen because they are opposed to protecting all alike in their rights of life, liberty, and property. No doubt every one desires that. What they do object to then is giving to the national government the power of protecting the rights of citizens. This they wish to be left in the hands of the states. No one will deny the right and the duty of

---

[1] Randall, *Globe*, p. 1057.   [2] *Globe*, pp. 1088-1095.

the United States to protect its citizens in foreign lands or on the high sea. Then why should it not also protect their rights in the several states? Is this not an anomaly? Gentlemen remember the case of Martin Koszta,[1] who, as a declared citizen of the United States, had his rights vindicated by prompt and summary action, when they were threatened by the government of Austria. But the United States, in the presence of the laws of South Carolina or Alabama, is powerless to protect the rights of its citizens within the limits of those states.

Though the bill of rights is not now binding upon the states, there are three provisions in the Constitution which show that it is the duty of the states to observe and enforce the bill of rights. In the first place, the Constitution declares itself to be the supreme law of the land. From this it results that the citizens of each state, being also citizens of the United States, ought to be entitled to all the privileges and immunities of citizens of the United States, in every other state; and all persons, now that slavery has been abolished, should be entitled everywhere to equal protection in their rights of life, liberty, and property. Second, the Constitution provides that the members of the several state legislatures and all executive and judicial officers, both of the United States and of the several states, shall be bound by oath to support it and all the rights secured by it. Finally, all state judges are especially bound by the United States Constitution, " anything in the constitution and laws of any state to the contrary notwithstanding."

The Constitution certainly imposes upon the states the duty of enforcing the bill of rights; but since they have been negligent and unmindful of their duty, it is now neces-

---

[1] For an account of the Koszta affair, see Moore, *American Diplomacy*, pp. 154-159.

sary that Congress be empowered to enforce by penal enactment those great canons of the supreme law.

Gentlemen who oppose this amendment, simply declare to those rebel states, go on with your confiscation statutes, your statutes of banishment, your statutes of unjust imprisonment, your statutes of murder and death against men because of their loyalty to the Constitution and Government of the United States.

That is the issue that is before the American people, and God helping me, without respect for persons in high places who show a disposition to betray this great cause, I will not betray it so long as it is given me to know the right.

Unless this amendment be adopted before the eleven seceded states are again admitted as integral parts of the Union, it will be impossible for the loyal minority in them to maintain a government there after the military is withdrawn. Then where will Congress derive the power, unless this or some similar amendment be adopted, to prevent the re-enactment of all those baneful laws discriminating against the colored people? The rule now is that the citizens must rely upon the state for their protection. If the rebel states are unqualifiedly admitted, some of their officials will violate their oaths as they have done before, and clothed with perjury, avenge themselves upon the loyal men for their fidelity to the sacred cause of the Constitution and the laws.

Sir, we are no longer permitted to doubt that whole communities are capable of so great perfidy. We are told they will be in terror of the prowess of your arms, and doubtless they will avoid an armed conflict again. But the point I desire to make clear is, that unless you put them in terror of the power of your laws, made efficient by the solemn act of the whole people to punish the violators of oaths, they may defy your restricted legislative power when reconstructed; they may dismember your Union and drive into banishment every loyal man in all the rebel states, and hold as their heritage a territory one-half as large as continental Europe, without firing a gun or daring again to commit the overt act of treason.

I speak in behalf of this amendment in no party spirit, in no spirit of resentment toward any state or the people of any state, in no spirit of innovation, but for the sake of a violated Constitution and a wronged and wounded country. I urge the amendment for the enforcement of those essential provisions of your Constitution, which declare that all men are equal in the rights of life and liberty before the majesty of the American law; and that no man, no matter what his color, no matter how poor, friendless or ignorant, shall be deprived of those rights without due process of law.

In spite of Bingham's plea, Congress, as has been seen, was not moved to adopt his civil rights resolution at this time. Before proceeding to the consideration of how it and the other provisions of the fourteenth amendment were adopted later, it is necessary to discuss two other matters with which the committee concerned itself. One of these was a resolution—occasioned partly by Johnson's veto of the Freedmen's Bureau bill and partly by the insistent demand for the admission of the Tennessee delegation—wherein Congress declared its power over everything connected with reconstruction. The other was the evidence, taken by the committee, relative to conditions in the South. These two questions will form the subject of the two succeeding chapters.

CHAPTER IV

UNITING THE REPUBLICAN CONGRESSMEN AGAINST THE PRESIDENT [1]

TENNESSEE was the only rebel state that, even according to the severe tests applied by Congress, needed no reconstruction by that body. Apparently if it had not been for fear of setting a precedent that later might have proved troublesome in the cases of the other ten states, her representatives and senators would have been admitted soon after the assembling of Congress. In order to understand how Tennessee came to be in a class different from the other rebel states, it is necessary to review briefly the political history of that state from the passage of the act of secession, May 6, 1861, to the meeting of the 39th Congress in December of 1865.

Statistics show that about 40,000 men, living principally in eastern Tennessee, voted against secession.[2] Unlike the " original " Union men in the other states, who, when once their state had seceded, threw in their lot with the Confederacy, the Union men of east Tennessee not only voted against secession but supported the Union cause throughout

---

[1] For part of the journal relating to this chapter, see *supra*, pp. 63 to 81.

[2] *House Reports,* 39th cong., 1st sess., no. 30, part i, p. 91. This volume, divided into four parts, contains all the testimony taken by the four sub-committees of the joint committee. (See *supra*, p. 47). Hereafter it will be referred to as *Testimony*, part i—Tennessee; part ii—Va., N. C., and S. C.; part iii—Ark., Ga., Miss., and Ala.; part iv—Fla., La., and Tex.

the struggle. During the first two years of the war, these men suffered many persecutions at the hands of the rebels. Had the Confederate government let them alone, it is probable that they would have remained neutral, for the east Tennesseean had no more love for the " Yankees " than he had for the large planters of the South. Such action on the part of that government, however, was impossible, as east Tennessee was one of the principal seats of war. When the Confederate congress passed its first Conscription act and attempted to enforce it in that section, thousands of Union men there left their homes and fled either into the mountains or into Kentucky, where they joined the Union forces and gradually fought their way back home again.[1]

On the 3rd of March, 1862, President Lincoln appointed as military governor of Tennessee, Andrew Johnson, who, during the three years he held that office, gained for himself a national reputation for courage and fidelity to the Union cause.[2] On September 19, 1863, Lincoln, in accordance with his cherished plan of establishing loyal civil governments in the rebel states whenever the expulsion of the Confederate forces seemed likely, authorized Johnson to exercise whatever powers might be necessary to enable the loyal people to organize such a republican form of government in Tennessee as would entitle her to the guarantee of the United States therefor.[3] Though Johnson was in thorough sympathy with Lincoln's plan, continued military contests and the disorder attendant thereon, rendered it impossible for him to make definite preparations for holding a convention until late in the fall of 1864. The convention was called to meet in Nashville on December 19th, but the re-

---

[1] *House Reports, op. cit.,* p. 115.
[2] *Ibid.,* pp. 1, 5.
[3] *Ibid.,* p. 5.

entrance of Hood's army into Tennessee after its disastrous campaign around Atlanta, caused the postponement of the convention. After Hood's army had been practically destroyed in the battles of Franklin and Nashville, and the power of the Confederacy had been forever broken in Tennessee, the convention was again called.[1]

It assembled on January 9, 1865, and proceeded to undo everything that had been done by the rebel legislature, and to create a new state government in harmony with the Government of the United States. In order to accomplish these purposes, it proposed for ratificatioin by the people an amendment to the state constitution for the abolition of slavery.[2] It further proposed what was called a " schedule " to the constitution, declaring that the adoption of the ordinance of secession and the convention between Tennessee and the Confederate government was an " act of treason and usurpation, unconstitutional, null and void;" that all laws passed by the rebel legislature were likewise null and void; that all debts incurred in aid of the rebellion were never to be paid; that the acts of Andrew Johnson as military governor, together with his appointments to office, were valid and binding.[3] The amendment and " schedule " were duly ratified by the people on February 22d, about 20,000 votes being cast for them and only a few hundred against.[4] Only those persons who swore loyalty to the United States and enmity to the Confederacy, were allowed to vote. An election for state officers was held on March 4th, at which the celebrated " Parson " Brownlow was chosen governor,

---

[1] *House Reports, op. cit.,* p. 6.

[2] The thirteenth amendment at this time had not been submitted to the states, as it did not pass Congress until January 31st. Rhodes, vol. v, p. 50.

[3] *Testimony,* part i, pp. 6, 7, 99.

[4] *Ibid.,* pp. 8, 9, 92.

and men noted for their "unconditional Unionism" were selected as members of the legislature.[1]

The new government was inaugurated on April 3, 1865. Among the acts passed by the legislature, demonstrating its loyalty, was one fixing the qualifications of voters. In general, it provided that all former civil and military officers under the Confederate government or the rebel government of Tennessee, should be disfranchised for fifteen years, and that all other rebel soldiers and sympathizers should be disfranchised for five years. It also ratified the thirteenth amendment, and provided that the freedmen should have the same rights as other people in civil, but not political, affairs.[2] The legislature also elected two United States senators, and at a general election held in August, eight members of Congress were chosen. Though at least two of these ten men for a short time at the beginning of the war had held commissions as judicial officers under the Confederate government, there were no objections to the delegation as a whole on grounds of personal disloyalty to the United States Government.[3]

When Congress met, the Tennesseeans were insistent that they be admitted to their seats. One of their number, Horace Maynard, who was well-known for his Union sentiments, had been selected by Johnson as an instrument with which to thwart Stevens in his purpose of excluding all the southern members. As has been seen, however, Stevens outgeneraled his adversary, and though Maynard made repeated efforts to obtain the floor, it was " imperatively and

---

[1] *Testimony*, part i, p. 98.

[2] *Ibid.*, pp. 30-32, 73, 99.

[3] *Globe*, p. 33. As a mark of special favor to the Tennessee members, the House allowed them the right to occupy seats in the hall, a privilege persistently denied the members-elect from the other seceded states.

peremptorily" refused him.¹ There was a strong feeling, however, among Republicans both in and out of Congress, that though the general rule of temporarily excluding the southern representatives was just, the Tennessee members ought to be excepted from its operation. One of the most difficult tasks that fell to the lot of Thaddeus Stevens was the fight he was forced to carry on against this sentiment within his own party and among his own followers.

The sub-committee² on Tennessee began taking testimony and examining witnesses on January 25th, and concluded its labors on February 13th. It took the depositions of most of the members of the Tennessee delegation, all of whom declared that their admission into Congress would strengthen the position of the loyalists, whereas their continued exclusion would diminish if not destroy their influence.³ Only eight other witnesses were called, five of whom were army officers⁴ stationed in Tennessee, and the other three, loyal citizens. Upon being asked whether in their opinion the complete restoration of Tennessee to her place in the Union would tend to strengthen the loyal government in the state or no, each of the eight answered, " yes," thereby confirming the opinion of the members-elect. The tenor of this testimony together with other pressure that was being brought to bear upon the committee⁵ made it impera-

---

[1] Letter of Maynard to the *Washington Chronicle*, copied in *New York Evening Post*, December 6, 1865; *Globe*, pp. 3 *et seq.*

[2] See *supra*, pp. 47, 48; this sub-committee was composed of Bingham, Grimes and Grider. The last was a Democrat, and Bingham and Grimes were not extreme radicals.

[3] *Testimony*, pt. i, pp. 110-128.

[4] Including Gens. G. H. Thomas and C. B. Fisk.

[5] See *New York Tribune*, February 19, 1866, for a letter written a few days before from Washington, in which the correspondent said there was a strong undercurrent in Congress among Republicans in

tive that some immediate action be taken in regard to admitting the Tennessee delegation.

Consequently, when the committee had disposed of the resolutions for amending the Constitution in regard to the basis of representation and civil rights, it began to devote its attention to the admission of Tennessee. In order to understand the close relation between this matter and the development of the breach between Johnson and Congress, it is necessary to make constant reference to the journal. On February 15th, the sub-committee on Tennessee, consisting of Bingham and Grimes, both conservatives, and Grider, a Democrat, reported a resolution stating simply that Tennessee had adopted a constitution republican in form and therefore was entitled to representation in Congress.[1] This resolution was discussed at this meeting and the next, February 17th, and though it was amended, its principle was not departed from. However, eight members of the committee apparently did not desire so simple a resolution, and just before the adjournment of this meeting voted that a new sub-committee be appointed to whom "the whole subject of Tennessee" should be referred.[2] This

---

favor of the unconditional admission of Tennessee. This, the *Tribune* opposed, saying: "Such action would mean the abandonment of the guarantee policy of the Republican majority in Congress; and that principle once abandoned, the majority will hopelessly flounder about in the mazes of arbitrary theories and special pleadings. Then, without a fixed policy to guide them, they will unconsciously yield point after point, until Tennessee, with all her good and laudable qualities, will prove the Trojan horse carrying all rebeldom concealed in her belly." This statement well expresses the reason why the extreme radicals strenuously objected to admitting the representatives from Tennessee.

[1] See *supra*, p. 63.

[2] See *supra*, p. 67.

new sub-committee was composed of Williams, Conkling, and Boutwell, all radicals.

As has been said, up to the appointment of this new sub-committee on Tennessee, the basis of the committee's discussion was a simple resolution, reciting the fact that Tennessee had adopted a constitution, republican in form, and was therefore to be admitted unconditionally to an equal position with the other states. That the three Democrats, and the four most conservative Republicans, Grimes, Harris, Bingham, and Blow, were in favor of such unconditional admission may fairly be inferred from the fact that they voted against the motion to raise a new committee on Tennessee. Had Fessenden, who was the most conservative of the eight Republicans who voted for the motion, changed his vote to the negative, no new committee would have been appointed, and it is not too much to suppose that a resolution for the admission of Tennessee without condition would have been carried at this or the next meeting of the committee. Had such action been taken by the committee and favorably considered by Congress, to that extent it would have been a virtual approval of the President's policy. It is fair to assume that those members of the committee who favored such action were desirous of working in harmony with the President and coming to some sort of understanding with him.

But harmony between the President and the conservatives was exactly what Stevens and his fellow-radicals were seeking to prevent. In order to understand what their purpose was in having the question of Tennessee's admission referred to this new radical sub-committee, it is necessary, though at the risk of some repetition, to review the relations between the President and Congress for the preceding two and a half months. Johnson suspected when the committee was appointed, that the whole proceedings both in the Republican caucus and in the House were revolutionary and a preconcerted design aimed at him and his policy of reconstruction.[1] He had hoped that the demand of Horace Maynard and his colleagues for recognition as duly qualified representatives from Tennessee, would frustrate the scheme of the radicals; but, as already said, Maynard was put aside.[2] When this move on the part of the President failed, he expected that the Senate would refuse to concur in the House resolution creating the joint committee on reconstruction; and his friends, the administration Republicans, certainly did their utmost to accomplish this result, but with slight success. Though some of the sting was taken out of the resolution,[3] its main purpose was accomplished; whereupon the President became thoroughly convinced that a deep and extensive intrigue, with Stevens and Sumner as the chief plotters, was going on against him.[4]

Andrew Johnson has been severely denounced[5] for not taking steps toward compromising with Congress, and viewed in the light of present knowledge, he certainly made a great mistake in not doing so. When it is remembered, however, that Congress from the beginning acted under the leadership of two men who were violently opposed to his policy and who publicly arraigned him in bitter terms, it is hardly to be expected that he, a man naturally combative,

---

[1] *Diary of Gideon Welles*, vol. ii, pp. 387, 388.

[2] See *supra*, pp. 142, 224. *Cf.* also Welles, vol. ii, p. 388. Welles thought the putting aside of Maynard was by common consent of that gentleman and the radical leaders. Maynard did, in fact, along with several of his colleagues, ally himself with the radicals when a definite break was made between them and Johnson. This would tend to prove the correctness of Welles' suspicion.

[3] See *supra*, ch. i, pp. 145 *et seq.*

[4] Welles, vol. ii, p. 398.

[5] Rhodes, vol. v, pp. 570 *et seq.*

and under unfriendly criticism, obstinate, would make overtures of peace to such a body. Moreover, the leaders of the conservative Republicans, Grimes and Fessenden, with whom he should have compromised, were unwilling to support him unless they could at the same time largely modify or even control his policy.[1] In spite of many assertions to the contrary, Andrew Johnson was not a weak man, and did not allow himself to be controlled by anybody. Hence Grimes and Fessenden found themselves drifting toward the radicals; and while they wished very much to avoid a rupture,[2] when it came, these two able and honorable men, as well as most other conservatives, naturally supported the radicals for a time, at any rate, in what they considered the lesser of two evils.

But so long as there was no open rupture between Congress and the President, there was always a possibility that the President might come to an understanding with the conservative Republicans in both houses, especially with those in the Senate. Such an understanding Stevens knew would defeat all his cherished plans for a thorough reconstruction of the southern states. It was therefore his policy to make, as soon as possible, an irreparable breach between the legislative and executive departments. It is almost certain that he correctly understood the character of Johnson, and believed that under stress of opposition and bitter denunciation, the latter sooner or later would retort in kind and thereby give his opponent exactly the opportunity he desired of bringing about the long-sought rupture. Therefore, during January and February, Stevens and his satellites embraced every opportunity that presented itself for raising

---

[1] Welles, vol. ii, p. 449.

[2] See *supra*, ch. ii, pp. 173 *et seq*. *Cf.* also Welles, vol. ii, p. 434, and *New York Herald*, February 20, 1866, Washington correspondence.

the ire of Johnson to the bursting point. They calculated that any violent speech of his against themselves could be so distorted as to make it appear that Johnson had gone over to the rebels. Then by insidiously appealing to prejudice they realized that they could overwhelm him before the bar of public opinion. A few incidents will illustrate the methods they employed in baiting their adversary.

On January 8th, Williams, of Pennsylvania, whom Gideon Welles described as "a revolutionary and whiskey-drinking radical,"[1] introduced a resolution stating that it was the sense of the House that the military should not be withdrawn from the South, until Congress " shall have ascertained and declared their further presence there unnecessary."[2] The resolution was passed as a party measure, though a large number of members abstained from voting when their names were called. Such a usurpation of executive prerogative by a branch of the legislative department was, as Welles points out, " purposely offensive;" and he foresaw that sooner or later the President would have " a square and probably a fierce fight with these men."[3]

On January 29th, there appeared in the papers an authorized utterance of the President, entitled, " Conversation between the President and a distinguished senator."[4] In this interview, Johnson expressed himself rather freely in regard to some measures then pending in Congress. This was the first time he had done so, and though he was guarded and moderate in his language, he left no room to doubt that he would veto a bill which the House had just passed, granting unqualified suffrage to the negroes in the

---

[1] Welles, vol. ii, p. 412.   [2] *Globe*, p. 137.
[3] Welles, vol. ii, p. 413.
[4] *New York Herald*, January 29, 1866. The " distinguished senator " was Dixon of Connecticut, one of the administration Republicans. Welles, vol. ii, p. 449.

District of Columbia. It should be remarked in passing that Sumner and the other radicals in the Senate, with all their keenness for universal suffrage, seem to have been aware that on the direct issue of enfranchising the great mass of ignorant negroes who, during the war, had drifted into Washington, they would hardly be sustained by the country. At any rate the bill was not pressed to a vote in the upper house. It was certainly most unfortunate for Johnson that it was not passed, for on this issue it is likely that he would have been sustained by the country, while certain defeat awaited him on such issues as the fourteenth amendment and the Civil Rights and Freedmen's Bureau bills.

At the time the interview was given out the House of Representatives was debating the proposed amendment on the basis of representation.[1] The President expressed himself as opposing the further amendment of the Constitution, but thought that if there was to be a change in the method of apportioning representatives, it should be according to the number of qualified voters in each state. The radicals professed to take great umbrage at this utterance by the executive, as an intrusion upon the prerogative of the legislative branch of the government.

Stevens, alive as always to the occasion, seized this as an excellent opportunity for saying something that would serve the double purpose of drawing from Johnson a further expression of his hostility to Congress, and at the same time creating an *esprit de corps* among his colleagues against executive encroachment. On January 31st, he rose in his place, ostensibly to debate the resolution for amending the Constitution, but in reality to read into the record and make comments on the much-discussed "conversation be-

[1] See *supra*, ch. iii.

tween the president and a distinguished senator." [1] He declared this utterance clearly was meant as a proclamation or command from the President, made and put forth in advance and at the time when Congress was legislating on the questions; made in violation of the privileges of the House; made in such a way that centuries ago, had it been made to Parliament by a British King, it would have cost him his head. "But sir," said he in concluding, " we pass that by; we are tolerant of usurpation in this tolerant government of ours." He then resumed his seat, patiently to await the echo of his words which he expected from the direction of the White House.

But no echo came immediately. Meanwhile the sentiment in favor of admitting the Tennessee delegation was growing apace, and even Stevens, with all his tenacity and influence, could hardly have withstood it much longer. There is no doubt that Johnson would have been very much pleased had the Tennessee representatives been admitted unconditionally, for he was most interested in his own state where he had been the principal instrument in putting the presidential policy of reconstruction into operation. Whether such unconditional admission of Tennessee would have been regarded by Johnson as a peace offering, and caused him to make concessions to the conservatives or no, it is difficult to tell with any degree of certainty.[2] At any rate, Stevens seems to have feared that it might lead to mutual concessions and an understanding between them. He therefore determined that if Tennessee must be admitted

[1] *Globe*, pp. 536 *et seq.*

[2] The correspondents for nearly all the New York dailies and weeklies believed the President would make concessions to Congress if that body would admit Tennessee. *New York World*, January 3, 1866; *The Independent*, January 4, 1866. *Cf.* also Welles, vol. ii, p. 434. Welles, however, did not think the President would concede anything, even though Tennessee were admitted.

it should be with such conditions as would put the President in an embarrassing situation. If he should sign the resolution admitting Tennessee with conditions additional to those which he had required, he would thereby commit himself to the fundamental principle of the radicals that his conditions were not sufficient; if, on the other hand, he should veto it, then the argument that the radicals were alone in their policy of excluding the rebel states, would lose its force.[1] Thus it is seen that the question whether Tennessee should be re-instated by a simple act declaring her entitled to representation, or by a resolution with several conditions attached, was significant.

On February 19th Conkling, from the select committee on Tennessee, reported a resolution providing that senators and representatives from that state should be entitled to admission upon certain conditions being complied with.[2] The conditions were that Tennessee should not pay her rebel debts, that she should forever maintain in her constitution the provision disavowing the doctrine of secession, that all rebels should be disfranchised for at least five years, and finally that the qualified voters of the state at a special election should accept the foregoing conditions.

No action was taken on Conkling's resolution, however, and the committee adjourned without deciding whether Tennessee should be admitted with or without conditions. It is probable that the settlement of the question was purposely deferred to await the announcement of the President's action on the Freedmen's Bureau bill, which it was expected would be made during the day.[3] His veto of that

[1] See Welles, vol. ii, p. 442, for this view of Stevens' intentions; also *New York World,* February 19, 1866.

[2] See *supra,* p. 68.

[3] This was a bill to continue indefinitely and enlarge the operation of the Freedmen's Bureau which had been established a year before. For its exact terms, see Flack, pp. 12-14.

bill alienated the conservatives and caused them to change their attitude in regard to preventing the radicals attaching conditions to the admission of Tennessee. In fact, it caused a loss of interest in the whole Tennessee question, as it gave Stevens an opportunity to commit Congress against the policy of the President without bringing in Tennessee at all.

In his veto message, Johnson not only expressed disapprobation of the Freedmen's Bureau bill's provisions, but went so far as to question the right of Congress to legislate on questions affecting so vitally the southern states while they were still unrepresented.[1] This attitude on the part of the executive so highly incensed every Republican congressman who was jealous of the prerogative of the legislative branch of the government, that when the committee met the next morning, February 20th, even the conservatives were ready to adopt a resolution proposed by Stevens in the following words:[2]

Be it resolved by the House of Representatives, the Senate concurring, that in order to close agitation upon a question which seems likely to disturb the action of the government, as well as to quiet the uncertainty which is agitating the minds of the people of the eleven states which have been declared to be in insurrection, no senator or representative shall be admitted into either branch of Congress from any of said states until Congress shall have declared such state entitled to such representation.

This resolution was adopted, all the Republicans voting in the affirmative, and it was ordered to be reported to the House immediately.[3]

Before following the progress of the above resolution

[1] For the text of message, see *Globe*, p. 915.
[2] See *supra*, p. 71.
[3] *Ibid.*, p. 72.

through Congress it is necessary to make a brief statement of the reasons that led Johnson to veto the Freedmen's Bureau bill, and to note the reception by the country of that veto. This was the first of a series of events—one leading to the other—that made the breach between him and Congress irreparable.

In the first place, Johnson certainly opposed the bill on principle, but as the New York *Sun*[1] pointed out at the time:

The difference between Congress and the President as to the contents of the bill is not sufficient to justify a veto. It is justifiable, however, on the ground that the President has a policy of his own for the restoration of the southern states, and Congress has an antagonistic policy of its own for the same purpose. It has been evident for some time that these conflicting methods must sooner or later come into collision, and the Freedmen's Bureau bill is simply the medium that has brought the opposing elements into contact. The President saw clearly that the bill was only the advance guard of a long procession of others that are even more obnoxious to him. He saw that his policy was being ignored by Congress and that that body was determined to force its own program upon the South. He knew it was impossible to avoid the issue eventually and he determined to meet it firmly at the outset.

Moreover, Johnson believed that the bill was championed principally by the radicals, who, in their commitee of fifteen, had intrigued against him and assumed to dictate the policy of the administration.[2] No doubt, he thought a large number of Republicans who were not classed as radicals would, now that the issue was clearly defined, come to his support. Johnson's great mistake was in thinking the

[1] *Globe*, February 21, 1866.
[2] Welles, vol. ii, p. 435.

Freedmen's Bureau bill a measure for which the radicals alone were responsible.[1] As a matter of fact, there were very few Republicans who did not desire such modification of the President's policy as would give protection and assistance to the newly-emancipated negroes. The Freedmen's Bureau bill was designed to render such protection and assistance, and since most conservative Republicans were committed to its principles, they could not now abandon them honorably and sustain the veto. The mere veto, had it been placed simply on the grounds of the inexpediency and unconstitutionality of the Freedmen's Bureau bill, would hardly have constrained the conservatives to go over to the radical position and support Stevens' declaratory resolution. They were forced into that position by that part of the President's veto message,[2] in which he expressed the opinion that it was highly improper for Congress to legislate upon a subject concerning almost solely those very states which were then unrepresented in that body.[3]

The response from the country showed the President had chosen badly in making the Freedmen's Bureau bill the issue on which he proposed to fight it out with the radicals. The great majority of the Republican papers were not supporters of the radicals, but desired to have the President and the conservatives come to a common understanding. They were unanimous, however, in their support of the principles involved in the Freedmen's Bureau bill.[4] The

[1] Welles, vol. ii, p. 435.

[2] *Globe*, p. 915.

[3] Fessenden stated that he had no particular interest in the Freedmen's Bureau bill, and would have felt inclined to sustain the veto had Johnson not taken this attitude in regard to the rights of Congress. *Globe*, p. 987.

[4] For a confirmation of this statement, see *New York Tribune*, Mar. 3rd, in which editorials on the subject of the veto are reprinted from

New York *Tribune* had all along expressed the hope that the President and Congress would act in harmony, and while it favored negro suffrage, it was distinctly unfriendly to the extreme measures advocated by Stevens and Sumner. It deeply lamented the President's veto and said regarding his action:

Mr. Johnson has made a grave mistake. He has relieved those who elected him of a great responsibility by taking it on his own shoulders. Hereafter, whatever wrongs may be inflicted upon or indignities suffered by the southern blacks, will be charged to the President, who has left them naked to their enemies. Time will show that he has thereby precluded a true and speedy restoration of the South, and inflicted more lasting misery on her Whites than on her Blacks.[1]

The *Chicago Republican* believed the veto meant an irreparable break between Congress and the President, and said:

The point at which the President deserts the Republicans is well defined. No other point could be worse for him, none could be better for those he abandons. The Republicans propose to fulfil the pledge of the nation by protecting the freed people against the unjust, discriminating, barbarous laws of the states lately in rebellion. That is the whole sense and purport of the vetoed bill. The President refuses his consent to a measure so just and necessary. He will give the luckless freedmen, no matter though they may have borne arms and suffered wounds for the nation, no other protection than that of the ferocious clutches from which they have but just been snatched. They shall have no safeguard, no law, no administration of justice, except such as the rebel states will afford

twenty-two Republican newspapers representing all parts of the country. All of them expressed regret that there was to be a conflict between the President and Congress.

New York Tribune, February 20, 1866.

them! That is the whole sense and purport of his veto. It is not a question of political rights. Negro voting has nothing to do with it. And on this monstrous proposition to deny to the freedmen all national protection against local legislation of an oppressive, discriminating, caste character, the President flouts and spits upon the earnest convictions of the loyal masses and makes an ostentatious appeal to the country.[1]

The *Boston Advertiser*, speaking more solemnly, said:

The grave character of the issue thus suddenly joined between the legislative and executive branches of our government is one which it was worth much serious effort to avoid, not for the interests of party which are temporary and inconsiderable, but for the sake of the national interests which are momentous and eternal. But if it indeed has come, we do not see how Congress can decline to meet it openly and firmly; relying upon the certain support of the great majority of the American people in a steadfast adherence to the course marked out alike by self-respect and by the demands of public safety.[2]

Harper's Weekly was one of the last of the Republican papers to give up hope that the President and Congress might be reconciled. It was not until after the veto of the Civil Rights bill that it was fully assured the President would yield nothing of his policy for the sake of acting harmoniously with the conservative Republicans. On April 14th, it announced that there was no longer room to doubt that the breach was beyond repair, and announced its departure from him in these words:

President Johnson must see that the Union party cannot accept the indiscriminate support of all his views and measures

[1] Quoted in *New York Tribune*, March 3, 1866.
[2] *Ibid.* Quoted in *New York Tribune*, March 3, 1866.

as the test of constitutional fidelity; and he makes a profound mistake if he regards the situation as a struggle between himself and Mr. Thaddeus Stevens. When he sees those who have as little respect for Mr. Stevens' wisdom as he has himself, gravely questioning his course, it is a fatal delusion if he sees only Mr. Stevens.

As has been said, the declaratory resolution was passed by the committee to rebuke Johnson for intimating in his veto message that the extent of the power of Congress over reconstruction was the right of each house to determine the election, returns, and qualifications of its own members; and for questioning the propriety of Congress legislating on matters pertaining to the southern states while they were unrepresented. Stevens, relying on the resentment occasioned by the veto message, believed he and his friends could push the resolution through both houses. If this could be accomplished, the breach between the President and Congress would be so widened as to make reconciliation almost impossible. The methods adopted by the radicals in railroading the resolution through the House on February 20th, and the incidents attendant thereon, marked that as the second important event in the progress of the rupture. A perusal of that day's proceedings, as faithfully recorded in the *Globe*,[1] will convince any one that thereafter there was not even the shadow of a chance that the President and the Republican representatives could ever be brought to act in harmony.

In presenting the declaratory resolution to the House, Stevens said:

Until yesterday [Feb. 19] there was an earnest investigation into the condition of Tennessee to see whether by act of Congress, the state could be admitted to representation; but since

[1] *Globe*, pp. 943-950; *cf.* also accounts in newspapers of February 21.

yesterday there has arisen a state of things which the committee deems puts it out of its power to proceed further without surrendering a great principle and the rights of this body to the usurpation of another power.[1]

The previous question was then called. The radicals either were or feigned to be in an angry state of mind. Should a Democrat protest against the proceedings, he was silenced with shouts of "Order! Order!" from all parts of the hall. Mr. Rogers hoped the resolution would not be driven through under gag law. (Order!) Mr. Eldridge (Dem.) submitted the point of order that the committee had no right to report its proceedings by piecemeal; and that the House ought not to receive any other than a final report from it. The point of order was overruled by the speaker.

Mr. Grider—I rise to a privileged question. I appeal to the courtesy of the gentleman from Pennsylvania to allow me to make one or two statements.

The Speaker—This is not a privileged question.

Mr. Grider—I make an appeal to the gentleman from Pennsylvania.

Mr. Stevens—There are earthquakes around me, and I tremble; I dare not yield.

Mr. Grider—I ask to be heard on this proposition and that it be postponed and printed. (Shouts of "Order! Order!")

The Speaker—The gentleman from Kentucky is not in order.

Mr. Rogers—I ask the gentleman from Pennsylvania to yield to me for a question. (Cries of "Order!")

Mr. Stevens—Not until after the vote is taken.

Mr. Rogers—Will he not allow me to be heard?

(Loud shouts of "Order!") This is gag law. (Renewed shouts of "Order!")

Mr. Randall (Dem.)—I rise to a question of order; that

[1] *Cf. supra*, p. 71.

this House has no constitutional power to dismember the Union, and no authority in law to destroy the rights of the states.

The speaker ruled against the point of order. The Democrats then spent an hour or two in making motions to adjourn, demanding the yeas and nays, tellers, and applying all other methods of delay known to parliamentary procedure. Mr. Eldridge, their floor leader, proposed to Mr. Stevens that if he would withdraw his demand for the previous question and allow debate, the Democrats would consent to go on with the business.

Mr. Stevens—It is simply the return of the rebels of 1861. I sat thirty-eight hours under this kind of a fight once, and I have no objection to a little of it now. I am ready to sit for forty hours.

Mr. Eldridge—I appeal to the gentleman from Pennsylvania to—(Cries of " Order!").

In vain did the Democrats plead for just one hour in which to debate the question.

Mr. Voorhees (Dem.)—Will the opposite side of this House allow me to make a proposition? (Cries of " No! No!")

Mr. Washburne hoped his side would hear Mr. Voorhees for a moment. Other radicals objected.

Mr. Eldridge—Will they allow nobody to make a proposition to them? (Cries of " No! No!").

After six hours, the Democrats saw the uselessness of continuing their dilatory tactics and gave up the unequal contest. The vote was then taken and the resolution passed 109 to 40, only eight Republicans voting with the Democrats. About 30 Republicans, however, had absented themselves, thinking thus to escape the responsibility of voting; but Thaddeus Stevens was too shrewd a party manager to allow so considerable a number of his colleagues to shirk. Therefore, on the next day he moved to reconsider the vote by which the resolution was passed, in order to allow these wavering gentlemen to place themselves on record. Most of them, under the influence of the party lash, were forced to vote in the affirmative.[1] The victory lay with the great radical; three-fourths of the members of the House of Representatives were irrevocably committed to his leadership against the policy of Andrew Johnson.

On February 21st, Fessenden, in the Senate, moved[2] the postponement of the regular order of business in order to take up the resolution for consideration. Objection was made, so, under the rules, it went over until the next legislative day, which, since the twenty-second was a holiday, was the twenty-third. In the meantime occurred the third, and what by most writers has been considered the most important event in the progress of the breach between Johnson and the Republicans in Congress. This was a speech delivered by the President on Washington's birthday.[3] In this speech, Johnson made a defense of his policy. Since that policy was being assailed, it was perfectly natural and proper that he should defend it. However, he made two mistakes. In the first place, he denounced the reconstruction committee as an irresponsible central directory that had assumed all the powers of Congress and was using them to keep the southern states out of the Union. This was an error in fact,[4] for, as has been seen, the committee previous

[1] *Globe*, p. 966.

[2] *Ibid.*, pp. 954-957.

[3] McPherson, *Reconstruction*, p. 58.

[4] For a fair and just defense of the committee, see Fessenden's speech cited *infra*, pp. 244 *et seq.*

to the veto of the Freedmen's Bureau bill was not controlled by the radical faction in it. His second mistake was one of policy. He arraigned by name Charles Sumner and Thaddeus Stevens as traitors, and classed them with Jefferson Davis and Robert Toombs as destroyers of the fundamental principles of the government. From his standpoint of zealous defender of the Constitution and the rights of the states, this was certainly not a misstatement of fact; but at that time, when it was not customary for the President to denounce members of a co-ordinate branch of the government, it was considered in bad taste. Though Johnson lost practically nothing with conservative senators by this personal assault on two men whom they themselves heartily disliked, he certainly must have lost popular support by it. Republicans of the rank and file were accustomed to hearing only rebels and copperheads speak disparagingly of such men as Stevens and Sumner, and it was easy to convince them that whoever did so belonged in one or the other of those categories. However, Johnson did injure himself among conservative senators by his derogatory remarks concerning the reconstruction committee. This is evident from the tenor of their speeches in the debate, which commenced on the succeeding day on the declaratory resolution. As its passage by the Senate constitutes the fourth event in the series, a brief account of the most significant points brought out in the debate is now in order.

After the morning hour on February 23d, Fessenden moved to lay aside the regular order of business and take up the consideration of the resolution.[1] Sherman (Rep.) objected. "The Senate," said he, "like the House three days ago, is now in a state of great excitement, and to de-

[1] *Globe*, pp. 981-983.

bate the resolution at present will needlessly irritate the controversy." Fessenden replied that he personally was calm, and that he was aware of no effort to get up a wrangle with the President. He had not tried to do so, but he believed that when the latter in a message to the Senate tells that body it has nothing to do with the matter of reconstruction, it is time the judgment of Congress be expressed on that subject. Though Sherman again pleaded for delay and other members spoke to the same effect, Fessenden's motion was carried, 26 to 19, five not voting.

Fessenden then made an elaborate speech advocating the resolution and defending the committee on reconstruction.[1] He declared his committee was not an "irresponsible central directory," as its members considered themselves merely as servants of Congress. It was created by Congress in order to obtain information in regard to conditions in the southern states. This information the Senate and House had a right to, and should obtain before agreeing to admit their representatives, even if they should be good and loyal men. He continued:

I had no particular interest in the Freedmen's Bureau bill and would have been inclined to sustain the veto had not the President in his message questioned the right of Congress to enact any law affecting the interests of the late Confederate states while they are not represented. To have voted to sustain the veto would have meant the endorsement of all the President said, including this last part of his message. I do not see how any senator could endorse this part of his message and at the same time retain his own self-respect and a proper respect for the rights of the Senate. I believe the President meant to say both in his message and his speech that the extent of the power of Congress is for it to judge of the credentials of representatives. For my part, I believe it is for

[1] *Globe*, pp. 985 *et seq.*

Congress and Congress alone to settle the question of whether those states are entitled to representation, and I believe it should do so without dictation or even advice from anybody.

I confess the committee was influenced by the President's message containing the foregoing ideas, when it saw fit to propose that Congress distinctly state its power over the subject of reconstruction. This resolution is substantially resuming the form of the original proposition as introduced into the House at the beginning of the session.[1] Though I did not originally think this part of the resolution necessary, I do now, because, under the circumstances of this case, with this attempted limitation of its powers with regard to its own organization, Congress is prepared to say to the executive and to the country: "Over this subject we have, and mean to exercise, the most full and plenary jurisdiction; we will be limited with regard to it by no considerations arising from the views of others, except so far as those considerations may affect the minds of individuals; we will judge for ourselves, not only upon credentials and the character of men, but upon the position of states that sent those men here." In other words, to use the language of the President, when the question is to be decided whether they obey the Constitution, whether they have fitting constitutions of their own, whether they are loyal, whether they are prepared to obey the laws; we will say whether those preliminary requirements have been complied with, and not he.

In concluding, Fessenden expressed a kindly feeling towards Johnson and said he did not believe the latter would intentionally injure any of the country's institutions. He thought his feelings in regard to Tennessee had carried him further in expressing his disappointment, than in calmer moments he would have been willing to go.

Three days later John Sherman made an able speech in

---

[1] See *supra*, p. 37.

opposition to the resolution.[1] He admitted the Senate's legal right to pass it but saw no use in doing so, as it certainly would neither quiet the public mind nor close agitation on the subject as the committee seemed to think. The true way to assert the power of Congress over reconstruction was to exercise it and say nothing about it. "Suppose," said he, "the two houses cannot agree on a plan of reconstruction, must these eleven states stand in their present isolated condition beyond the pale of civil law until they can agree upon some proposition? Should the two houses thus tie each other's hands?" He didn't think so. In fact they couldn't do so. For if the majority in either house, even after the passage of the resolution, should desire to exercise its undoubted power to admit senators or representatives from the southern states, the other house could not prevent it.[2] After twitting the members of the committee for their long delay in formulating a plan of reconstruction, he passed on to the most interesting part of his speech, wherein he commented on Johnson's past actions and, as Rhodes says, "held out the olive branch" to him.[3]

He regarded it as a great misfortune that Congress and the President had come to no agreement in regard to a plan of reconstruction before the war had ended, and he maintained that in all essentials Johnson had followed the policy suggested by the Wade-Davis bill. Congress could complain of nothing in Johnson's actions up to and including the veto of the Freedmen's Bureau bill. He regretted the 22d of February speech, but realized that the gentlemen whom Johnson had denounced by name had given him cause

---

[1] *Globe*, appendix, pp. 124-133.

[2] Fessenden later admitted that Sherman was correct in his contention as to the power of each house. *Globe*, p. 1143.

[3] Rhodes, vol. v, p. 579.

to be greatly provoked, and he intimated that they richly deserved what had been said of them.

He believed Tennessee and Arkansas were then in a condition warranting the readmission of their delegations to seats in Congress. The weakness of the position of Congress was not that any one denied its power, but that it held no lantern to the ex-rebels; no mode by which they could get back into the folds of the Union. Let the reconstruction committee, instead of asserting the power of Congress, report a resolution fixing the manner by which the southern states may come back into the Union, by which their loyal sons might be represented in Congress.

Fessenden defended the committee from the charge of delay, and declared that nearly all the information which the committee wanted was in the hands of the President; that although the House and Senate had both asked him to furnish it to the committee, he had not seen fit to do so. It was therefore necessary that the committee obtain information for itself independently. This would necessarily take time; hence if there were any delay the blame should be imputed not to the committee but to the President.[1]

Several other senators spoke on the resolution but only a few of the points brought out by them need be noticed here. Dixon, an administration Republican from Connecticut, put his finger on the main difficulty when he showed that it was the question of negro suffrage and the desire of his party associates to add to their political strength thereby, that really prevented the immediate readmission of the southern members to their seats in Congress. Any other reasons given for their continued exclusion were insincere and manufactured for the occasion. He then appealed to all members of his party whose actions were not prompted

[1] *Globe*, p. 1147.

by partisan motives, and who were not obsessed with the idea of universal negro suffrage, to join with him in taking up immediately the question of admitting the southern representatives. They should consider in the case of each state whether it is in the Union, whether it has a legislature, whether its people are loyal, whether the public safety will permit its admission and whether the men elected are fit to be admitted.[1]

Nye, a Republican from Nevada, quoted the words of Cobden to the effect that the American conflict had been an "aristocratic rebellion against a democratic government." Since the battle had been between those two opposing principles, he contended that a settlement should be made in accordance with the exact issue on which the contest had been waged. He therefore favored the passage of the resolution and hoped that Congress would continue to exclude the southern states, until a "nationalizing and democratizing" policy of reconstruction could be formulated for them.[2]

Stewart, also a Republican of Nevada, who had voted to sustain the President's veto, but later went over to the radicals, stated that the resolution contained an untruth. "When and by whom," said he, "were eleven states declared in insurrection?" Lincoln's proclamation of August 16, 1861, said: "I do hereby declare that the inhabitants of certain states and parts of states . . . are declared in a state of insurrection against the United States." He protested against putting the late President in a false position, for if there was any point upon which he was careful, it was always to speak of *inhabitants,* and not *states, in insurrection.* That had always been Lincoln's theory, the theory on which the war had been fought, and had been incorporated as a principle in the Union platform. "If this

[1] *Globe,* pp. 1039 *et seq.*   [2] *Globe,* pp. 1069 *et seq.*

resolution be correct, it means that if a portion of the people of a state go into insurrection, that state shall be excluded from representation just so long as Congress may elect. I do not say that principle ever will be applied to any other section, but I ask you, are you willing so to apply it?"[1]

Reverdy Johnson opposed the resolution on the ground that it would delay still further the restoration of the Union. When his opponents talked about danger to the government resulting from the admission of the southern representatives, he feared that they were confusing their party with the government. The mass of the southern people were honest and had accepted the results of the war in good faith; he was therefore certain the admission of their representatives would, instead of endangering the country, prove the surest way to the establishment of its peace and prosperity.[2]

The vote was taken on March 2nd, and the resolution passed, 29 to 18, Sherman, in spite of his speech, voting in the affirmative.[3] Its adoption by the Senate had a significance quite different from that of the House. In the latter body it was in the nature of an ultimatum to Andrew Johnson from the radicals that they meant to wage war upon him and his policy, and they clearly indicated that they had no desire to co-operate with him. The conservative Republicans in the Senate, who held the balance of power, meant to tell him, kindly but firmly, that they could not endorse his policy *in toto*; that he must pay some respect to the prerogative of the legislative branch of the government. This is the interpretation one naturally puts on Fessenden's opening speech. In closing the debate, he clearly told the radicals in the House, that the majority in the Senate had a

[1] *Globe*, pp. 1079 *et seq.*   [2] *Ibid.*, pp. 1107 *et seq.*
[3] *Ibid.*, p. 1147.

perfect legal right, in spite of the resolution, to act independently and admit members from the southern states whenever they might see fit. Moreover, he warned them that if matters should go so far as to show that they were acting unreasonably, wilfully, or from temper, so as to produce improper delay, he would advocate the Senate's reversing its action in regard to the resolution.[1]

Andrew Johnson occupied an excellent strategic position during the early days of March. Two courses of action lay open before him. In the first place he could vigorously maintain his stand upon the firm ground of the justice and sufficiency of his policy of reconstruction. Had he chosen this course he should have recognized at once the fact that the Republican party had, as a body, gone on record against him. This he should have announced boldly to the public and called to his support every man both in public and private life, regardless of past party affiliations, who desired an immediate restoration of the Union on the principles so definitely enunciated by his predecessor and himself. He should have reorganized his cabinet so as to have secured a body of men as his advisers, distinguished for their patriotism and ability, in perfect accord with his policy, and aggressive in action. In a day when patronage was a justifiable weapon to use in a political fight, and when politicians played the game largely for the spoils, he should have wielded this cudgel on behalf of his friends to the discomfiture of his foes. True, this is the course of action which he did eventually pursue, but not with sufficient vigor and not until it was too late to be effective.

His second course of action, as heretofore said, would have been to come to an understanding with about a dozen naturally conservative men in the Senate. This he never

[1] *Globe*, pp. 1143 *et seq.*

had a better opportunity to do than at this very time. In the contest over the declaratory resolution, Johnson retained the entire following that had sustained his veto. In addition, John Sherman rendered him a partial support, while Lane of Kansas went entirely over to his side. The latter, on February 26th, had introduced a resolution providing that the credentials of the Arkansas and Tennessee senators be taken from the desk and referred to the judiciary committee, so that they might be acted upon immediately. This resolution was lost by a vote of only 27 to 18, the absentees being about equally divided between the advocates and opponents of the measure.[1] Thus a further defection of five or six Republican senators from the policy of exclusion would have meant the entire frustration of the radicals' plans. These half-dozen recruits Johnson could easily have secured by signing the Civil Rights bill, which was designed to render inoperative the southern "black codes."

Conservatives of the type of Grimes, Fessenden, and Trumbull desired only three conditions before agreeing to admit properly qualified men from the southern states. One was that the basis of representation be changed; but after proposing what seemed to them a fair adjustment of that question, to have it ruthlessly spurned by the extreme radicals so thoroughly disgusted them that it is quite probable they would have been willing to abandon the proposition altogether.[2] The second condition was that the negroes in the South be secured in their civil rights. The third, and to them the most important condition, was that the President vindicate their contention that Congress did have au-

---

[1] *Globe*, pp. 1025-1027.

[2] See *supra*, p. 205. The exceedingly acrimonious debate on this proposition between the extreme radicals and conservatives, as respectively represented by Sumner and Fessenden, occurred between March 2nd and March 9th.

thority over the rebel states while they were still unrepresented, and over the question of reconstruction. These men had been trained in that old school of politics which taught the strict separation of governmental powers and the rigid independence of the legislative, judicial and executive departments. Their honesty, and their fidelity to the principle of the equality of the co-ordinate branches of the government, caused them to uphold the prerogative of the legislative against the overgrown pretensions of the executive; as later, the same principle caused them to vote against the conviction of Andrew Johnson when his removal would have aggrandized the legislative to the serious detriment of the executive. As previously indicated, these last two conditions—guaranteeing the negroes' civil rights and the prerogative of Congress—the President could have fulfilled by approving the Civil Rights bill.

Before entering upon the last phase of the breach between Johnson and Congress, something must be said of a sort of compromise, which for a short time appeared to give some promise of being successful. Its purpose was to get all the factions of the Union party, including the President, the conservatives and the radicals, to unite in adopting a common policy of reconstruction. Indeed its author hoped it would prove acceptable to the southern people and even to the Democrats. This all-embracing scheme was embodied in a resolution introduced into the Senate on March 16th, by Stewart of Nevada.[1] After reciting the fact that negro

[1] *Globe*, pp. 1437, 1438. Stewart was a cosmopolitan sort of person who had settled in Nevada only a short while previous to its admission as a state. He was the son-in-law of Henry S. Foote, a former member of the Confederate Congress from Mississippi, but who was then living in New York. It was supposed at the time that he had suggested the plan to Stewart, but this was denied by both men. Foote approved the plan, however, and thought if it should be offered in good faith it would be accepted by the South. See letter of Foote in *New York World*, March 23, 1866.

suffrage was the principal stumbling-block in the way of a speedy restoration of the Union, it provided:

1. That each of the states, whose people were lately in insurrection, shall be recognized as having resumed its former relations with this government, and its chosen representatives shall be admitted into the two houses of the national legislature whenever said state shall have amended its constitution so as, 1st to give the negroes equal civil rights; 2nd to repudiate its war debts; 3rd to yield all claims for slaves liberated; 4th to provide for the extension of the elective franchise to all persons upon the same terms and conditions, making no discrimination on account of race, color or previous condition of servitude: provided, that those who were qualified to vote in the year 1860 by the laws of their respective states shall not be disfranchised by reason of any new tests or conditions which have been or may be prescribed since that year.

2. That when the aforementioned conditions shall have been complied with and ratified by a majority of the present voting population, a general amnesty shall be proclaimed.

3. That all the loyal states be respectfully requested to incorporate in their constitutions an amendment corresponding with the one above described.

4. That it is not intended to assert a coercive power on the part of Congress in regard to the regulation of the suffrage in the different states, but only to make an appeal to their own good sense and love of country, with a view to the prevention of serious evils now threatened.[1]

Stewart's resolution was referred to at the time as a plan to restore the Union on the basis of universal amnesty and universal suffrage. As a matter of fact, it practically invited the South, so far as negro suffrage was concerned, to adopt the principle of the present day " grandfather clause." Nevertheless it was a sincere attempt to solve in a patriotic

[1] The resolution as here printed is somewhat abridged.

way the knotty problem of reconstruction and as such received respectful consideration from thoughtful people who were not carried away by racial or sectional prejudice. Stewart was not a great man nor was he, as a general rule, free from party bias, but it is not too much to say that his was the only plan of reconstruction ever offered by a man in public life which took into consideration the feelings of the people both of the South and of the North. Had it been adopted, the great amount of bitterness, suspicion, and misunderstanding which was engendered by the actual process of reconstruction would most certainly have been avoided.

In explanation of his resolution, Stewart said he had carefully observed events since Congress assembled, and had come to the conclusion that a proposition of this kind corresponded with the prevailing sentiment in Congress and also in the country as indicated by the public press. Not having heard from the southern states on the proposition, he believed it but fair and just that the best terms Congress was willing to grant should be submitted for them to adopt or reject. His plan was neither coercive nor odious in its provisions, and at the same time it avoided the long delay attendant upon a constitutional amendment. By his method of procedure alone could the South be heard from during the first session of Congress, and should his offer be refused there would be plenty of time to adopt other measures. He pointed out that what he proposed in the way of negro suffrage accorded with the telegram sent to Governor Sharkey of Mississippi by the President, in which he recommended that negroes possessing certain educational or property qualifications be allowed to vote. He therefore believed that he could be depended upon to give the proposition his hearty support.

At the conclusion of his speech some of the extreme radicals gathered around Stewart and welcomed him as a new convert to the doctrine of universal suffrage.[1] As a matter of fact, he had been very careful to refrain from expressing himself as to the propriety of allowing the negroes to vote. At the same time, all of the radicals, except Henry Wilson, who congratulated him refrained from committing themselves to the doctrine of universal amnesty.

Stewart's plan was well received by the country. Speaking on his resolutions a week or so later, he said they had been indorsed by practically every important Union newspaper in the North, and that he had received numerous letters from prominent persons, including ex-Governor Andrew, of Massachusetts, urging their adoption.[2] Moreover, at least three prominent southerners favored the proposition as a final settlement.[3] The New York *Sun*[4] and *Tribune*[5] both gave it their hearty indorsement and hoped that it would be adopted. Even such radical journals as the *Nation*[6] and the *Independent*[7] recognized its justice but doubted if the South would accept it in good faith and sincerity. Finally Andrew Johnson does not seem to have been entirely hostile to the idea.[8] His veto of the Civil Rights bill, however, put its adoption as a compromise measure beyond the realm of possibility; and though, in a somewhat modified form, it will be referred to again, it will be rather as one of the suggested congressional plans of reconstruction than as a compromise.

---

[1] *Globe*, pp. 1438, 1439.
[2] *Ibid.*, pp. 1753, 1754. *Cf.* Stewart's *Reminiscences*, ch. xxii.
[3] *Ibid.* A. H. Stephens, Henry S. Foote, Gov. Sharkey of Miss.
[4] *Ibid.*, March 19, 1866.
[5] *Ibid.*, March 17 and 21, 1866.
[6] *Ibid.*, March 22, 1866.
[7] *Ibid.*, March 29, 1866.
[8] Welles, vol. ii, p. 457.

It is now in order to give an account of the final events in the progress of the breach between Johnson and Congress; and towards its consummation as in its beginning, the question of Tennessee's restoration was vitally involved.

On March 5th, the committee after considerable discussion finally adopted a resolution admitting Tennessee which contained essentially the same conditions as that which Conkling had reported on February 19th.[1] This resolution Bingham reported to the House on the same day (March 5th) it was adopted by the committee.[2] He asked that it be recommitted and stated that he would bring it up again within a fortnight. As a matter of fact, over four months elapsed before he did so. The disposal made of it by Congress at that late date does not concern us here, but it will be considered below in another connection.[3] There are two reasons which may explain why the Republicans on the committee, after reporting the resolution, allowed action on it to be deferred for so long. Neither of these reasons is absolutely susceptible of proof, however, and it is generally unsafe to speculate on the motives of men when one has no direct documentary evidence to sustain his statements. Nevertheless two hypotheses are here suggested, but with the qualifying remark that either, neither, or both may be incorrect. The former involves the motives of the conservatives, while the latter has to do with those of the radicals.

Bingham, who had charge of the resolution and who on account of the similarity of his and Fessenden's views, was probably influenced by him, asked that it be recommitted, in order to await, no doubt, the action of the President on the

---

[1] See *supra*, p. 68 and p. 75.
[2] *Globe*, p. 1189.
[3] Chap. vii.

Civil Rights bill. His object in reporting it was to let Johnson see that Congress was serious in the demand that its power over reconstruction be recognized. Had the Civil Rights bill been signed, it seems clear that the conservatives would have made every effort to pass the Tennessee resolution forthwith.[1] Without directly approving it and without contradicting his former statements, he might have allowed it to become law by reason of the "ten day lapse," [2] and thereby tacitly agreed to the assertions made by Congress of its prerogative. If he had done this, as he should have, the conservatives would have begun to pass similar resolutions with regard to such states as Arkansas, North Carolina, and Georgia,[3] which according to the evidence then being taken, were most deserving of consideration. If the conservatives in the House had not been able to obtain a majority for such resolutions, and they probably could not have done so at first, their friends in the Senate doubtless would have acted alone, and eventually the majority of the representatives of necessity would have joined them.

That men like Fessenden and Grimes in the Senate and Bingham and Blow in the House had in mind the adoption of such a policy as is above outlined, would seem to be proved by: (1) the abhorrence in which they held the extreme radicals and the reluctance with which they eventually were led to act with them; (2) the general tenor of their speeches, especially those of Sherman and Fessenden in the Senate; (3) the fact that in committee they passed

[1] Welles, vol. ii, pp. 441, 442.

[2] The New York *World* of February 17th advised the President to allow the resolution for admitting Tennessee, if containing obnoxious conditions, to become law by this means. From a statement made to Welles, March 3rd, he had evidently decided to accept the advice. Welles, vol. ii, p. 443.

[3] Men like A. H. Stephens, however, would hardly have been admitted.

the resolution for admitting Tennessee, which they certainly meant should be acted on by Congress in case the Civil Rights bill were signed; (4) that the committee, controlled by conservatives,[1] took no steps whatever toward formulating a congressional plan of reconstruction until after the veto and repassage of the Civil Rights bill; and this in spite of the fact that radicals both in and out of Congress, who considered the breach with the President final after the 22nd of February speech, were making a persistent demand that the committee report a plan counter to that of the President.

If the purpose of the conservatives was as above stated, the question naturally arises as to why Thaddeus Stevens voted for the resolution and favored having it reported to the House. The probable answer is that he expected by making public the resolution with its conditions and declarations obnoxious to Johnson to arouse still further his pugnacity and obstinacy and thereby cause him to veto the Civil Rights bill, as the radicals wished him to do. Stevens did not desire to have the resolution passed, however, for as previously stated he did not wish to have a precedent set to which persons advocating the admission of other states might refer. Moreover, like most other Republicans probably, he knew that one and perhaps both of the Tennessee senators would help to sustain the President's vetoes. Finally, the anger raised in Johnson's breast at first seeing the language of the resolution, might be partially allayed by passing it; for he so very much desired the admission of Tennessee that even he would hardly have been disposed to

---

[1] I class as conservatives, Fessenden, Grimes, Harris, Bingham and Blow, who, with the three Democrats, constituted a majority. Conkling and Williams, though later violent radicals, at this time tended to be conservative. Fessenden as chairman controlled the time of the committee's meetings.

quarrel a great deal with the method of its accomplishment. Though Stevens was correctly interpreting the attitude of Johnson towards the Tennessee resolution,[1] he must have felt alarmed at the possible rupture which might grow out of the differences between radical and conservative senators in regard to the amendment on the basis of representation, the debate on which was still continuing with much acrimony.[2] Moreover, Stevens doubtless knew what the intentions of the conservatives were to be with regard to the other states in case the President accepted the Civil Rights bill and the Tennessee resolution. And early in March it seemed to most observers that he would certainly sign the former[3] and give his tacit consent to the latter.[4] Indeed, there is little doubt that when the bill was being considered in the Senate, it was his intention to sign it. At least three senators so understood his attitude, and one of them, Trumbull, its author, thought it had been framed in entire harmony with Johnson's views and with what he had been doing for the protection of freedmen in their civil rights throughout the South.[5] Finally every member of his cabinet except two, advised him, in fact urged him, to sign the bill.[6]

Why did he not do so? The answer is that Thaddeus Stevens understood what the effect of his signing the bill would be and therefore set himself the task of preventing

[1] Welles, vol. ii, p. 444.

[2] See *supra*, p. 205.

[3] Rhodes, vol. v, pp. 581-583.

[4] See *supra*, p. 257, note 2.

[5] *Globe*, p. 1760. The other two senators were Sherman and Stewart; see Sherman, *Letters*, p. 276, and Stewart's *Reminiscences*, pp. 198-200.

[6] Welles, vol. ii, pp. 463, 464. Rhodes, vol. v, p. 583, note 4, says McCulloch was for the veto; Welles says McCulloch hoped the President could see his way clear to sign the bill. Seward and Welles advised the veto.

it. His method of accomplishing this result was to wield with such telling effect the weapons of sarcasm and slander that his antagonist would be forced to fight back with whatever weapon he could lay his hand on easiest.

During the early days of March the House for the first time was taking a brief recess from discussing reconstruction. Every Saturday, however, was given over to general debate on the President's message, when new members had an opportunity to deliver their maiden speeches, which were generally filled with sentiment for delighting their admiring "folks back home." The old and well-known members who could talk at any time, did not as a rule attend these debating sessions, but on Saturday, March 10th, Thaddeus Stevens was in his seat. Though everybody knew what his views on reconstruction were, he rose ostensibly to debate that much-discussed question.[1] He begged the pardon of the members for imposing upon them a speech prepared several weeks before when radical ideas were not so common. He feared his opinions would now appear stale and ultra-conservative in comparison with some that recently had been expressed. After these introductory remarks, he declared in a very serious tone that he had no feelings of hostility toward the President and expressed for him friendship and respect. He remembered the courageous and patriotic course he had pursued during the war and for his past record he could say nothing except in the highest praise.

What followed these laudatory words can best be understood and its spirit best preserved by the epitome of a page from the old Congressional *Globe*.

Mr. Price [radical of Iowa]—When I remember that the press for the last few weeks has been repeating the name of a

[1] *Globe*, pp. 1307-1310.

certain " Thaddeus Stevens " as having been used by the President in a recent speech at the White House, and when I hear a gentleman whom I suppose to be the Thaddeus Stevens referred to, speak in such terms in favor of the President, I wish to know whether he is the same gentleman (laughter).

Mr. Stevens—Does the gentleman suppose the speech to which he refers was a fact? (Laughter.) What I am going to say now, I do not wish to have reported. It is a confidential communication, and I presume gentlemen will not violate the confidence I repose in them (renewed laughter). Sir, that speech was one of the grandest hoaxes ever perpetrated. I am glad to have this opportunity to exonerate the President from ever having made that speech (renewed laughter). It is a part of the cunning contrivance of the copperhead party, who have been persecuting our President since the 4th of March last. Why, sir, taking advantage of an unfortunate incident which happened on that occasion [1] (laughter), they have been constantly denouncing him as addicted to low and degrading vices. To prove the truth of what I say about this hoax, I send to the clerk's desk to be read, a specimen of this system of slander, printed in the leading paper of the Democratic party. (The clerk read as follows from an editorial in the New York *World* of March 7, 1865.)

" The drunken and beastly Caligula raised his horse to the dignity of a consul. The consulship was scarcely more disgraced by that scandalous transaction than is our Vice-Presidency by the late election of Andrew Johnson. That office has been adorned in better days by Adams and Jefferson, Calhoun and Van Buren. And now to see it filled by this insolent, drunken brute, in comparison with whom even Caligula's horse was respectable! And to think that only one frail life stands between this insolent, clownish, drunkard and the Presidency! May God bless and spare Abraham Lincoln."

Mr. Stevens—We never credited this slander. But our ene-

---

[1] Johnson is said to have been under the influence of alcohol when inaugurated as Vice-President.

mies, being unable to fix such odium upon our President by evidence which the lawyers would call *aliunde,* they resort to another expedient. If my friend before me (Bingham) were trying a case *de lunatico inquirendo,* and if the outside evidence were doubtful, he would lead the alleged lunatic to speak upon the subject of the hallucination, and if he could be induced to gabble nonsense, the intrinsic evidence of the case would make out the allegation of insanity. So, Mr. Speaker, if these slanderers can make the people believe that the President ever uttered that speech, then they have made out their case (laughter). But we all know he never did utter it. They had wrought it up in such a cunning way, however, as to impose upon the people. They even went into attendant circumstances in minute detail. For instance, they said he was accompanied by a former rebel mayor of this city and the counsel for the assassins of the late President. Now I know the gentleman is satisfied it is all a hoax.

If any doubt remains as to whether this episode was prearranged and the slanderous remarks were made by Stevens with malice aforethought, the opinion of Gideon Welles[1] should be convincing. Welles had a remarkable faculty for understanding the character and interpreting the motives of men.

Thaddeus Stevens has to-day made a blackguard and disreputable speech in the House. Beginning with the false assertion that the speech was prepared two months ago, and continuing with the equally false assurance that an interlude, or byplay, which was introduced was unpremeditated, this wretched old man displayed more strongly than in his speech those bad traits of dissimulation, insincerity, falsehood, scandal-loving, and defamation that have characterized his long life. The radical managers and leaders were cognizant of his speech, and had generally encouraged it, but I shall be disap-

---

[1] *Diary,* March 10, 1866, vol. ii, pp. 451, 452.

pointed if they do not wish the vain old man had been silent before many months. The people may not in the first excitement and under the discipline of party be enabled to judge of the conspirators correctly who are striving to divide the Union, not by secession but by exclusion. It is clearly a conspiracy, though not avowed.

Whether Welles, in thinking Stevens' speech indicated the existence of a conspiracy to divide the Union, was right or not, there is little room for doubt that the speech itself was intended to prevent an understanding between Johnson and the conservatives. Welles was under the same delusion as Johnson in thinking the Freedmen's Bureau and Civil Rights bills were fathered by the radicals. Since Stevens' speech stimulated Welles' combativeness, how much more must it have fired the same sort of spirit in Johnson! Certainly it must have determined him, in spite of the advice of his best friends, to veto the Civil Rights bill. Therefore, on March 27th, he returned it to the Senate without his signature, but a week or so later it was re-passed by a two-thirds majority in both houses, and thus became law, the objections of the President to the contrary notwithstanding.[1] The breach between Johnson and Congress was completed. The conservatives were now forced to unite with the radicals in enunciating what purported to be a congressional plan of reconstruction.

Before following its development in the committee and in Congress, a brief examination should be made of the evidence which was supposed to show why such a separate plan was necessary.

[1] Flack, pp. 35-40.

CHAPTER V

Testimony Taken by the Committee—The Raison d'etre of the Fourteenth Amendment

The sub-committees which were appointed on January 15th[1] began taking testimony about January 20th, and continued their labors until about the end of April. There had been some discussion as to the feasibility of allowing these committees to travel through their respective districts and examine witnesses in the localities visited, but this plan was not followed, and all witnesses were examined in Washington.

This was the first enquiry by congressional committee into conditions in the South after the cessation of hostilities, but it was not the last; for from this time until the close of the Reconstruction period in 1877, whenever any extraordinary event occurred in any portion of the southern states, Congress took it upon itself to appoint a committee of enquiry. The report of the findings of these periodic investigating committees generally served a double purpose—first as an excuse for some proposed legislation, and second, as a kind of chamber of horrors where the crimes of southern "rebels and traitors" against "loyalists" were exhibited as an ominous warning to the northern voter to put none but loyal men on guard. So the testimony taken by the joint committee on reconstruction served as the *raison d'être* of the fourteenth amendment and as a campaign document for the memorable election of

[1] See *supra*, p. 48.

1866. 150,000 copies were printed in order that senators and representatives might distribute them among their constituents.[1]

It seems strange to us now how little each section really knew of the other, and how eagerly the people of the North especially perused all sorts of information concerning conditions in the South. That this testimony was read by the people generally in the North, is proved by the fact that the newspapers of the time published copious extracts from it, as it was made public, together with editorial comments upon it. Moreover, nearly all the larger newspapers had kept one or more correspondents traveling through the South and making daily reports of what they saw and heard there. To us who are accustomed to news columns almost, if not entirely, free from partiality and political bias, it is a source of wonder how not the views only but the news of these correspondents varied with the political alignment of the proprietors and editors of their respective journals.

The evidence that was given before the committee is by no means free from bias, and in many instances it is *ex parte*. In the winter of 1865-66, there were in Washington a large number of army officers who had seen service in the South, Freedmen's Bureau agents, so-called southern refugees, both black and white, as well as congressmen-elect from the southern states, who were awaiting admission to their seats. It was from these people that the sub-committees summoned their witnesses. The first three classes mentioned were hoping that Congress would undo the work of the President in the South, and provide for the establishment of governments there after the manner of the existing governments in Tennessee and Missouri, where none could vote but loyalists. Consequently in giving their tes-

[1] *Globe*, pp. 3325, 3326.

timony they never lost sight of the idea of influencing in this direction such legislation as would follow.

The agents of the Freedmen's Bureau, and to some extent the army officers, were of the type who later became, under the operation of the Reconstruction acts, genuine "carpet baggers;" while the refugees in response to the same stimuli developed into full-grown " scalawags." The real southerners, on the other hand, in general did their cause no good, but harm rather; as they after the manner of their class at that time, and being encouraged by the position of the President, were inclined not to take, as a matter of course and as results of the war, whatever changes Congress might see fit to make in the fundamental law of the land; but seized the opportunity afforded them on the witness stand to give expression to their outworn political philosophy. A perusal of Alexander H. Stephens' testimony will illustrate the truth of this statement.[1] It is no exaggeration to say that Stephens' political philosophy, as given before the committee in April of 1866, is a political curio. In a nutshell, it is that a state may secede at will, may return to its allegiance at will, and having so returned, is entitled to resume its former relations without submitting to any conditions precedent. However prevalent such political philosophy then was in the South, it was not very palatable to those northern people who desired that all the fruits of the war should be harvested before southern members were again admitted into Congress.

As has been seen, there was not entire unanimity, however, among Republicans as to what the "fruits of the war" were, but even the most conservative believed that all of the guarantees later embraced in the fourteenth amendment should be included. These guarantees, it will be remembered, were four in number: (1) Equality of civil

[1] *Testimony*, part iii, pp. 158-166.

rights, without regard to race or color; (2) The guarantee of the validity of the United States debt, including debts incurred for payment of pensions and bounties, the repudiation of all rebel debts and a constitutional denial of the validity of claims for slaves emancipated or property destroyed during the war; (3) Exclusion of the more prominent rebels from office; (4) A more equitable basis of representation, so that the vote of a southern " traitor " should not equal the votes of two loyal soldiers in the North. The questions asked the witnesses generally had a bearing on these matters and were intended to show the necessity for some such guarantees as the foregoing. Numerous resolutions proposing amendments to the Constitution and containing one or more of these guarantees, had been introduced into Congress during December of 1865 and January of 1866. So the testimony served not to create in the minds of the committee and of Congress any new ideas as to what measures ought to be passed, but simply to confirm them in the opinion that these four guarantees introduced previous to the taking of the testimony were necessary.

Since the first measure which Congress proposed to pass was that one giving equal civil rights to the negroes, it was necessary that the sub-committee produce evidence, showing that no such equality then existed and that as a consequence the rights of the freedmen in the South were not respected. Therefore, one of the first and most important questions asked of almost every witness was in regard to the condition of the freedmen and the treatment accorded them by the whites. Of a hundred and twenty-five persons who were asked whether there was not general hostility and even frequent cruelty towards the freedmen on the part of southern whites, eighty-nine replied in the affirmative, while only thirty-six gave a negative answer.[1] A still

[1] *Testimony*, part iv, pp. 171-173.

further proof that these "wards of the nation" could not be entrusted with safety to the tender mercies of their former masters, is attested by the fact that seventy-three witnesses emphatically declared that the presence of the Freedmen's Bureau and of United States troops was necessary in the South, while only nine denied the existence of any such necessity.[1] These witnesses said, moreover, that so long as equality of civil rights was denied the freedmen, United States authority must be continued; but if the negro were given free entrance to the witness stand, and some said, to the ballot-box, he would be able to protect his own interests without outside assistance. That this hostility towards the negroes was not caused by their alleged shiftlessness and general tendency to idleness and crime, but rather by the natural prejudice and ill-temper of the whites, is indicated by the fact that fifty-nine witnesses declared their belief in the fitness and disposition of the freedmen for free labor, while only four thought that slavery was the only condition to which they were adapted.[2] Eleven persons testified that the southern people were hostile to the idea of free labor, while only four thought that they were reconciled to it.[3] Before reading such typical parts of the testimony as is given below one should remind himself that while possibly the witnesses did not as a rule perjure themselves, they gave neither a fair nor a complete picture of conditions in the South during the winter of 1865-66. As has already been said, a great many of them expected to benefit themselves by persuading Congress to pursue a course of legislation favorable to their own political ambitions. Moreover, their inquisitors likewise had personal ends to serve and were bent upon proving by the evidence that their

[1] *Testimony*, part iv, pp. 170-171.
[2] *Ibid.*, pp. 173-174.
[3] *Ibid.*, part iv, p. 174.

favorite nostrums were the correct prescriptions for the maladies in the body politic of the South. Therefore, as a revelation of the actual social, economic and political conditions in the South the testimony is not very reliable, and hence it is not analyzed primarily with the idea of making such a revelation. The purpose of the analysis is to present the more or less questionable facts which served the double purpose of corroborating the ideas of the members of Congress as to the proper mode of reconstruction, and promoting the defence of these ideas before the people.

The following extracts from the testimony in regard to the treatment of the freedmen will tend to show why Congress was determined to pass such measures as the Freedmen's Bureau bill, the Civil Rights bill, and the civil rights resolution for amending the Constitution.

Dr. Daniel Norton (colored), of Yorktown, Va., upon being asked what the whites would do with the negroes in case the military force and Freedmen's Bureau should be removed, replied:[1]

I do not think that the colored people would be safe. They would be in danger of being hunted and killed. The spirit of the white against the black is much worse than it was before the war; a white gentleman with whom I was talking made this remark: he said he was well disposed toward the colored people, but that finding that they took up arms against him, he had come to the conclusion that he never wanted to have anything to do with them, or to show any spirit of kindness toward them.

Rev. William Thornton (colored), of Hampton, Va.[2]

Question. What acts of unkindness can you mention?
Answer. Some days ago an old gentleman named Hough-

---

[1] *Testimony*, part ii, p. 52.   [2] *Ibid.*, p. 53.

ton, a white man living in the neighborhood of my church, was in the church. In my sermon I mentioned the assassination of Mr. Lincoln. Next day I happened to meet Houghton, who said to me, "Sir, as soon as we can get these Yankees off the ground and move that Bureau, we will put you to rights; we will break up your church, and not one of you shall have a church here." Said I, "For what? I think it is for the safety of the country to have religious meetings, and for your safety as well as everybody else's." "We will not have it, sir," said he, and then he commenced talking about two classes of people whom they intended to put to rights, the colored people and the loyal white men. I asked him in what respect he was going to put them to rights; said he, "That is for myself."

Question. Is he a man of standing and condition in the neighborhood?

Answer. He owns property there.

Question. Is he a rebel?

Answer. Oh, yes.

Question. Can you speak of any acts of violence committed by the whites upon the blacks?

Answer. Yes, sir; about three weeks ago a colored man got another one to cut some wood for him, and sent him into the woods adjoining the property of a Mr. Britner, a white man. The colored man, not knowing the line between the two farms, cut down a tree on Britner's land, when Britner went into the woods and deliberately shot him as he would shoot a bird.

Question. Was he not indicted and punished for that?

Answer. They had him in prison.

Question. Is he not in prison now?

Answer. I heard that they had let him out last Sunday morning.

Question. Do you know any other instances of cruelty?

Answer. I have church once a month in Matthews county, Virginia, the other side of the bay. The last time I was over there an intelligent man told me that just below his house a lady and her husband, who had been at the meeting, received thirty-nine lashes for being there, according to the old law of Virginia, as if they had been slaves. This was simply because they were told not to go to hear a Yankee darky talk. They said he was not a Yankee but a man born in Virginia, in Hampton.

Question. Why did they not resist being flogged?
Answer. They are that much down.
Question. Did they know that they had a right to resist?
Answer. They dare not do it.
Question. Why.
Answer. I do not know. On the 1st of January we had a public meeting there, at which I spoke. The next night when I was coming from the church, which is about a mile and a half from my house, I met a colored man who told me that there was a plot laid for me; I went back to the church and got five of my church members to come with me. I afterwards learned that a fellow named Mahon, a white man, had determined, for my speech that day, to murder me the first chance.

Question. Did that come to you in so authentic a form as to leave no doubt upon your mind?
Answer. I believe he made the threat. The next day he said to me, " We hope the time will soon come that these Yankees will be away from here, and then we will settle with you preachers." That gave me to understand that the threat was made.

Mr. Ezra Heinstadt, a loyalist attorney of New Orleans, La.[1]

Question. Would it or not, in your judgment, be safe for the loyal people of Louisiana, both white and black, to withdraw from that state at this time the military power and supervision of the Federal Government?
Answer. I unhesitatingly say that I do not consider it would be safe for them to do so. My opinion is that if the

[1] *Testimony*, part iii, p. 24.

entire force of the Federal Government were withdrawn from the state of Louisiana the Union men, as we call those who were loyal during the rebellion, would be driven from almost all the rural portions of the state at least, if not from the city of New Orleans, and the condition of the blacks would, to a certain extent, be worse than it was when slavery existed there, for they would be controlled by force in such a way as to be left very little liberty whatever.

Question. What is the feeling there generally among those who have been in the rebellion as to managing the blacks properly without physical compulsion?

Answer. The general impression is that it cannot be done; that the negroes will not work unless by the application of physical force to compel them to do so.

Question. Suppose the power of the Federal Government were withdrawn, in your judgment what would be the course of the people in legislating in regard to the blacks? Would they seek in spirit to restore a system of servitude, or would they in good faith carry out the spirit of the emancipation amendment of the Constitution?

Answer. As to that I would refer you to the enactments of the legislature of Louisiana recently in session. They passed most stringent laws, making it a highly penal offence for any one to do anything that might be construed into encouraging the blacks to leave the persons with whom they had made contracts for labor; and also making it a misdemeanor for the blacks to do so, subjecting them to be arrested as vagrants and sold as such during the remaining portion of the time for which they had contracted, and giving the preference in buying them at such rate to the persons with whom they had made contracts. There have been several instances in the parishes where the local authorities have passed most stringent ordinances upon the subject, but which have been overruled by the military authorities. I will refer here to what was done in one instance. When Brigadier-General Fullerton assumed the control of the affairs of the Freedmen's Bureau in the city of New Orleans, some time during last fall—I do not remember the exact date—he issued an order that all persons of color in and about the city of New Orleans who did not produce evidence immediately of being employed should be arrested as vagrants. The consequence was that in the course of twenty-four or forty-eight hours a very large number of colored persons who were found upon the streets without evidence of employment with them were put in prison. After that state of things had continued for some forty-eight hours the order of General Fullerton was revoked by order of General Canby, the commander of the department, and those persons were set at liberty. I will make this general statement, that from the habits, the universal and long continued habits of life of the white population of Louisiana in the government of slaves, it is very generally believed by them that the negroes will not work—that they will become an idle and thriftless population unless their labor can be controlled by force; that is the general impression. My own opinion upon that subject, formed from long experience in Louisiana, and a pretty general acquaintance with the planting interests, is that in a short time, when the negroes shall experience the necessity of labor in order to live, they will become an industrious population. A great deal of the labor of the city of New Orleans is now being performed by them.

Question. Are the negroes now willing to work for those who they believe treat them kindly, and give them fair wages?

Answer. Well, sir, so far as my observation extends—and I have looked into this subject considerably—the disposition of the negroes generally is to go to work for those who will treat them properly and pay them a fair compensation.

Question. What is the prevailing sentiment among the rebels in regard to allowing negroes to become landholders in the state?

Answer. There is a very general opposition to that, as well as to the education and moral improvement of the negro race. But the opposition to negroes holding property is not so great in Louisiana as it is in some of the adjoining states, from the fact that from time immemorial free negroes have been landholders in Louisiana. I will add that this is more particularly directed against those negroes who were lately slaves than against what we call in Louisiana free colored persons, of whom there have been a very large number in the state for a great many years.

Question. Judging from your observation and means of information, what would you suggest as the suitable remedy to be employed by the Federal Government for the evils to which you have referred as existing in the state of Louisiana?

Answer. The first great requisite, that which I imagine would have the best influence in settling the state of things in Louisiana, would be to maintain for some years a rigid administration of the Freedmen's Bureau to protect the blacks in their rights, as well as to see that they complied with the reasonable and proper contracts they might make. I consider that such an establishment would stand as a barrier to the encroachments of one class upon the rights of the other. In regard to political matters, I consider that it would be a solecism in government for us to have states containing different classes of population, one class of which, almost equal in numbers to the other class, being entirely debarred from the exercise of the elective franchise.

Major General Edward Hatch,[1] who had been stationed in Mississippi and Alabama after the close of the war, gave the following testimony:

Question. What is the disposition of the people there towards the colored population?

Answer. The poorer classes of the white people have an intense dislike towards them. So far as any love, or regard or care for the negro, or the slave, I have never seen any of it, and do not believe it ever existed, except so far as his former money value may have caused care for him. There are men in Mississippi who are willing to accept the state of affairs as

---

[1] *Testimony*, part iii, p. 5.

they are now, and to employ the negro and pay him a fair reward for his services. But a great portion of the people of Mississippi are not of large enough views to understand this matter. They wish to control the negro and his labor in such a way that he will be compelled to remain with them for never less than a year, and upon their own terms.

Question. According to your observation, what is the disposition of the negroes in reference to working, if they can be assured of pay for their work?

Answer. We have always found them very ready to work. I have seen no instance where they were not willing to work when they have been assured of their rights. The superintendent, who by the way was a northern man, of the work of opening the Mobile and Ohio railroad, told me that the negro men whom he had to work for eight dollars a month and army rations worked as well as any men; that men never worked better. We issued the rations to those negroes working on that road. We issued no rations to indigent negroes, though we issued a large amount of rations to indigent whites; also a large amount of Confederate corn that we had taken, and I run one or two mills to grind corn to feed them. We never issued a ration to an indigent negro while I was there.

Question. Why not.

Answer. They never asked for any. I stopped issuing to the whites, but they made so many complaints that I was ordered to commence issuing again. They were in a starving condition, as the armies, the Confederate as well as our own, had gone over the country and nearly eaten it up. I have always found the negro ready to work when he was assured that he would be paid according to his contract.

Question. As a general thing, would northern men be kindly received who might go to Mississippi to live?

Answer. No, sir; there is a very intense antipathy towards northern men in all Mississippi, with perhaps an occasional exception. I have heard them say that no northern man should come there and work their plantations and live among them, unless he was an overseer under them, or something of that kind; that he could not come there and expect to own a plantation. There is no doubt at all that there is an intense hatred felt towards northern men. They may from policy sometimes perhaps consent to use a northern man for some purpose. But in the portion of the state where I have been I have seen no evidence of good feeling towards northern men.

Question. Is there a disposition among the people of that state to discourage the negro from purchasing land?

Answer. From all that I heard the people say, I should say that the disposition was to discourage the negro from purchasing land. The owners of the large plantations do not wish to cut up their plantations at all, and all the good land in Mississippi is generally owned by the large planters. The valley of the Tombigbee contains a very large negro population, and the planters have always hoped to work their plantations with the negroes since the surrender. I suppose that at one time they found a great deal of trouble in doing so. The negroes were afraid to contract with their old masters for fear they would be brought into slavery again, although they knew they were free. Their masters wanted to work the negroes for $75 a year, although they used to pay $200 a year for their work. The negro was shrewd enough to understand the difference in price, and thought it strange he was not worth as much as before. We found the negroes willing to go to work on their old plantations whenever they were assured that they would be paid. I myself told the negroes at the time of the surrender that it would be much better for them to go back on the plantations to work, and that they would be secured under their contracts as long as I was there and the troops were there; and a large portion of the negroes did so. This was some time before the Freedmen's Bureau took charge of them.

The testimony of former provisional Governor James Johnson, of Georgia,[1] while general in its nature, was perhaps fair and impartial.

---

[1] *Testimony*, part iii, p. 129.

Question. The object of the committee is to ascertain the condition of Georgia, and the sentiments of the people with reference to this Government; how far they are loyal, and how far they are disloyal; and we would be glad to have you give your opinions upon that subject, and any facts you may have.

Answer. The condition of public affairs in Georgia, in my estimation, is improving now, and has been improving for some time past. Our people are becoming better satisfied, with the lapse of time, and their passions are gradually abating. As an evidence of this fact, I could point to the legislation of the state on particular subjects; the provisions which are being made by law for the protection of freedmen, and securing them in their rights. While I say that our people are gradually improving, it is due to truth that I should say there are individual exceptions. We have some bad men among us, whose passions have not yet abated; but there are not a great many of them. Immediately after emancipation went into actual effect, there was some hostility manifested towards the negroes, by some classes of persons. But that hostility is abating, particularly on the part of those who formerly owned slaves. I would qualify this general remark, by saying that, whilst it is true of the most, there are individual exceptions; there are individual cases of outrage and wrong perpetrated upon the freedmen. But such acts do not meet the approval of the great masses of our people. This being true, that there are violent men, evil-disposed men, as a matter of course they easily associate themselves together; and a few men can do a great deal of harm and make a great deal of noise. For this reason, in my judgment, a few troops of the United States should still be kept in Georgia for the present, for the purpose of keeping in restraint these evil-disposed men to whom I have referred. These troops are further necessary to aid and assist the Freedmen's Bureau, whilst it remains, in my judgment. And, in my opinion, it is proper, at present, that that bureau, or something akin to it, should be continued in the state for a time. In my judgment, when the district and circuit courts of the United States are properly organized in the state, and when our own legislature shall have perfected their system of laws in reference to negroes, then the bill which has already passed one branch of Congress, which proposes to declare and secure the civil rights of persons, if passed by the other branch, will dispense with the necessity of the presence of the Freedmen's Bureau, or of the troops of the United States. But until that is done, I think it is proper that both should be continued.

General Robert E. Lee.[1]

Question. How do the people in Virginia, the secessionists more particularly, feel toward the freedmen?
Answer. Every one with whom I associate expresses kind feelings towards the freedmen. They wish to see them get on in the world, and particularly to take up some occupation for a living, and to turn their hands to some work. I know that efforts have been made among the farmers, near where I live, to induce them to engage for the year at regular wages.
Question. Do you think there is a willingness on the part of their old masters to give them fair living wages for their labor?
Answer. I believe it is so. The farmers generally prefer those servants who have been living with them before. I have heard them express their preference for the men whom they know, who had lived with them before and they wish to get them to return to work.
Question. Are you aware of the existence of any combination among the whites to keep down the wages of the negroes?
Answer. I am not. I have heard that, in several counties, land owners had met in order to establish a uniform rate of wages; but I never heard, nor do I know, of any combination to keep down wages, or establish any rate which they did not think fair. The means of paying wages in Virginia are very

---

[1] *Testimony*, part ii, p. 130.

limited now, and there is a difference of opinion as to how much each person is able to pay.

Question. How do they feel in regard to the education of the blacks? Is there a general willingness or a general unwillingness to have them educated?

Answer. Where I am, and have been, the people have exhibited a willingness that the blacks should be educated, and they express an opinion that that would be better for the blacks and better for the whites.

Question. General, you are very competent to judge of the capacity of black men for acquiring knowledge; I want your opinion on that capacity as compared with the capacity of white men?

Answer. I do not know that I am particularly qualified to speak on that subject, as you seem to intimate; but I do not think that he is as capable of acquiring knowledge as the white man is. There are some more apt than others. I have known some to acquire knowledge and skill in their trade or profession. I have had servants of my own who learned to read and write very well.

Question. Do they show a capacity to obtain knowledge of mathematics and the exact sciences?

Answer. I have no knowledge on that subject. I am merely acquainted with those who have learned the common rudiments of education.

Question. General, are you aware of the existence among the blacks of Virginia, anywhere within the limits of the state, of combinations having in view the disturbance of the peace, or any improper and unlawful acts?

Answer. I am not. I have seen no evidence of it, and have heard of none. Wherever I have been they have been quiet and orderly, not disposed to work or rather not disposed to any continuous engagement to work, but just very short jobs, to provide them with the immediate means of subsistence.

Question. Has the colored race generally as great a love of money and property as the white race possesses.

Answer. I do not think it has. The blacks with whom I am acquainted look more to the present time than to the future.

Question. Does that absence of a lust of money and property arise more from the nature of the negro than from his former servile condition?

Answer. Well, it may be, in some measure, attributable to his former condition. They are an amiable, social race. They like their ease and comfort, and, I think, look more to their present than to their future condition.

No doubt a more important factor in determining Congress to provide for equality in civil rights was the black codes passed by the southern legislatures during the winter of 1865-66. These codes were not, as a rule, read into the testimony. Alex. H. Stephens, however, offered an extract from an act passed by the Georgia legislature declaring the rights of persons of color. This act is not typical of the black codes, but is here inserted to show that under favorable circumstances the southern states would doubtless have dealt justly with the negroes, without the stimulus of an amendment to the Federal Constitution on civil rights.[1]

Question. What, at present, are the relations subsisting between the white people and black people, especially in the relation of employer and employed?

Answer. Quite as good, I think, as in any part of the world that ever I have been in between like classes of employer and employee. The condition of things in this respect on my return last fall was very different from what it was when I left home for my present visit to this city. During the fall, and up to the close of the year, there was a general opinion prevailing among the colored people that at Christmas there would be a division of the lands, and a very general indisposition on their part to make any contracts at all for the present year. Indeed,

---

[1] *Testimony*, part iii, p. 160.

there were only very few contracts, I think, made throughout the state until after Christmas, or about the first of January. General Tillson, who is at the head of the bureau in the state, and whose administration has given very general satisfaction to our people, I think, was very active in disabusing the minds of the colored people from their error in this particular. He visited quite a number of places in the state, and addressed large audiences of colored people; and when they became satisfied that they were laboring under a mistake in anticipating a division of lands after Christmas and the first of January, they made contracts very readily generally; and since that time affairs have, in the main, moved on quite smoothly and quietly.

Question. Are the negroes, generally, at work?

Answer. Yes, sir; they are generally at work. There are some idlers, but this class constitutes but a small proportion.

Question. What, upon the whole, has been their conduct? Proper, under the circumstances in which they have been placed, or otherwise?

Answer. As a whole, much better than the most hopeful looked for.

Question. As far as you know, what are the leading objects and desires of the negro population, at the present time, in reference to themselves?

Answer. It is to be protected in their rights of persons and property—to be dealt by fairly and justly.

Question. What, if anything, has been done by the legislature of your state for the accomplishment of these objects?

Answer. The legislature has passed an act, of which the following is a copy:

("No. 90.)

"An act to define the term 'persons of color,' and to declare the rights of such persons.

"Sec. 1. *Be it enacted, etc.*, That all negroes, mulattoes, mestizoes, and their descendants having one-eighth negro or African blood in their veins, shall be known in this state as 'persons of color.'

"Sec. 2. *Be it further enacted,* That persons of color shall have the right to make and enforce contracts, to sue, be sued, to be parties and give evidence, to inherit, to purchase, and to have full and equal benefit of all laws and proceedings for the security of person and estate, and shall not be subjected to any other or different punishment, pain, or penalty, for the commission of any act or offence, than such as are prescribed for white persons committing like acts or offences."

The third section of this act simply repeals all conflicting laws. It was approved by the governor on the 17th of March last.

Question. Does this act express the opinions of the people and will it be sustained?

Answer. I think it will be sustained by the courts, as well as by public sentiment.

The next matters with which the committee concerned itself were the questions settled by section iv of the fourteenth amendment, viz., the guarantee of the validity of the National debt, the declaration of the invalidity of the rebel debt, and of all claims for slaves and damages done to the property of rebels during the war. Of fifteen witnesses who were asked whether there was an expectation among southerners of compensation for slaves emancipated and property destroyed during the war, twelve replied in the affirmative, and three in the negative.[1] Twenty-eight witnesses declared there was a general reluctance to pay taxes and the National debt, and thought that if it were paid, the Confederate debt should also be paid, while only one thought otherwise.[2] Some of the typical answers in reply to these questions follow:

General A. L. Chetlain, of Galena, Illinois, who had been serving in Alabama since Lee's surrender:[3]

[1] *Testimony,* part iv, p. 169.   [2] *Ibid.,* p. 175.
[3] *Testimony,* part iii, p. 150.

Question. Do you know anything of the expectations of the people in regard to payment for their slaves and compensation for their losses during the war?

Answer. They talk very freely in regard to an effort being made by their members, when once in Congress, to get pay for all the negroes they have lost, or that have been freed under the President's proclamation. They also expect that a majority in Congress will be secured, after the admission of their members, to give the disabled soldiers of the South the benefits of the pension act. They also speak freely of the matter of claims. They say that, now that they are pardoned and again in the family, they expect the Government will pay them for the damages which they sustained by Sherman's, Grierson's and Rousseau's raids.

Judge John C. Underwood, of New York, whom Lincoln made federal judge of the district court in Virginia:[2]

Question. Let me put a hypothetical case to you. Suppose that by means of a combination with the so-called Democratic party, *alias* copperhead party, *alias* conservative party, they, the rebels, should again obtain political power in Congress, and in the executive department; suppose this to be the result of a combination between the ex-rebel party in the South and this so-called Democratic party in the North; what would be the effect of that ascendancy upon the rebel states? What measures would they resort to.

Answer. They would attempt either to accomplish a repudiation of the National debt, or an acknowledgment of the Confederate debt, and compensation for their negroes. I think these would be their leading measures, their leading demands; and I think if either the rebel debt could be placed upon an equality with the National debt, or both could be alike repudiated, they would be satisfied. But the leading spirits would claim compensation for their negroes, and would expect to get it by such a combination.

[1] *Testimony*, part ii, p. 8.

Homer A. Cooke,[1] a former quartermaster in the United States army, who had been stationed in North Carolina:

Question. How do the ex-rebels feel about the payment of the Federal war debt? If it was left to them to vote *yes* or *no* on the question of paying it, what way would they vote generally?

Answer. They would vote *no*, without doubt.

Question. It would not be a very close struggle?

Answer. It would be about as unanimous as the vote in this district on the question of negro suffrage.

Question. Suppose the question were referred to them whether or not they would pay the rebel war debt, how would they vote there generally, *yes* or *no*?

Answer. I think their vote would be in the affirmative, to pay it; because the mass of voters are under the influence of a few men, and those men are directly interested in the debt, as they hold the bonds.

Brigadier-General C. H. Howard,[2] an inspector in the Freedmen's Bureau, and brother of Gen. O. O. Howard, testified as to conditions in Georgia and Florida:

Question. What is the general feeling, according to your observation, in regard to the payment of the Confederate rebel debt, or the state rebel debt, in any of those states?

Answer. I think there is a pretty universal feeling in favor of paying the state rebel debt, but for pretty obvious reasons they would not be willing to shoulder any further the Confederate debt.

Question. How do they feel in regard to the payment of the Federal debt for carrying on the war?

Answer. Their feeling is unquestionably opposed to it; but still they generally expect to be compelled to aid in the payment.

[1] *Testimony*, part ii, p. 204.   [2] *Testimony*, part iii, pp. 39, 40.

Question. Suppose the question was left to the votes of the constituents in South Carolina, Georgia, and Florida. Suppose the electors at the polls were voting on the question of paying the Federal debt, would they vote for it?

Answer. They would not; I think not.

Question. Would they then, knowingly and willingly, elect representatives to Congress who would vote to pay the Federal debt, supposing that question should be made an issue at the polls or in the caucus?

Answer. If that question were the main issue?

Question. Suppose it to be the sole issue?

Answer. If it were the sole issue, I have no doubt that the man who advocated the payment of the Federal debt would lose his election. But there might be personal considerations in favor of candidates which would affect that question very much. Your question has brought to my mind something which has been quite frequently expressed to me directly, and has been told to me by northern men, as being found to be the invariable sentiment—that the Government of the United States should take measures to pay for the slaves.

Question. Do they seem to entertain that expectation.

Answer. A large number of men in the interior seem to think that since the late indication of the sentiments of the Government (as being conciliatory and disposed to grant them favors) some measure would be taken to remunerate them for the loss of their slaves. I would not say that was very unanimous or universal, but I found that there were quite a number thinking that way.

Question. What is the foundation of that expectation—any party combinations?

Answer. Not that I know of. I have an idea that the expectation would never have arisen in the form of an expectation but for a certain policy which they think has been put in operation by the Government. They regard it as a change of policy since the first establishment of peace.

There was a feeling among congressmen, that the leaders

in the rebellion should be disfranchised or at least disqualified from holding offices of trust under the state or national governments. Among the questions asked the witnesses was one to bring out the fact that the people of the South had been and still were to a very large degree under the influence of their leaders, and that in order to build up there a loyalist party, it was necessary to strip these leaders of as much of their influence as possible. Forty-three persons out of forty-five gave it as their opinion that the President's special pardons and leniency to these leading rebels had had a very bad effect upon them and had caused them —humbled and meek at the close of the war—to assume again all their former hauteur and insolence toward the North.[1] Fifty witnesses out of sixty-four believed that these leaders, and under their influence, the public generally, continued to hold to their old secession principles and states' rights doctrines; that they had submitted to Federal authority only under a feeling of compulsion, and that in case of a war between the United States and some foreign power, these leaders would be willing to fight against the United States, especially if they should see any chance by so doing of rehabilitating the Confederacy and securing their independence.[2] Twenty men, who were asked if the southern politicians did not hope to regain the balance of power in the Union by means of a split in the Union party, and by co-operation with the northern Democrats, replied unanimously in the affirmative.[3] Several other witnesses declared that much of the hostility, so prevalent in the South toward the Union and Union men, was studiously engendered by the violent language used by politicians and newspaper editors.[4]

[1] *Testimony*, part iv, pp. 175, 176.
[2] *Ibid.*, pp. 176, 177.   [3] *Ibid.*, p 180.
[4] *Testimony*, part ii, pp. 120, 121, 123.

The following extracts from the testimony will serve as concrete illustration of what was said by witnesses in reply to questions bearing on these general matters.

The indefatigable John Minor Botts,[1] of Virginia, after entertaining the committee with an account of Lincoln's negotiations with the Virginia secession convention just prior to the fall of Fort Sumter, was interrogated as to the present feeling of the ex-rebels in Virginia towards the United States Government.

Answer. At the time of the surrender of General Lee's army and the restoration of peace I think there was, not only a general, but an almost universal acquiescence and congratulation among the people that the war had terminated, and a large majority of them were at least contented, if not gratified, that it had terminated by a restoration of the state to the Union. At that time the leaders, too, seemed to have been entirely subdued. They had become satisfied that Mr. Lincoln was a noble, kind-hearted, generous man, from whom they had little to fear; but when he was assassinated, and Mr. Johnson took his place, they remembered Mr. Johnson's declarations in the Senate of the United States before the war, his own treatment during the war by the secession party, and his declarations after he came to Washington as the Vice-President of the United States, in one or more speeches, but especially in a speech in which he declared that treason was a crime which must be punished. They felt exceedingly apprehensive for the security of their property, as well as for the security of their lives; and a more humble, unpretending set of gentlemen I never saw than they were at that time. But from the time that Mr. Johnson commenced his indiscriminate system of pardoning all who made application, and from impositions which, I have no doubt, were practiced upon Mr. Johnson in pardoning the worst class of secessionists among the first, they be-

---

[1] *Testimony*, part ii, pp 120, 121, 123.

came bold, insolent, and defiant; and this was increased to a very large extent by the permission which was, immediately after the evacuation of Richmond, given by General Patrick, the Democratic copperhead provost marshal of the army of the Potomac, to the original conductors of the public press before the rebellion to re-establish their papers, I believe, without restriction or limitation, upon any of the proprietors; since which time, I think, the spirit of disloyalty and disaffection has gone on increasing day by day, and hour by hour, until among the leaders generally there is as much disaffection and disloyalty as there was at any time during the war, and a hundred-fold more than there was immediately after the evacuation and the surrender of the army. This is the conclusion to which my mind had been brought by the licentiousness of the press, and by communications which are made to me from all parts of the state, either verbally or by letter, from the most prominent and reliable Union sources. If I were to judge from anything I have ever heard personally from these gentlemen, I should not think there was any very great difference between their loyalty and yours or mine; but I hear of it elsewhere, and I see evidence of it daily, not only in the public press, but in the proceedings of the so-called legislature of the state. It is no more a legislative body than we compose one here now. I believe if the leaders and the public press could be restrained in their expressions and inculcations of disloyalty with the masses of the people we should have no trouble whatever.

Lieutenant W. L. Chase, an officer of the Freedmen's Bureau, stationed in Culpeper county, Virginia, testified:[1]

Question. In case of war between the United States and a foreign power, what side would these men espouse, do you think?

Answer. I think that a great many of those who entertain

[1] *Testimony*, part ii, p. 96.

these bitter sentiments would go with the foreign country in preference to the United States. My views were in accordance with those of Mr. Johnson when I went there, believing that his policy in reference to reconstruction of the states was just; but from my experience, I am inclined to be very radical.

Question. What do you think has really been the effect of that liberal policy on the minds and hearts of secessionists there?

Answer. I think it has been the cause of their demanding what they had no right to demand, and of making them more bitter towards the Government generally, especially to the people of the north.

Question. Does it make them more outspoken and insolent in their language towards the Government of the United States?

Answer. I believe it does, from what I can learn. After the fall of Richmond and the surrender of Lee's army, people were in a state of terror. They expected almost total annihilation. They found out that nothing of that kind was going to happen; and turned right around.

Question. Do they not respect the laws of the United States down there?

Answer. They do not like to if they can avoid it.

J. W. Alvord, an agent of the Freedmen's Bureau, testified in regard to his experience in Virginia and other southern states.[1]

Question. Now state what, among the rebel people, is the general feeling towards the Government of the United States?

Answer. It is hostile, as it seems to me, in the great majority of the southern people; I mean that part of them who were engaged in the rebellion. There is evidently no regret for the rebellion, but rather a defence of it, and only a submission to the circumstances of the case as a conquered people. They

---

[1] *Testimony*, part ii, p. 243.

everywhere defend the principles on which the rebellion was commenced.

Question. They still insist that those principles were right?

Answer. Yes, sir; they seem to feel that peace was brought about by an arrangement which allowed them the equal condition of belligerents, and in possession of all that they previously had had of government privileges. They everywhere insist upon the immediate restoration of such privileges, and that they shall be readmitted as states into the Union. They complain bitterly of the treatment they are receiving in being kept out.

Sufficient evidence has now been quoted to show that the motive actuating the members of the committee was as stated above, to fortify their preconceived opinions in regard to the following matters: First, that an amendment to the Constitution was necessary to give the negroes equal civil rights, it being shown that without such an amendment the lives, liberty, and property of the freedmen would not be protected or respected. Second, another amendment that would guarantee the validity of the National debt, repudiate the rebel debt and claims for slaves emancipated and property destroyed. Third, an amendment that would either disfranchise for a time the whole rebel population, or at least disqualify the leaders of the rebellion from holding any office of trust or emolument under the national or state governments. In addition to these it followed that, since almost the entire white population of the South was disloyal, still another amendment was necessary to readjust the basis of representation in such a way as to give to that section as little power as possible in the National Congress and in the electoral college. Some members of the committee, especially Boutwell, Stevens, and Washburne, were anxious to substitute for this last proposition one that would give the suffrage to all the negroes, which together with a wholesale disfranchisement of the rebels, would insure the election of loyal members of Congress from the southern states. The testimony certainly proved that the negroes were almost the only loyal element in the South, and could be depended upon, under proper tutelage and influence, to vote "right," but the more timorous members of the committee were afraid at that time to take so bold a step, especially as in most of the northern states the colored people did not enjoy the right of suffrage; and propositions to admit them to the franchise were not popular.

Thus fortified in their opinions by the evidence as to what measures they should recommend to Congress in order to secure "the fruits of the war," the committee was now ready to put them into proper language as resolutions of amendment to the Constitution. How these various propositions were combined into one resolution and became a part of the Constitution as the fourteenth amendment will form the subject-matter of the next chapter.

CHAPTER VI

THE FOURTEENTH AMENDMENT

CONGRESS having refused to adopt the President's reconstruction policy and having failed to compromise with him, was now under the necessity of formulating a policy of its own. It had long been criticized for rejecting the policy of the President, and at the same time proposing no plan of its own. This criticism at first was made only by the opponents of Congress, but when it became evident to all that harmony of action between the executive and legislative branches of the Government was impossible, supporters of the latter began to grow impatient because it did not offer some alternative method of its own for restoring the rebel states. Radicals, both inside and outside of Congress, began to fear that unless the various differences among the Republican members were harmonized and some common policy agreed upon, that of the President would inevitably become permanent for sheer want of a substitute. Radical newspapers and journals were especially urgent that a plan counter to the President's be evolved and immediately announced by Congress.

The *Nation* in an editorial on April 20th, gave expression to this demand. It declared:

The people are willing to keep the southern states out of the Union until certain conditions are complied with, but they want to know what those conditions are going to be. Congress has agreed upon none. The only thing Congress has agreed on is keeping the southern states out for the present, but this is simply the excavation for the foundation for the new building. The public is anxiously waiting to see the structure rise and is tired of hearing the builders wrangle over the style of architecture. More serious work than we have yet had must now begin. If it does not—if a greater willingness is not displayed by individuals to serve in the more obscure positions and to unite on some comprehensive plan—we greatly fear that the coming fall will find the public thoroughly out of patience with Congress and quite ready to let the President and his friends have their own way.

The New York *Tribune*, after the veto of the Civil Rights bill, became daily more and more insistent that Congress adopt a policy of its own, and towards the middle of April made one of its characteristically frantic appeals to Congress for immediate and comprehensive action. It suggested that the Stewart resolutions might be a good basis to begin on.[1]

These resolutions had been somewhat modified since they were first introduced on March 16th.[2] On April 4th, Stewart had again brought them forward, with only a few slight verbal changes.[3] He urged that now since Congress had definitely rejected the policy of the President it must enunciate one of its own. The outside world was saying that Congress did not intend to adopt any policy whatever; that there was no sincerity on its part; that the only object it had in pretending to favor restoration was to use senators and representatives for other purposes. Isolated propo-

---

[1] *N. Y. Tribune*, April 21, 1866.

[2] See *supra*, ch. iv, p. 253.

[3] *Globe*, pp. 1753, 1754. Though Stewart voted to sustain the veto of the Freedmen's Bureau bill, he says he did so only because the President agreed to sign the Civil Rights bill. When Johnson failed to keep his agreement Stewart became one of his most bitter enemies. *Reminiscences*, pp. 197-201.

sitions for amending the Constitution would no longer answer the demands of the situation. Whatever plan might be adopted must cover the whole subject and operate as a permanent settlement of the reconstruction question. He respectfully submitted his resolutions, no longer as a compromise, but as such a distinct and comprehensive congressional plan as he thought the occasion demanded. He hoped for their immediate consideration and adoption, and moved to take them out of the hands of the joint committee and make them the special order for the next day, but the Senate did not accept his suggestion.

On April 12th, Stewart introduced a resolution for amending the Constitution.[1] It consisted of two sections; the first provided for impartial suffrage, and equality in civil rights, and the second declared invalid claims for slaves emancipated. This was accompanied by a simple legislative resolution which declared, that "whenever any one of the eleven states shall have ratified the foregoing amendment, then such state shall be recognized as having resumed its former relations with this Government, and a general amnesty shall exist in regard to all persons in such state who were in any way connected with the late insurrection."

On April 16th, when the committee for the first time met with the definite purpose of evolving a distinct congressional plan of reconstruction, Stewart was invited to meet with them and discuss his proposition.[2] At this meeting, he no doubt urged the same considerations which he had previously brought to the support of his proposition in the Senate.[3] While he and some others continued to insist that it be made the basis of congressional action, it is not surprising that he failed to have it adopted. For in the end

[1] *Globe*, p. 1906.   [2] See *supra*, p. 82.
[3] See *supra*, p. 254.

the determination of the congressional plan of reconstruction was not left to the most able and statesmanlike congressmen, but to mere politicians who acted almost entirely from motives of party advantage. It is true Stewart's plan contemplated giving the negroes the vote, but it also gave to the whites amnesty. The radicals correctly reckoned that the dominant race, by imposing educational and property qualifications for voting, would disfranchise a sufficient number of negroes to retain control of the southern state governments and obtain a greater proportion of power in the National Government than it had ever before possessed. To the minds of the radicals, good party men as they were, nothing could be more offensive. According to their ideas, if the rebels were to control in the South, southern influence in the National Government should be reduced to a minimum; if negro suffrage were granted and representation allowed to remain according to population, reconstruction should be so ordered that the " party of the Union " might at least divide with the Democrats the delegations from the southern states in Congress and the electoral college. In other words, the proposition for negro suffrage reduced itself to this: though admirable in theory, its practical application would be baneful if the political benefits from it were to accrue to the hated rebels and despised copperheads; on the other hand, it would be not only admirable in theory but excellent in practice should it result in placing loyal Unionists in control of the ex-rebel states. But at that time the radicals dared not enact so " thorough " a reconstruction measure as would accomplish this desirable result. Therefore, since the Stewart plan would neither diminish the number of southern representatives nor give any considerable portion of them to the radicals, it was worthless as a partisan measure and hence was rejected.

The next proposition considered by the committee also

came from an outsider, Robert Dale Owen. Owen was the son of Robert Owen, one of the great English radicals of the second quarter of the 19th century. Robert Dale Owen was hardly less known than his father as a reformer and humanitarian. He had come to America only a few years before the outbreak of the Civil War, and quite naturally had interested himself in the slavery question, and after the war, in the general welfare and future development of the negro race. Fortunately, he has left an account of how he came to propose a plan of reconstruction, how it was endorsed by Thaddeus Stevens, how it was first adopted by the committee, and why it was finally rejected.[1]

The proposition follows:

A joint resolution proposing an amendment to the Constitution, and to provide for the restoration to the states lately in insurrection of their full political rights.

Whereas it is expedient that the states lately in insurrection should, at the earliest day consistent with the future peace and safety of the Union be restored to full participation in all political rights.

Therefore, be it resolved by the Senate and House of Representatives of the United States of America in Congress assembled (two-thirds of both Houses concurring), that the following article be proposed to the legislatures of the several states as an amendment to the Constitution of the United States, which, when ratified, by three-fourths of said legislatures, shall be valid as part of the Constitution, namely:

Article—

Section 1. No discrimination shall be made by any state, nor by the United States, as to the civil rights of persons because of race, color, or previous condition of servitude.

---

[1] Owen's account may be found in the *Atlantic Monthly* for June, 1875, under the caption, "Political Results from the Varioloid." For the action of the committee on Owen's plan, see *supra*, pp. 83 *et seq.*

Sec. 2. From and after the fourth day of July, in the year one thousand eight hundred and seventy-six, no discrimination shall be made by any state nor by the United States, as to the enjoyment by classes of persons of the right of suffrage, because of race, color or previous condition of servitude.

Sec. 3. Until the fourth day of July, one thousand eight hundred and seventy-six, no class of persons, as to the right of any of whom to suffrage discrimination shall be made by any state, because of race, color, or previous condition of servitude, shall be included in the basis of representation.

Sec. 4. Debts incurred in aid of insurrection or of war against the Union, and claims of compensation for loss of involuntary service or labor, shall not be paid by any state nor by the United States.

Sec. 5. Congress shall have power to enforce by appropriate legislation, the provisions of this article.

And be it further resolved, that whenever the above recited amendment shall have become part of the Constitution, and any state lately in insurrection shall have ratified the same, and shall have modified its constitution and laws in conformity with the first section thereof, the senators and representatives from such state, if found duly elected and qualified, shall, after having taken the usual oath of office, be admitted as such:

Provided, That no person who, having been an officer in the army or navy of the United States, or having been a member of the Thirty-sixth Congress, or of the Cabinet in the year one thousand eight hundred and sixty, took part in the late insurrection, shall be eligible to either branch of the National legislature until after the fourth day of July, one thousand eight hundred and seventy-six.

It seems fitting that Owen should tell his own story of his relations with the committee and the fate of his proposition.[1]

---

[1] *Atlantic Monthly,* June, 1875: "Political Results from the Varioloid."

Throughout the winter of 1865-66 I had watched, with anxious interest and with some misgivings, the doings of Congress and of her reconstruction committee....

Toward the close of March—the committee still inactive—I became, to borrow the Quaker term, greatly "exercised" in regard to this matter; and I visited Washington, resolved to do what in me lay toward the judicious settlement of so vital a question; not concealing from myself, however, that an outsider, intermeddling in congressional action, must make up his mind to encounter, from members, a certain amount of impatient opposition.

After sounding several of my personal acquaintances in the House and Senate, also Governor Morton (not yet senator), I called, early one morning, on my friend Thad. Stevens (as we were wont to call him), then chairman, on the part of the House, of the reconstruction committee and read to him the following: [Then follows Owen's proposed amendment: see *supra*, p. 83.]

"Read that to me again," said Stevens, when I had concluded.

I did so, and inquired if he had an hour to spare.

"I have nothing half so important to do as to attend to this. Take your own time."

Then I set before him, succinctly, the chief reasons for the policy embodied in my amendment. "The freedmen," I said, "ought to be regarded as the wards of the Federal Government."

Stevens—Our very first duty is to them. Let the cursed rebels lie on the bed they have made.

Myself—But we cannot separate the interests and the fate of the negro from those of the planter. If we chafe and sour the whites of the South, the blacks must necessarily suffer thereby.

Stevens—Is that your reason for proposing prospective suffrage?

Myself—Not the chief reason. The fact that the negro is, for the present, unprepared wisely to use the right of suffrage, and, still more, incapable of legislating with prudence, is not less a fact because it has occurred through no fault of his. We must think and act for him as he is, and not as, but for lifelong servitude, he would have been. We seclude minors from political rights, not because they are unworthy, but because, for the time, they are incapable. So of foreigners; we grant them the privileges of citizenship only after five years' probation.

Stevens—I hate to delay full justice so long.

Myself—Consider if it be not for the freedman's welfare and good name that he should be kept away from the duties and responsibilities of political life until he shall have been, in a measure, prepared to fulfill these with credit to himself and advantage to the public service. He thirsts after education, and will have it if we but give him a chance, and if we don't call him away from the schoolroom to take a seat which he is unfitted to fill in a legislative chamber. If he occupies such a seat prematurely—perhaps before he can read a word of the Constitution—and becomes a nuisance or a laughing-stock, we, in case we mismanage our African wards, ought to bear the blame.

Stevens—You seem to take it for granted that as soon as the negro is admitted to political rights, he will set up as legislator.

Myself—In South Carolina and Mississippi the blacks outnumber the whites; and in Louisiana, Alabama, Georgia, and Florida, the numbers approach equality. The negro can count, if only on his fingers; and knows well enough when he has the power. Are we reasonable if we expect from uncultured freedmen self-restraint and abnegation of political aspirings which we never find among ourselves?

Stevens—If the negroes don't rule, impenitent traitors will. Isn't that as bad?

Myself—I think not; and if either are to make a mess of it and lose character, I'd rather it should be the planter.

Stevens—But if they dictate the laws, what security have the freedmen against outrage and virtual return to slavery.

Myself—This. We shall have invested them, beyond repeal by law, with political rights, if it be prospectively only; and their former masters will feel that they have now to deal with men who, in a few years, will be able to control elections, make governors and congressmen, and confer office on whom they please.

Stevens picked up my manuscript, looked it carefully over, and then, in his impulsive way, said: " I'll be plain with you, Owen. We've had nothing before us that comes anywhere near being as good as this, or as complete. It would be likely to pass, too; that's the best of it. We haven't a majority, either in our committee or in Congress, for immediate suffrage; and I don't believe the states have yet advanced so far that they would be willing to ratify it. I'll lay that amendment of yours before our committee to-morrow, if you say so; and I'll do my best to put it through."

I thanked him cordially, but suggested that, before he did so, it would perhaps be well that I should see Senator Fessenden and other prominent members of the reconstruction committee on the subject; to which he assented.

Then I laid before him, as supplement to my article xiv, a draft of a joint resolution to amend the Constitution, and to provide for the restoration to the states lately in insurrection of their full political rights. [Here follows Owen's resolution for restoring the southern states. See *supra*, p. 84.]

Stevens flared up at this. " That will never do! Far too lenient. It would be dangerous to let these fellows off on such terms."

I reminded him that if the ex-rebel states (as they surely would) postponed negro suffrage till 1876, then, according to the third section of my article, instead of sixty-six representatives in Congress (as under the apportionment then in force), they would be entitled under a purely white basis of representation, to forty-two representatives only. " Surely," said I, " you can manage that number, even if they should happen to be ultra secessionists."

" Perhaps we could," replied Stevens. " But you forget

the Senate. The eleven insurrectionary states would be entitled to their twenty-two senators, suffrage or no suffrage."

I admitted the force of this; and I failed to bring him over to my views of a clement policy. He had been terribly stirred up, like so many others, by the assassination of Lincoln, and he was ruled by an embittered feeling toward the South.

I found Senator Fessenden, who was chairman of the reconstruction committee on the part of the Senate, the very reverse of Stevens. Cold, deliberate, dispassionate, cautious, he heard me patiently, but with scarcely a remark. At the close, while assenting to the importance of the subject, he withheld any opinion as to my amendment; asked me to leave the manuscript with him, said he would give it careful attention and would be glad to see me again. When, two days later, I called upon him, he told me, in guarded and general terms, that he thought well of my proposal, as the best that had yet been presented to their committee. Washburne (E. B.) agreed to my amendment, with some enthusiasm. Conkling approved it. So, strongly, did Senator Howard. So, in a general way, did Boutwell. So, qualifiedly, did Bingham, observing, however, that he thought the first section ought to specify, in detail, the civil rights which we proposed to assure; he had a favorite section of his own on that subject. All the Republican members of the committee received the proposal more or less favorably. The Democrats held back.

Owen then goes on to tell how his plan was adopted by the committee and ordered to be reported to Congress.[1] Out of courtesy for Fessenden, however, who was sick of the varioloid, the report was held back for a couple of days in order that he, the chairman, should have a part in making the most important report of the session.[2]

Stevens' recital to Owen of the reasons why the com-

[1] *Cf. supra*, p. 99.
[2] See *supra*, p. 100. This was the reason for Williams' motion.

mittee abandoned his plan shows the extent to which political expediency had weight in the formulation of the congressional plan of reconstruction.

"Our action on your amendment" [said Stevens] "had, it seems, got noised abroad. In the course of last week the members from New York, from Illinois, and from your state too, Owen—from Indiana—held, each separately, a caucus to consider whether equality of suffrage, present or prospective, ought to form a part of the Republican programme for the coming canvas. They were afraid, so some of them told me, that if there was "a nigger in the wood-pile" at all, (that was the phrase), it would be used against them as an electioneering handle, and some of them—hang their cowardice!—might lose their elections. By inconsiderable majorities each of these caucuses decided that negro suffrage, in any shape, ought to be excluded from the platform; and they communicated these decisions to us. Our committee hadn't backbone enough to maintain its ground. Yesterday, the vote on your plan was reconsidered, your amendment was laid on the table, and in the course of the next three hours we contrived to patch together —well, what you've read this morning."

I was silent, thinking to myself how often in this riddle of a world, results of the most momentous import turn on what seem to us the veriest trifles. But, mortified as I was, I could not help smiling when Stevens, after his characteristic fashion, burst forth, "*Damn the varioloid! It changed the whole policy of the country.*"

One should be on his guard against taking too seriously Owen's feeling that Stevens committed himself almost wholly to his plan of reconstruction. As a matter of fact, he accepted only the Owen amendment and advocated a much more stringent bill than Owen's for disfranchising the rebels and for restoring the southern states.[1] Stevens cer-

---

[1] See *supra*, pp. 116, 119.

tainly cared but little for the fourteenth amendment as actually adopted and never intended that it should serve as a permanent settlement of the reconstruction question. No doubt the Owen plan was much more pleasing to him as a final adjustment than what the committee actually reported. To Stevens, however, this final report was to serve merely as a party platform, and as such, he gave it his cordial support.

Owen's proposition is the forbear of the present fourteenth amendment, but after the members of the committee decided to dodge the issue of negro suffrage, they changed it in many particulars at their meeting on April 28th,[1] and it is hardly recognizable in the proposition which they finally adopted, and reported to the House and Senate on April 30th.[2] This proposition read as follows:

A joint resolution proposing an amendment to the Constitution of the United States.

Be it resolved by the Senate and House of Representatives of the United States of America in Congress assembled (two-thirds of both Houses concurring) that the following article be proposed to the legislatures of the several states as an amendment to the Constitution of the United States, which, when ratified by three-fourths of said legislatures, shall be valid as part of the Constitution, namely:

Sec. 1. No state shall make or enforce any law which shall abridge the privileges or immunities of citizens of the United States; nor shall any state deprive any person of life, liberty or property without due process of law; nor deny to any person within its jurisdiction the equal protection of the laws.

Sec. 2. Representatives shall be apportioned among the several states which may be included within this Union according to their respective numbers, counting the whole number of

---

[1] See *supra*, pp. 100 *et seq.*
[2] *Globe*, pp. 2286-7, 2265.

persons in each state, excluding Indians not taxed. But whenever in any state the elective franchise shall be denied to any portion of its male citizens not less than twenty-one years of age, or in any way abridged, except for participation in rebellion or other crime, the basis of representation in such state shall be reduced in the proportion which the number of male citizens shall bear to the whole number of such male citizens not less than twenty-one years of age.

Sec. 3. Until the 4th day of July, in the year 1870, all persons who voluntarily adhered to the late insurrection, giving it aid and comfort, shall be excluded from the right to vote for representatives in Congress and for electors for President and Vice-President of the United States.

Sec. 4. Neither the United States nor any state shall assume or pay any debt or obligation already incurred, or which may hereafter be incurred, in aid of insurrection or of war against the United States, or any claim for compensation for loss of involuntary service or labor.

Sec. 5. The Congress shall have power to enforce by appropriate legislation the provisions of this article.

At the same time the committee adopted and reported two bills: one to provide for restoring to the states lately in rebellion their full political rights, the other declaring the leading rebels ineligible to office under the Government of the United States.[1]

On May 8th, Stevens opened the debate on the resolution for amending the Constitution.[2] In epitome his speech was as follows: The proposition was not all the committee desired and it fell far short of his individual wishes. However, nearly everybody on the committee believed it was all that could be obtained at the present time. To him it was a matter of great regret that the first amendment on the

[1] For the disposition made of these bills see *infra*, ch. vii.
[2] *Globe*, pp. 2459-60.

basis of representation had been slaughtered in the "house of its friends by a puerile, pedantic criticism and by a perversion of philological definition."[1] The section of this amendment on that question was not so good as that, but was at least a step in the right direction.

Section 1 simply meant that whatever law punishes or protects a white man should operate in the same way upon the black man. This would abolish the existing discriminations in all those states where there were black codes. It was true that this end was already accomplished by the Civil Rights act, but he feared that so soon as the Democrats should again obtain control of Congress, they would repeal that law; hence the necessity for this civil rights section of the amendment.

Section 3, the penal section, was the most important of all, its only drawback being its extreme leniency. It should prove the most popular among the people as it prohibited the rebels from voting until after 1870. This was the mildest of all punishments ever inflicted upon traitors. "I might not consent to the extreme severity denounced upon them by a provisional governor of Tennessee—I mean the late lamented Andrew Johnson of blessed memory—but I would have increased the severity of this section." Of the fourth section, Stevens said, "None dare object to it, who is not himself a rebel."

In a brief peroration he requested every friend of justice, every friend of the Union, and every friend of the final triumph of the rights of man and their extension to every human being, to sacrifice his peculiar views; and instead of vainly insisting upon the immediate operation of

[1] Referring to Sumner's "scholarly" speech in opposition. See *supra*, ch. iii, p. 205.

all that is right, to accept what is possible, and "all these things shall be added unto you."

The third section was attacked in the House by both conservative Republicans and the Democrats. Blaine thought it would lay the National Government open to the charge of bad faith, and suspected that since Congress had previously given the President the power to pardon certain rebels, their subsequent disfranchisement would seem to be inconsistent if not unjust.[1] A Democrat suggested that it looked a little foolish to proceed on the theory that a rebel, after being branded as an outlaw and disfranchised for four years, would at the end of that time be converted into a true and loyal citizen, perfectly qualified to be entrusted with the franchise.[2] Continuing in language the truth of which may now be seen, he said:

The committee have had the opportunity, in the most important period of our history, to have inscribed their names among the first statesmen of the age, by a liberal and enlightened policy, which would have bound all sections of the country together in the strong bond of mutual friendship and restored Union. That opportunity they have allowed to pass. Stripped of all its disguise, the measure is a mere scheme to deny representation to eleven states; to prevent indefinitely a complete restoration of the Union and perpetuate the power of a sectional party.

Garfield profoundly regretted that the public virtue had not been found such that the party could come out on the plain, unanswerable proposition that every adult citizen of the United States should enjoy the right of suffrage.[3] However, he would accept what he could get, but he hoped

---

[1] *Globe*, p. 2460. [2] Finck, *Globe*, p. 2462.
[3] *Globe*, pp. 2462-2464.

the House would see fit to eliminate section 3, as it would be difficult and impracticable of enforcement. It must either remain a dead letter or an army must be maintained in the South in order to see that it be not evaded.

Most of the debate in the House on the merits of the amendment dealt with the first and second sections on civil rights and the basis of representation, respectively. The arguments for and against these two propositions having been analyzed when they were considered as separate amendments, and as no new points were brought forward, it is not now necessary to dwell further upon them. The principal interest that attaches to the passage of the amendment through the House turns upon the third section. Practically every Republican who spoke upon the question expressed himself either against the principle of that section or against the practicability of its enforcement. It looked as though it would be stricken out, when, just before the vote was to be taken, Stevens again came to its defense.[1] The third section was the vital proposition of them all, and without it he did not care the snap of his finger whether the amendment were passed or not. If it should be eliminated there would be no friends of the Union on his side to carry into operation the other provisions. The other side of the House would be filled with yelling secessionists and hissing copperheads.

Give us the third section or give us nothing. Do not balk us with the pretense of an amendment which throws the Union into the hands of the enemy before it becomes consolidated. Gentlemen say I speak of party. When party is necessary to sustain the Union, I say rally to your party and save the Union. I do not hesitate to say at once, that section is there

[1] *Globe*, pp. 2533, 2545. For a suggested interpretation of Stevens' anxiety for the retention of this section, see next chapter.

to save or destroy the Union by the salvation or destruction of the Union party. Gentlemen tell us it is too strong—too strong for what? Too strong for their stomachs but not for the people. It is too lenient for my hard heart. Not only to 1870, but to 18,070 every rebel who shed the blood of loyal men should be prevented from exercising any power in this Government. Gentlemen here have said you must not humble these people. Why not? Do not they deserve humiliation? If they do not, who does? What criminal, what felon deserves it more, sir? They have not yet confessed their sins; and He who administers mercy and justice never forgives until the sinner confesses his sins and humbles himself at his footstool. Why should we forgive any more than He.

This speech is one of the best examples of Stevens' invective powers, and was confessedly for the purpose of arousing the partisan spirit. Nevertheless, there were enough Republicans opposed to the third section, who, together with the Democrats, could have stricken it out, had not about a dozen of the latter believed it good party tactics to make the whole amendment as obnoxious as possible, and so voted with the radicals rather than with the conservatives. As it was, the section was retained by the narrow margin of 84 to 79.[1] Among the Republicans who favored its elimination were Blaine, Garfield, Raymond, Hayes, and Bingham and Blow of the committee. All other Republican members of the committee voted for its retention as did also those two Democratic tacticians Rogers and Grider. Had this section been stricken out by the House, it is almost certain that there would have been no penal section in the fourteenth amendment, as the Senate certainly would not have reinserted it. In such case, Congress might have drafted a real plan of reconstruction.[2]

---

[1] *Globe*, p. 2545.

[2] Just what I mean by this statement will be explained in ch. vii.

By a vote of 128 to 37, the House on May 10th, passed the amendment as it had been reported by the committee.[1]

As has been said, Fessenden reported the amendment and accompanying bills to the Senate on the same day (April 30th) that Stevens had introduced them into the house. Although no formal action was taken by the upper House until several days after the amendment had passed the lower, two preliminary attempts to substitute some other proposition for that of the committee were made. On May 2d, Dixon, who still classed himself as a Republican, gave notice of his intention to offer as a substitute for the whole plan of the committee the following:

Resolved, That the interests of peace and of the Union require the admission of every state to its share in public legislation whenever it presents itself in an attitude of loyalty and harmony, but in the persons of representatives whose loyalty cannot be questioned under any constitutional or legal test.

Dixon explained that his resolution was couched in words employed by the President in the veto message of the Freedmen's Bureau bill. What the country needed and expected from Congress was a practical scheme for hastening the re-establishment of all the states in their full constitutional relations. The plan of the committee must inevitably delay indefinitely this result, for it was impossible to believe that any person in his right mind could expect that the southern states would accept the amendment. No self-respecting people would voluntarily disfranchise themselves even though it be for only a short term of years. But granting that they would do so, how could men who talk so much about a republican form of government be encouraged to look for the fruits of peace from such a policy? Certainly

[1] *Globe*, p. 2545.

the extremes to which partisan passions had been inflamed in Tennessee by the disfranchisement of the greater part of the population there, did not encourage practical men to desire a similar wholesale disfranchisement in the other southern states. The section in regard to the rebel debt was unnecessary, as the southern people certainly would not assume it in their poor condition, and it was absurd to think of any political party going before the people on a platform demanding that it be paid by the National Government. Likewise, section 1 was unnecessary, as the civil rights act gave to each citizen who might be denied justice by state courts the power to appeal to the United States courts. These latter were commanded with all their machinery to interfere in his behalf, and in the case of an emergency to employ the military power to secure him justice.

To Dixon, Sumner replied that he would favor his proposition had Dixon not forgotten that four million slaves had been declared freemen by the power of the National Government, and the same power should secure to them that freedom. Dixon very properly retorted that the amendment secured them nothing which they did not already possess.

It was not until May 14th, that the amendment was again considered in the Senate. On that day Stewart moved that the punitive section be stricken out, and offered an additional proposition for defining citizenship.[1] No action was taken on his motion, however, and it was not until May 23rd, nearly two weeks after the amendment had passed the House, that the Senate seriously undertook its consideration. Even then some of the radicals thought it should be further postponed, for as Sumner confessed, the longer final reconstruction was deferred the more radical it would

[1] *Globe*, p. 2560.

be.¹ Fessenden had not fully recovered from his attack of varioloid, and hence was unable to open the debate as his position of chairman of the committee reporting the amendment entitled him to do. This duty devolved upon Howard.

The objects of the first section, he again pointed out, were (1) to make the prohibitions of the so-called bill of rights binding on the states and compel them to respect these great fundamental guarantees, and (2) to abolish all class legislation in the states and do away with the injustice of subjecting one caste of persons to a code not applicable to another.² He regretted the second section, and himself very much preferred that Congress should be given direct authority to bestow equal suffrage on all male citizens in every state. Nevertheless, he defended it as being expedient and considered it an improvement on the previous proposition on the basis of representation, as it would operate uniformly throughout the Union.³ The third section he had opposed in committee.⁴ His principal objection to it was that it would accomplish nothing, for the rebels under it would still be allowed to vote for members of the state legislature, who in turn could select the presidential electors. Personally he preferred a section prohibiting all persons who had participated in the rebellion and were then (1866) over thirty years of age from holding either a state or Federal

---

[1] *Globe*, pp. 2763, 2764.

[2] *Globe*, pp. 2764-2768. Though the objects of the civil rights amendment were stated in ch. iii, p. 217, I again restate them in the words of Howard in order to show that in the minds of the members of the committee the meanings of the first and second forms of this amendment were identical. They considered the change merely a verbal one and intended in both cases to confer upon Congress power to enforce by positive legislation equal civil rights.

[3] Contrariwise, *cf.* Stevens, *supra*, p. 304.

[4] This was Howard's statement in the Senate, but the record does not bear him out in it. See *supra*, pp. 105, 106.

office. At this point Clark, of New Hampshire, arose and read a substitute for section 3 and gave notice that at the proper time he would offer it. This substitute embodied the principles of the bill declaring certain persons ineligible for office, which had been framed and reported by the committee.[1] Howard said he would support this substitute, and it did in fact later become section 3. He realized there was not much danger that the rebel debt would ever be paid by anybody. Nevertheless, so long as it remained in quasi-existence it might be a subject of political squabbling and party wrangling.

Wade suggested that the amendment be changed by replacing section 2 with the old resolution on the basis of representation, which had previously been defeated.[2] He also thought the amendment would be strengthened by omitting the punitive section and by adding to section 4 a clause declaring valid the National debt, including debts incurred for payment of pensions and bounties. In section one he desired to substitute for the word *citizens*, the words *persons born in the United States or naturalized by the laws thereof*. He explained that the word *citizen* had no exact meaning in the United States, and feared that if the Democrats obtained control of the Government they would in all probability put a different construction upon it from that given it by the Republicans.

On May 24th, Stewart, keenly disappointed that his own proposition had not been accepted by the committee, delivered what is by far the most interesting and statesmanlike speech that was made on the general subject of reconstruction at any time during the session.[3] The amendment, said

[1] See *supra*, p. 119.
[2] *Globe*, pp. 2768-2771.
[3] *Ibid.*, pp. 2798-2804.

he, had been urged because of its expediency; but as a matter of fact no man really knew what was expedient, because every one was liable to estimate the sentiments of the whole country by the views of a few friends or a small portion of his constituents, modified by his own peculiar ideas and wishes. Apparently there was very little difference between Union men as to what ought to be done if they had the power to do it. He was of the opinion that it was expedient to do right and that it was easier to agree as to what was right than as to what would be likely to return A or B or C to Congress. " The Union party agree that all men are entitled to life, liberty, and the pursuit of happiness, and they will endorse any necessary means to secure those inalienable rights to every American citizen." The more direct and positive the plan, the better. All digressions from principle would involve the Union party in new difficulties and increase its embarrassments. The President's plan of restoration was unsatisfactory, because it ignored the civil rights of four million loyal citizens guilty of no offense but fidelity to the Government and excluded them from constitutional liberty. Nevertheless, he had hesitated at the beginning of the session to condemn that plan because no better one seemed likely of adoption. Since then, however, two noble sentiments had become manifest upon which the people of the North might unite—protection for friends of the Union, and mercy to a fallen foe. Mercy pleaded generous amnesty; justice demanded impartial suffrage. Both principles were buried beneath an ocean of prejudice, but he firmly believed that the only solution of the problem was one based upon these two humane and just principles, having as they did the support of an enlightened press and public opinion. To those who criticized him for advocating negro suffrage when formerly he had opposed it, he replied, in the language of Lincoln, that he adopted " new views whenever they appear to be true views." If all those who had changed their opinions during the preceding six years should vote for his proposition, the others could vote as they pleased.

The world moves, and those who do not perceive it are dead to the living issues of the day. I have always advocated the necessity of taking the world as we find it, and following the logic of events. The development of new facts is constantly exploding old theories. The trouble is that some men do not seem to comprehend the new facts. . . . In advocating this plan I am profoundly impressed with the conviction that if this Union is ever restored, it must be done with impartial suffrage and general amnesty.

Stewart declared, however, that he realized that there were two obstacles in the way of adopting his proposition, both based upon passion and prejudice, and each nearly insurmountable. One was hatred of rebels, and a demand that they be disfranchised; the other was hatred of the negroes and a demand that they be disfranchised.

The great mass of the people of the South are either rebels or negroes, and if we yield to either demand the struggle is not ended. The party left in power, whether it be black men or white men, will soon display all the meaner qualities of despotism, intolerance, arrogance and above all a fierce hatred for the democratic protective principle of the equality of man. If we yield to both these demands, and disfranchise both blacks and whites, what will become of our free government, for which we were willing to sacrifice the last dollar and the last man?

Let justice be done, and then it becomes the duty of every loyal man to invoke mercy even for those who have attempted the destruction of our free institutions. We will then reflect that the South is not alone responsible for slavery and all its woes; that the North and civilized Europe have all played a part in planting this vile institution upon the most favored section of our common country, and the whole nation has been clothed in sackcloth and ashes because of the great crime. When the evil is removed and the rights of man acknowledged, we will cease to enquire who is most to blame, or who is most guilty, but we will labor to forget the past in view of the bright prospect of peace and justice.

Immediate and universal suffrage may not be wise, but what danger can there be in allowing all the negroes to vote with like educational and moral qualifications with the whites hereafter to become voters? The white men who have been in this rebellion must also have the ballot and full enfranchisement, or they must be driven out of the country, for if you retain them here disfranchised enemies, the extraordinary powers necessarily devolving upon the few whom you trust with political rights must make them tyrants. Every attempt to govern a state by a minority, however loyal that minority may be, is a mockery on republican institutions and will inevitably produce anarchy and discord. There will be no peace in Maryland, Missouri, or Tennessee until the people are enfranchised.

In conclusion, he declared the world would brand the Republicans as factionists and their efforts as a struggle for partisan power if they relied on expediency rather than on justice.[1]

Sherman moved to replace sections 2 and 3 with clauses providing respectively for apportioning representation according to male voters and direct taxes according to property values in each state.[2]

Five days elapsed before the Senate again, on May 29th,

---

[1] My purpose in quoting thus at length from Stewart's speech, and *infra* from that of Hendricks, I shall try to make clear in the succeeding chapter.

[2] *Globe*, p. 2804.

resumed consideration of the amendment. On each of those five days the Republican senators spent several hours in caucus, in which they finally adjusted their differences in regard to the terms of the amendment.[1] The net result of these caucuses was the fourteenth amendment in its present form. It will be noted that the principal changes made were in the first, third, and fourth sections. To the first section was added the clause defining who are citizens of the United States, which was for the purpose, as Howard said, of removing all doubt on that question.[2] The original third section was stricken out, and in its place was incorporated a section embodying the principles of the bill declaring certain persons ineligible to office.[3] In the fourth section Wade's suggestion as to declaring the validity of the National debt was inserted.[4] In addition two or three verbal changes were made. On May 30th, Reverdy Johnson, who perhaps understood southern sentiment better than any other man in the Senate, declared emphatically that the new third section would be just as objectionable to the southern people as the old one, and he was absolutely sure that the southern states would reject the amendment and principally on account of this section.[5] "Do you want to act upon the public opinion of the masses of the South? Do you not want to win them back to loyalty? And if you do, why strike at the men who, of all others, are most influential and can bring about the end which we all have at heart?"

The death of Gen. Winfield Scott caused two or three

---

[1] See *infra*, p. 317. See also newspapers for May 25 to 29. So far as I know the secret proceedings of this caucus have never come to light. Though nearly fifty years have passed, neither in memoirs, nor in letters published or unpublished, has any senator then present made a statement of what went on in this caucus.

[2] *Globe*, p. 2890. [3] See *supra*, p. 119.
[4] See *supra*, p. 312. [5] *Globe*, p. 2902.

more days delay in the consideration of the amendment and it was not until June 4th that the discussion on it was resumed. On that day Thomas A. Hendricks, who was then a Democratic senator from Indiana, delivered his well-known philippic against the policy of deciding in a party caucus upon so grave a matter as a constitutional amendment, designed to alter the fundamental principles of our Government.[1] He pointed out that the first report of the joint committee had been defeated, and this second one when first presented to the Senate seemed doomed to the same fate.

A second defeat of a party program could not be borne; its effects upon the fall elections would be disastrous. A caucus was called and we witnessed the astounding spectacle of the withdrawal for the time, of a great legislative measure, touching the Constitution itself, from the Senate, that it might be decided in the secret councils of a party. For three days the Senate chamber was silent but the discussions were transferred to another room of the capitol, with closed doors and darkened windows, where party leaders might safely contend for a political and party policy.

He then showed how an actual minority of the Senate, by such proceedings, could pass a constitutional amendment. There were forty-nine members, thirty-nine Republicans and ten Democrats. In caucus twenty Republicans voting for the amendment could bind the other nineteen. Hence the amendment may pass the Senate though there be only twenty men out of forty-nine who really favor it.

So carefully has the obligation of secrecy been observed that no outside persons, not even the sharp-eyed men of the press, have been able to learn one word that was spoken, or one vote given.

[1] *Globe*, pp. 2938-2942.

If section 2 fixes the principle that those who do not vote should not be voted for, why are foreigners in northern states represented though they must remain without a vote for at least five years? If in Maryland, West Virginia, Tennessee, and Missouri the majority are treated as unfit to vote, why shall the minority vote for them? Come now let candor and truth have full sway, and answer me; is it not because you believe that the few in these states now allowed to vote will send radicals to Congress, and therefore you allow them to send full delegations that it may add to your party's political power? Why, if the principle be right that none but voters ought to be represented, do you not say so. If, as you will say, the negroes ought to have the right of voting, why do you not in plain words confer it upon them, instead of trying to coerce the states by this indirect measure to give it to them?

To the argument that by the result of the war the representation of the South would be increased, he gave two answers: (1) the slaves were not made free by the voice of the South, but by the constitutional amendment that was demanded by the North, and the North could not well complain of the consequences of her own act; (2) he was willing to continue the old three-fifths arrangement in regard to the representation of negroes so long as they were not enfranchised.

Against the third section common sense alone was sufficient argument. Such a harsh and sweeping measure would include many excellent men whose services in the work of reconstruction would be of the greatest value to the country. Some of these men had displayed heroic courage in standing out against the secession movement, and though afterwards they were forced by the logic of events to yield obedience to, and to serve, the established government *de facto*, they had always at heart been Union men and therefore should not be proscribed. As a penalty for crime the measure was *ex post facto,* and if passed as an ordinary law it would therefore be unconstitutional. " Mr. President," said he, " do you think there will enough good come of this to justify us in departing from the principle which is found in the Constitution of the United States and of every state in the Union, that a man shall be punished only according to the law in force at the time the act is done?"

Though the amendment was debated for three more days during which a number of Republicans expressed their dissatisfaction with it as a settlement of the reconstruction question, any effort to make any further changes in its provisions met with the opposition of a party governed absolutely by King Caucus. In vain did Doolittle, whom the Republicans called the apostate, plead with his former associates that they allow the various sections to be sent separately to the states for ratification.[1] It was of no avail that Cowan, another apostate, vehemently assailed his old friends and charged them with surrendering their individual principles and acting from motives of party alone.[2] On June 8th the vote was taken and the amendment passed thirty-three to eleven, four Democrats and one Republican being absent.[3] Five days later, Thaddeus Stevens in the House arose and announced in a sad voice that the members of the majority party had decided to concur in the Senate's amendments.[4] That was the end. What has been called the congressional plan of reconstruction was completed.

[1] *Globe*, pp. 2991, 3040.
[2] *Ibid.*, pp. 2989-2991.
[3] *Ibid.*, pp. 3040-3042.
[4] *Ibid.*, pp. 3144-3149.

CHAPTER VII

DID CONGRESS HAVE A PLAN OF RECONSTRUCTION?

It is impossible to give a categorical answer to this question. Most writers have regarded the fourteenth amendment as the plan of Congress for restoring the southern states to their places in the Union. Rhodes for instance, calls it a "magnanimous offer" to the South. As a matter of fact, there are grave doubts as to whether it *was* an "offer," and each individual who takes the trouble to read the records, is at liberty to form his own opinion as to its magnanimity. The same author is also of the opinion that, with the possible exception of the third section, the amendment was marked by statesmanship of a high order; and when he considers that there were no executions or confiscations, even the third section does not lack in generosity. Finally, he implies that the southern states were blameworthy for not taking advantage of the offer "eagerly and at once."[1]

The purpose of this chapter is not controversial, and it is not my intention to attempt to refute Mr. Rhodes or any other writer who has held opinions similar to his. Since, however, this is a history of the reconstruction committee, and if there were a congressional plan, it must have been the creation of that committee, an inquiry into the extent to which the fourteenth amendment

[1] *Rhodes*, vol. v, pp. 602-610.

may be regarded as such a plan of reconstruction would seem to be necessary and proper. In order to make this inquiry, I shall examine four matters which tend to throw light upon the question. These matters are: (1) The formal report of the chairman of the committee; (2) The action by Congress on the bill for restoring the southern states, which was reported by the committee,[1] and the attempted modifications of that bill; (3) The action taken by Congress in finally passing the committee's resolution for the restoration of Tennessee;[2] (4) The opinions expressed in regard to the question, by members of Congress, their outside supporters and opponents.

It will be remembered that the committee instructed Fessenden to prepare a formal report which was to be in the nature of a defense of the measures which the committee presented to Congress on April 30.[3] This Fessenden did, and after he had submitted it to his colleagues on the committee,[4] he presented it to the Senate on June 8, and on the same day Stevens presented it to the House.[5]

The report maintains that the people of the rebel states had risen in insurrection against the United States, severed their political relations as states with the Union, renounced their allegiance and established *de facto* governments for themselves. In support of their enterprise they had levied war on the United States for four years

---

[1] See *supra*, p. 117.
[2] See *supra*, pp. 63 *et seq*.
[3] See *supra*, p. 114.
[4] See *supra*, p. 120.
[5] *Globe*, pp. 3038, 3051. The report in full may be found in vol. ii, *Reports of Committees*, 1st sess., 39th Cong.; also in McPherson, p. 88 *et seq.;* and in Fessenden's *Life of Fessenden*, vol. ii, p. 67 *et seq*. In my analysis of the report no further page references will be given. The language of the report will be closely followed.

and had finally laid down their arms, not because they were convinced that their action had been a crime of which they repented, but because they were physically unable to prolong the struggle. The committee agrees with the President, that at the close of the war the rebel states were utterly devoid of civil governments, but as to whose duty it is to rehabilitate them, it does not agree with him. Moreover, it is urged that the conflict had taken on the proportions of a civil war of the greatest magnitude, which, by the law of nations, gave the conqueror the right to exact security from the vanquished against the renewal of the conflict.

The foregoing argument is nothing more nor less than the "conquered province" theory of Thaddeus Stevens, but the committee does not definitely commit itself to that theory. It argues that is not necessary to discuss the question as to whether the rebel states are in or out of the Union, but is willing to grant the "profitless abstraction" that they are still within the Union, thus committing itself to the "forfeited rights" theory.[1] Following this theory, it holds that even though the rebel states are still in the Union, they have placed themselves by the act of rebellion in a condition which abrogates the powers and privileges incident to states and denies them all pretense of right to enjoy such powers and privileges.

The argument then closely follows Sumner's "suicide" theory, maintaining that a state has certain duties to perform as a member of the Union, and if it faithfully discharges those duties, certain privileges and rights belong to it. If, however, the state attempts to evade discharge of its obligations, then Congress has the

---

[1] For an explanation of these theories, see Dunning, *Essays*, p. 99 *et seq*.

power to force it to the performance of its duty; but the state's privileges and rights are forfeited and cannot be restored to it until every condition which Congress sees fit to impose has been complied with, and the state shown proofs of an earnest desire to return to its former allegiance. This theory is applied by the committee as the basis of the refutation of those people—principally the President—who are urging that Congress is violating the great principle of taxation only with the consent of the taxed by imposing laws and taxes upon the southern states without allowing them representation in the law-making body.

It is not within the province of this analysis to discuss at length the committee's justification of sections 1 and 2 of the fourteenth amendment, as such justification has been considered above.[1] Suffice it to say that the committee felt that it was only justice to the colored loyalists in the South, and to the northern people themselves, that the rebel states be required to ratify such amendments before they be re-admitted to representation in Congress. The committee then prescribes the method of proceeding which a rebel state should follow. First, a convention should be assembled under competent authority. Such authority ordinarily emanates from Congress, but the committee is not disposed to criticise the President for his action in this regard. Second, the convention should proceed to form a constitution which should contain a refutation of the deadly heresy of secession, a recognition of the validity of all laws passed by Congress since the rebellion began, and finally, should incorporate all the principles embodied in the thirteenth and fourteenth amendments to the United States Consti-

[1] Chapters iii, v and vi.

tution. The constitution thus formed should be submitted to the people for ratification. Fourth, in case the people adopt the constitution, a legislature should be called, which may proceed with the election of senators and make provision for the election of representatives in accordance with the laws of Congress regulating representation. Fifth, proof that such action had been taken should be submitted to Congress for approval. It is interesting to note that with the exception of the prescription of negro suffrage and military rule, the foregoing is essentially the method of procedure laid down by Congress in the Reconstruction acts of 1867.

The committee then declares that in no case have the afore-mentioned plan of procedure and conditions been complied with, therefore one of two alternatives must be adopted by Congress. In the first place, it could waive all formalities and admit the states lately in rebellion at once, trusting that time and experience would set all things right. However, in the face of the evidence already reviewed relating to the prevalence of southern disloyalty, the committee does not feel that it would be justified in recommending such a course to Congress. In fact, it is declared that to allow such unrepentant rebels as for the most part have been elected by constituencies who believe in the right of secession as much as ever, to take their place in Congress without any guarantee of their own or their constituents' loyalty, would be a simple method of transferring the scene of war from the field of battle to the halls of Congress, where the conquered rebels, through their representatives, would seize upon the very government they had fought to destroy. Such a course would be a disaster of greater magnitude than the surrender of Grant to Lee, and Sherman to Johnston, would have been; for in the latter event, new armies could have been raised, but to allow the rebels in coalition with their friends at the North to take control of the government, would be even more infamous than that anti-coercive policy which permitted the rebellion in the beginning to take form and gather force.

Therefore the committee is forced to adopt the second alternative and summarizes the answer to the inquiry as to whether "the so-called Confederate states or any of them are entitled to be represented in either house of Congress," in the following paragraph:

The conclusion of your committee therefore is that the so-called Confederate states are not, at present, entitled to representation in the Congress of the United States; that before allowing such representation, adequate security for future peace and safety should be required; that this can be found only in such changes of the organic law as shall determine the civil rights and privileges of all citizens in all parts of the republic, shall place representation on an equitable basis, shall fix a stigma upon treason and protect the loyal people against future claims for the expenses incurred in the support of rebellion and for manumitted slaves, together with an express grant of power to Congress to enforce those provisions. To this end they offer a joint resolution for amending the Constitution of the United States, and the two several bills designed to carry the same into effect.

The report was highly satisfactory to the radical politicians, who realized that upon its reasoning they must defend their position before the country. In fact, it seems to have been written principally for the purpose of a campaign document, and it had the peculiar quality of suiting all the varying degrees of Republican sentiment. To the conservative it implied that the Johnson state governments in the South were competent to ratify a constitutional amendment, and if they should do so the southern delegations would be admitted to Congress. But in no place did the report definitely say those states were to ratify the amendment, nor does it expressly recommend that their representatives and senators be admitted in case they should do so. On the other hand, it seemed to prove, and doubtless to the complete satisfaction of the extreme radicals, that those state governments were not legally constituted, and it allows the inference to be drawn that Congress alone can provide the machinery for creating such legal governments, and nowhere is it said that Congress might not yet exercise its authority in that regard. Moreover, from an examination of the evidence, Fessenden, the author of the report, finds that nearly every white person in the South is disloyal, and for that reason, Congress found it unwise "to waive all formalities" and admit the southern representatives at once. Constituencies composed of such persons, said he, are unfit to be represented. Nowhere does he express the opinion that the adoption of the fourteenth amendment would make them any more loyal, and hence fit for representation.

The most, then, that can be said for the report is that it implies a congressional plan of reconstruction, but does not absolutely affirm that the committee's chief measure, the fourteenth amendment, was to serve as the only additional condition to be imposed upon the southern states, precedent to the admission of their delegations into Congress. It is quite true that Fessenden personally hoped and perhaps expected that such would be the case, but as already pointed out, he was writing primarily not his own opinions but such ideas as would be serviceable to all sorts of Republican congressmen in their appeal to the people for re-election.

But the report did recommend to Congress the adoption of the bill for restoring the southern states.[1] Let us see whether that recommendation was adopted.

The history of this bill in the House and in the Senate, its various postponements, and proposed amendments to and substitutes for it, will, even at the risk of tediousness, be given in detail in order to show that the majority of the Republican party were at no time willing to promise unreservedly to restore the southern states upon their ratifying the fourteenth amendment.

It will be remembered that Stevens and Fessenden introduced this bill into their respective houses at the same time they reported the fourteenth amendment. In the house, a motion was made and carried that the consideration of the bill be postponed till May 9.[2] This was on April 30, and the next day Boutwell offered to amend the bill so that only Arkansas and Tennessee were promised admission after duly ratifying the amendment and even they only after "they shall have established an equal and just system of suffrage for all male citizens within their jurisdictions not less than twenty-one years old."[3]

On May 2, Williams, in the Senate, proposed that the bill be so amended as to admit Tennessee and Arkansas immediately upon their ratification of the amendment, even though it had not become a part of the Constitution.[4] He further proposed that in case the amendment had not received the ratifications of three-fourths of all the states by March 4, 1867, but had been ratified by any of the remaining nine rebel states, such state

---

[1] See *supra*, p. 117. This bill provided that whenever a rebel state ratified the fourteenth amendment, and it had become part of thè Constitution, said state should be entitled to representation in Congress.

[2] *Globe*, p. 2287. [3] *Ibid.*, 2313.

[4] *Ibid.*, p. 2332 *et seq.*

should be admitted on that date, provided its constitution had been changed so as to conform to the principles of the amendment.

In explanation Williams said that should the rebel states ratify the amendment there was little doubt that enough of the loyal states would do likewise to make it a part of the Constitution. But in case the loyal states should not do so before March 4, 1867, he saw no reason to postpone longer than that date the admission of the insurgent states in case they had ratified the amendment by that time. Tennessee and Arkansas, because of the character of their constitutions and laws, were entitled to be excepted, and to have a preference over the other rebel states.

Though the House had postponed the bill for restoring the southern states until May 9, it was not until the 15th that it was reached in the regular order of business. Stevens moved to postpone it for two weeks more in order, as he said, to give the Senate time to act on the amendment.[1] Bingham was immediately on his feet with a vehement protest against further delay. He hoped action would be taken on it at once and declared the country expected Congress to present its whole plan of reconstruction as soon as possible. Moreover, he had the same idea as to Tennessee as Williams, and desired that the bill be acted on immediately in order that her representatives might be seated before the end of the session, as he had no doubt that her legislature would ratify the amendment as soon as given an opportunity to do so. Price, another representative from Ohio, and a friend of Bingham, was even more strenuous in objecting to the postponement of the bill, and radical Republican

[1] *Globe*, pp. 2598–2600.

as he was, more than intimated that Congress was trying to go before the country without committing itself to a plan of reconstruction, though leaving the implication that it had such a plan. He hoped his party would act with sincerity and not leave itself open to the charge of duplicity. Conkling, who was under the influence of Stevens, disavowed on the part of those who desired postponement any intention of acting in bad faith, and agreed that Congress ought to have a definite plan. However, he concurred in Stevens' opinion that the bill ought not to be acted on until the Senate should pass the amendment, as some changes might be necessary should the Senate, as seemed likely, modify any of the amendment's provisions. Though Stevens' motion received hardly half of the Republican vote, it was carried with the assistance of the Democrats, who thought it was good party politics to prevent their adversaries agreeing upon a definite plan of reconstruction.

Before proceeding further with the consideration of the bill it may be profitable to speculate for a minute upon Stevens' motives in having it postponed at this time. It is probable that he would have had no particular objection to passing the bill for restoring the southern states had he felt sure the Senate would adopt the amendment without striking out or materially modifying his beloved third section.

For Stevens no doubt knew, as every body must have known, that the southern people, though humiliated, would not voluntarily disfranchise themselves even for the sake of obtaining representation in Congress. Therefore he was not afraid to promise admission to the southern states on condition of their doing something which he knew they would not do. But he must have been pretty thoroughly convinced even as early as the fifteenth of May that his punitive section would not be allowed to stand, as it had very few, if any, friends in the Senate. Consequently, he was doubtless sincere in desiring to have the consideration of the bill postponed until after the Senate should have taken final action on the amendment.

Stevens as a shrewd, practical politician doubtless believed that in order successfully to contest the coming elections, his party must not be left open to the charge of being simply obstructionists and having no plan of reconstruction of their own. But when the Republican senators in caucus changed the third section from the old form to the new, he was no longer willing to risk passing the restoration bill, for he could have been by no means sure that the southerners, in their great desire again to take part in the National Government, would not be willing to debar a relatively few persons from holding a comparatively small number of offices in order to obtain their ends. It happened that at just that time he was being urged on by such journals as the *Nation* and the *Independent*,[1] to believe that radical sentiment was developing with sufficient rapidity in the North so that his party might safely go before the country in November in the advocacy of a "thorough" reconstruction for the South.

Therefore, on May 28, Stevens introduced into the House what was the first bill for the real *reconstruction* in contradistinction to *restoration* of the southern states.[2]

---

[1] See issues during all of May and June of these two papers in which the opinion was consistently expressed that the people were ready and anxious to support Congress in a plan of reconstruction based upon equal and exact justice. They therefore urged that Congress adopt such a plan.

[2] This was House bill 623. *House Journal*, p. 657. Nowhere is the bill printed in full, but an abstract of it may be found in the *Nation*, June

In fact, it was in the nature of a substitute for the restoration bill which we have been considering. Briefly stated, it recognized the Johnson governments as *de facto* and valid for municipal purposes only. They were compelled in their respective states to call conventions, the members of which were to be elected by all male citizens of whatever race or color. Citizens, however, in this instance would include only the negroes and a very small percentage of the whites, for by one of the sections of the bill, all persons who had held office under the government of the so-called Confederate States or who had taken an oath of allegiance thereto were declared to have forfeited their citizenship. In order again to become citizens and be qualified to vote, they must be naturalized just as other foreigners. Furthermore, it was required that the constitutions and laws to be framed must place all citizens upon an equality in respect to civil and political rights, and should such equality ever in the future be denied by the repeal of the laws establishing it, the guilty state would forthwith lose its right to representation. Finally, when any state should have complied with the provisions of this bill, its representatives and senators would be admitted into congress. Stevens' bill was ordered to be printed, but no further action was taken upon it at the time.

On the next day, May 29, the two weeks for which the committee's restoration bill had been postponed having elapsed, it again came up for consideration.[1] Ashley of Ohio, who later became notorious as an advo-

---

5, 1866. In terms and principles it was very similar to a bill introduced by Stevens early in the second session of the 39th Congress, and which was an immediate forerunner of the Reconstruction act. See *infra*, chap. viii, p. 358.

[1] *Globe*, p. 2878 *et seq*.

cate of impeachment, offered an amendment which provided that before the southern states could be readmitted a new election for all state and national officers must be held.[1] The amendment further provided that before a state's claim for admission could be considered all these offices must be filled with men other than those disqualified by the new third section of the fourteenth amendment as adopted by the Republican senators in caucus. He stated that personally he very much preferred some sort of bill that would secure the franchise to the negroes, but he was not himself prepared to offer such a bill, as he did not know how best to proceed in order to accomplish that end. Nevertheless he was fervent in his desire that Congress, before adjourning, should work out some plan whereby every loyal man in the South, whether white or black, should be given the right to vote. In spite of his own preferences, however, he would support the committee's bill if nothing better could be had, but he hoped that at least his amendment would be adopted.

Latham, of West Virginia, thought that Congress ought to say at once whether it expected to accept the Johnson governments as legitimate or not.[2] For himself, he firmly believed that they were illegal as then existing, and proposed that the reconstruction committee be charged with the duty of making an investigation with a view of ascertaining in what way they should be modified so as to qualify them to pass upon the fourteenth amendment.[3] His speech concluded the consideration of the bill for that day, and the next morning some one moved that it be postponed until June 4, the assigned reason being that Stevens was ill and not able to take charge of the debate. The motion was adopted without a division.

[1] *Globe*, p. 2881 *et seq.* [2] *Ibid.*, p. 2886.
[3] *Ibid.*, pp. 2904–2906.

It may be said with almost entire certainty that after May 29 the bill had no chance whatever of becoming law. For it was on this day that the Republican senators, after several conferences in caucus, announced the material modification already noted in the third section of the fourteenth amendment.[1] The second section of that amendment was a bitter pill for Sumner and the four or five other extreme radical senators who had so persistently denounced the original amendment on the basis of representation and had been instrumental in defeating it.[2] It must have been with extreme reluctance that Sumner agreed to vote for a provision which, only four months before, he had declared was a "compromise of sacred human rights." He never pretended that he would consider the fourteenth amendment as a final plan of reconstruction,[3] and on this very day (May 29) he offered to amend the restoration bill so as to compel the southern states not only to ratify the fourteenth amendment but also to provide in their constitutions for universal suffrage.[4] There can be little doubt that in order to have him and his immediate followers withdraw their opposition to section 2, the Republican caucus virtually promised him either to incorporate his amendment in the restoration bill or allow that bill to be consigned to a permanent place on the table. As a matter of fact the latter disposition was made of it, for we hear no more of it in the Senate.

But in the House, it was a different matter. In that body was a considerable minority of Republicans, who either from motives of natural conservatism or through fear of having their places successfully contested, were

[1] See *supra*, chap. vi, p. 316.
[2] See *supra*, chap. iii, p. 205.
[3] Rhodes, vol. v, pp. 609, 610.
[4] *Globe*, p. 2869.

anxious to have Congress definitely commit itself to this bill. This was especially true of the Ohio members and the representatives of other doubtful states like Connecticut, Indiana and parts of New York. But even here the efforts to have it disposed of were not so persistent after May 29th, as they previously had been. It was debated in a more or less desultory way from time to time throughout the remainder of the session. On June 4, Wilson of Iowa, chairman of the House judiciary committee, and a man of some ability and following, declared that Congress would not do its duty either to the loyal whites or the blacks in the South unless it empowered the latter to assist the former in obtaining control of the rebel states and holding them for the party of the Union.[1] After Wilson's speech, the bill was again postponed for ten days.

In the meantime, on June 11, Kelley of Pennsylvania introduced a substitute for the restoration bill.[2] Like Stevens' bill, it provided that the existing southern state governments should be recognized as valid for municipal purposes, but they were not to be allowed to pass upon the fourteenth amendment. In order to have their states restored to full fellowship in the Union, they must call conventions whose members were to be elected by all men twenty-one years old or over, who could read the Constitution. These conventions should frame constitutions, which must provide for equal civil rights and impartial suffrage. The first legislatures elected under the new governments might properly ratify the fourteenth amendment, and whenever they should do so, universal amnesty for all citizens therein would forthwith be declared, and their representatives and senators would

[1] *Globe*, pp. 2947–2949.   [2] *Ibid.*, p. 3090.

immediately be admitted into Congress. This was the first and last of Kelley's bill, and it is only mentioned here to show the diverse opinions that were held as to what sort of legislation should be enacted by Congress on the subject.

The restoration bill was debated from June fourteenth to twentieth. One Republican regretted to find that there was a disposition among his colleagues to postpone action on the bill.[1] Personally he thought it was a just measure, and he hoped that Congress would not adjourn and go before the country without a complete plan of reconstruction. George W. Julian made a long and impassioned speech, and as an original abolitionist, pleaded that the southern states be not readmitted until universal suffrage had been secured in them.[2] He pointed out that the House, earlier in the session, had by a vote of more than two to one passed a bill giving the negroes the right to vote in the District of Columbia. He believed that Congress had just as much power in the rebel states as in the District and he hoped that his colleagues would not recede from the advanced position they had previously assumed. In uttering these words, he was enunciating the same opinion as was expressed by three-fourths of the Republicans who spoke on the question. On June 20, Stevens suggested that the bill be disposed of by taking a vote immediately.[3] To this Banks objected, and moved that it be laid on the table.

His motion was carried, 75 to 20. There it lay till July 20, when Stevens with a certain mock earnestness called it up,[4] asked that it be put on its passage, and attempted to shut off debate by moving the previous ques-

---

[1] Windom, *Globe*, p. 3166 *et seq.* [2] *Globe*, p. 3208 *et seq.*
[3] *Ibid.*, p. 3303 *et seq.* [4] *Ibid.*, p. 3981.

tion. His followers, however, knew their master too well not to understand when he was serious and when he was trifling, so they obligingly failed to second the previous question. Some one objected that the bill had not been printed.

The fact that this measure, which was indeed the capstone of the great and much-heralded congressional plan, had been allowed to languish for nearly three months without any of its friends taking the trouble to have it printed, speaks eloquently for the lack of interest in it. After some discussion a motion was made that it again be laid on the table. Bingham and a few of his faithful followers called for a division. The yeas and nays were taken. The result showed 101 yeas, 35 nays, and 46 not voting. Thus sank into eternal sleep the luckless restoration bill. Of those who had framed it and jauntily announced it as an earnest of Congress' sincerity in offering the fourteenth amendment to the rebel states as terms for their readmission, Bingham alone[1] was willing to keep the faith.

Thaddeus Stevens, however, was as honest as Bingham. The latter desired to go before the country on the unequivocal platform of the fourteenth amendment. Neither did Stevens wish to equivocate, however, for he was quite willing to appeal to the country on his reconstruction bill as the main issue. He, therefore, on July 25, called up that bill and asked for a direct vote on it.[2] The vast majority of the 39th Congress were as unwilling to commit their political fortunes to Stevens' radical plan as they were frankly to embrace Bingham's conservative one. Consequently, they overwhelmingly voted

---

[1] Blow, who doubtless would have voted with Bingham's thirty-five, was absent.

[2] *Globe*, p. 4157.

to lay it also on the table. On July 28, the last day of the session, Stevens was allowed to bring up his bill for the purpose of amending it and making some remarks on it. His amendment put upon the President the duty of calling the conventions in the rebel states, and hence the existing governments were not recognized even for municipal purposes. The old man's speech was one of the ablest and most pathetic of his whole career. After reading it, it is impossible to doubt the sincerity and honesty of the man as he pleaded so eloquently with his colleagues that they go with him all the way in his plan for re-creating the very social and industrial, as well as political, institutions of the South. With tears in his eyes he begged them, should death overtake his racked and diseased frame ere the time should again come for their reassembling, to go forward and perfect and carry out the general principles of reconstruction which he had so frequently expounded to them.

From the foregoing account of the disposition made of both Bingham's and Stevens' bills we may draw the conclusion that the great majority of Republican congressmen were, on the one hand, unwilling to promise in good faith that they would require nothing further of the southern states than the ratification of the fourteenth amendment, and on the other, afraid to enter the approaching campaign on so radical an issue as that involved in Stevens' bill. But unless they should do something, they would still leave themselves open to the charge that they had no plan of reconstruction; for, passing the fourteenth amendment alone and saying nothing as to what the result would be if the southern states should ratify it, certainly could not have been regarded as a plan of reconstruction, even by the most gullible and simpleminded people. In this situation, it was fortunate for Congress that the state of Tennessee ratified the fourteenth amendment on July 19.[1] This event gave the politicians the exact opportunity they desired; for, by admitting Tennessee, they could leave the implication to be drawn, that should the other rebel states do what Tennessee had done, they too would be admitted. The radicals were well aware, however, in their own minds, that this was exactly what the other states would never do; for though they might conceivably ratify the fourteenth amendment, no one thought for a moment that they would ever evidence the same loyalty which Tennessee had shown.[2]

Within a few minutes after a telegram was received in Washington by certain members of Congress that Tennessee had ratified the amendment, Bingham moved[3] to reconsider the vote by which the joint resolution for admitting Tennessee had been recommitted on March 5.[4] The motion was agreed to, whereupon Stevens moved to lay the Tennessee resolution on the table, but other radicals, who apparently desired to save themselves the embarrassment of having their votes recorded on that proposition, moved an adjournment in order to accomplish the same result. Though the motion to adjourn was defeated, it received a majority of the Republican vote, but the conservative minority, together with the Democrats, were sufficient to defeat it. Stevens then attempted

---

[1] Dunning, *Reconstruction, Political and Economic*, pp. 69, 70.

[2] See *supra*, chap. iv, p. 223. I do not wish to be understood as implying that every Republican who voted for the admission of Tennessee did so purely from such sordid motive as is here intimated. I do believe, however, it was such a motive that influenced those that voted for Tennessee's admission, but did not vote for Bingham's restoration bill.

[3] *Globe*, pp. 3948-3950.

[4] See *supra*, chap. iv, p. 256.

dilatory tactics, in which he was supported by Boutwell, Morrill, and sometimes Conkling and about thirty or forty other extreme radicals. Bingham moved to substitute for the original committee resolution a new one, which simply stated that whereas Tennessee had ratified in good faith the articles of amendment proposed by Congress, and had in other ways shown to the satisfaction of Congress her return to allegiance to the Government, laws and authority of the United States, therefore, resolved, that the state of Tennessee be declared restored to her former practical relation to the Union, and again was entitled to be represented. Having done this, Bingham allowed an adjournment.

On the next day, the resolution was again brought forward for consideration, and Bingham moved the previous question.[1] Boutwell asked that he be allowed to amend the resolution so that Tennessee could only be admitted after having granted impartial suffrage, but Bingham refused to yield for that purpose, but was willing to allow Boutwell a few minutes in which to make some remarks on the proposition.

Of this opportunity Boutwell availed himself. He said he was not ignorant of the fact that the votes of the House already taken foreshadowed its purpose to pass the pending joint resolution for the admission of Tennessee. Moreover, he recognized the reason for this action as being the approach of a great political struggle in which his party associates seemed to feel that the passage of this resolution would give them strength. This he did not consider to be the case, for he thought the country would be more likely to sustain them if they pursued a policy looking towards equal and exact justice

[1] *Globe*, p. 3975 *et seq.*

to all men, than if they should make a compromise of sacred human rights. He admitted that he was not troubled as some seemed to be by the news that the proceedings of the Tennessee legislature upon the question of ratifying the constitutional amendment seemed to be irregular.[1]

His objections then were not technical, but vital and fundamental. In the first place the Tennessee government was not republican in form. He did not assert that it was necessary for every man to vote in order to have a republican form of government, but where terms and conditions are imposed, they should be of such a reasonable nature that it would be possible for the great majority of men to meet the requirements of the law. The House by passing this resolution was recognizing as republican in form the government of a state in which over 80,000 male citizens were for themselves and their posterity forever deprived of taking part. Such an act would be not only unjust, but in direct violation of that constitutional injunction which imposes upon Congress the duty of guaranteeing to each state a republican form of government.

Though he believed Congress had positive power to grant the franchise to the negroes in the rebellious states, he was then merely appealing to the negative power of Congress, by which he meant that Tennessee and the other southern states should be excluded from representation until they should perform this act of justice to the negroes. He admitted that the negroes were disfranchised in a majority of the northern states, and though

---

[1] The "irregular proceedings," alluded to by Boutwell, were the arrest and forcible detention in their seats of two members of the Tennessee assembly whose presence was required in order to constitute a quorum. See Fertig, *Reconstruction in Tennessee*, pp. 77-79.

he regretted the fact, he was inclined to excuse it on the ground that the injustice was not of such magnitude as to endanger the peace and safety of the country. In the case of the rebellious states, however, there seemed only the alternative of the National Government imposing equal suffrage on the one hand, and civil and social war on the other.[1] He then went on to show that though Tennessee had an adult male population of something like 200,000, only about 60,000 could vote, 80,000 of the remainder being blacks and 60,000 rebels. He did not complain of the disfranchisement of the latter group, but he did protest against that of the former, and principally for the following amazing reason: "That the continuation of this state of affairs invited and rendered necessary a combination between the 80,000 negroes and the 60,000 rebels. The latter forgetting their past prejudices, and the loyal blacks forgetting the disloyalty of the rebels, will join hands and overturn the government of the state."

Boutwell's concluding argument was either the raving of a diseased imagination or the subtle appeal of a wily politician to the laboring classes in the North to support negro suffrage for the South, while maintaining their natural predilections in regard to that question in their own states.

And what you are doing today for Tennessee you are invited hereafter to do for the other ten states of the South. There is only one alternative. It is this; that the 4,000,000 colored people shall escape from the tyranny which you authorize the southern oligarchs to exercise over them. And I bid the peo-

---

[1] This and the succeeding statements by Boutwell seem almost puerile, but they are only typical of the direful prophecies of what would happen in case "equal and exact justice" were not meted out to the negroes.

ple, the working people of the North, the men who are struggling for subsistence, to beware of the day when the southern freedmen shall swarm over the borders in quest of those rights which should be secured to them in their native states. A just policy on our part leaves the black man in the South where he will soon become prosperous and happy. An unjust policy forces him from home and into those states where his rights will be protected, to the injury of the black man and the white man both of the North and the South. Justice and expediency are united in indissoluble bonds, and the men of the North cannot be unjust to the former slaves without themselves suffering the bitter penalty of transgression.

He then acknowledged that his opposition to the admission of Tennessee was very much greater because he feared that it would serve as a precedent for the admission of the other ten states on the same terms, and in his opinion it would be ruinous to admit those states without exacting negro suffrage as a condition precedent.

As has been stated before, Bingham and his immediate follower, Blow, were the only members of the committee who were really desirous that their party should present a sincere plan of reconstruction to the country, and to that end had insisted that all the measures reported by the committee be considered and passed in their entirety. In debating the fourteenth amendment, Bingham had said the purpose for which the committee was organized would not be attained if only the amendment were sent to the people.[1] "For myself," said he, "I cannot approach the discussion of this great question which concerns the safety of all in the spirit of a partisan. . . . The want of the Republic today is not a Democratic party, is not a Republican party, is not any party save a

[1] *Globe*, p. 2541 *et seq.*

party for the Union, for the Constitution, for the supremacy of the laws, for the restoration of all the states to their political rights and powers under such irrevocable guarantees as will forevermore secure the safety of the Republic, the equality of the states, and the equal rights of all the people under the sanction of inviolable law."

But, as we have seen, he failed in having the House adopt his restoration bill. He hoped, however, by having a majority of his party vote for the admission of Tennessee, thereby to commit them, if not to the letter, at least to the spirit of that bill. That he himself would regard the admission of Tennessee in the nature of a precedent for admitting the other southern states under similar conditions, is evident from the general tone of his speech on the Tennessee resolution.[1] In closing the debate on that resolution, he said it was true that Tennessee excluded the negroes from the exercise of the elective franchise, and though he regretted it, he was bound to say that since the majority of the loyal states did the same thing he was at a loss to understand how gentlemen could advance that as a reason for denying Tennessee representation in the House.

We are all for equal and exact justice, but justice for all is not to be secured in a day. That statesman is wisest and most faithful to duty who will seize this opportunity to restore a state to its proper place in the Union, and thereby add one additional vote in aid of the final ratification of that amendment which provides for the protection of each citizen by the combined power of all. Would gentlemen esteem it nothing if the majority of the people of the other ten states lately in rebellion should imitate the example of Tennessee, and sol-

[1] *Globe*, p. 3978 *et seq.*

emnly ratify the amendment declaring that no state shall deny to any person within its jurisdiction the equal protection of the laws, and giving Congress power to enforce this righteous decree? . . . I tell you gentlemen that the American people will no more tolerate vassal states hereafter in this Republic than vassal men. If the majority of the people of Ohio have the right to control the political power of the state, the majority of the people of Tennessee have the same right. I ask gentlemen to weigh well the question when they come to vote, whether Tennessee shall be rejected only because the majority exercise the same power as to colored suffrage claimed for and exercised by all the other states? . . . One great issue has been finally, and I trust forever, settled in the Republic: the equality of all men before the law. Another issue of equal moment is now pending: the equality of the states. That is the issue between the gentleman [Boutwell] and myself. . . . I say these states must be equal before the law. They must have equal representation in the Senate, and they must each be represented according to their whole representative population in the House. It matters not whether the states have been in rebellion or may have been struggling to maintain the Constitution and the Union, the rule is the same, and I trust ever will remain, that the states like the people, are to be equal before the law.

The vote was then taken on the resolution and resulted in an overwhelming temporary victory for Bingham. Only twelve of the radicals had the hardihood to vote against the measure, the others, including Stevens, voted for it as a matter of political necessity. As a rule the Democrats also voted in the affirmative, though the language of the preamble was distasteful to them.[1]

---

[1] *Globe*, pp. 3980, 3981. One Democrat said : "I spit on the preamble, and vote *aye* on the resolution." Another facetiously remarked that he was paired with himself on the question, since he opposed the preamble but favored the resolution, therefore he would not vote at all.

On the next day (July 20) the resolution came up in the Senate but was immediately referred to the judiciary committee.[1] On July 21 it was reported back to the Senate, but with a complete change in the preamble. This now recited everything that had been done in Tennessee in the way of disfranchising rebels, etc., in addition to the ratification of the fourteenth amendment, and then the resolution declared that the state was entitled to representation because of *all* the foregoing conditions.

From this the implication may be clearly drawn that the judiciary committee desired it to be understood that Tennessee was to be admitted not merely because she had ratified the fourteenth amendment but also because of a great many other acts of loyalty which she had performed. Therefore, in case the other ten rebel states should ratify the fourteenth amendment, it would not necessarily follow that they would be forthwith admitted to representation, for it could be quite truly said that they had not shown the same evidence of loyalty in other ways that Tennessee had.

Moreover, the judiciary committee's preamble reasserted the positive power of Congress over the whole subject of reconstruction. Sherman objected to this on the ground that Congress had several times before asserted its power over the subject, and thought that it was unwise to do so again in this case, as it would only provoke a veto from the President and thereby cause additional delay. Trumbull, on the other hand, believed that for Congress not to assert its power on every occasion would be to surrender its position because of executive opposition. To B. Gratz Brown of Missouri, who like Boutwell in the House maintained that, since Ten-

[1] *Globe*, pp. 3987-4008.

nessee denied the negroes the right to vote, her government was not republican in form, Trumbull replied that if that were the case he (B. Gratz Brown) had no business in the Senate, since according to the same test Missouri's government was no more republican than that of Tennessee. Fessenden, while protesting that he was perfectly willing that Tennessee should be admitted before the fourteenth amendment had become a part of the Constitution, was not willing to have the other ten states admitted until it had been ratified by three-fourths of all the states. Therefore he desired that either the preamble recite the reasons for making an exception in the case of Tennessee, or that it be stricken out altogether, so that the Tennessee resolution would serve as a precedent for nothing whatever.

Sumner offered an additional resolution which was to the effect that Tennessee should not be admitted until she had enfranchised the negroes, but he could muster only four votes in favor of his proposition. Cowan declared that the restoration of Tennessee was an abandonment by the majority of their ground that they would not admit members of Congress from the lately rebellious states without guarantees. He thought that the whole debate on the resolution was a mere piece of political manoeuvring. "I ask in all seriousness whether there is a sane man in this body who believes that an amendment to the Constitution ratified against the will of the members of the Tennessee legislature, is worth in that state the paper it is written on? The ultimate power is with the people, and all these barriers that you attempt to build up between the people and their servants are as mere straw and chaff. Some day they must give way, and certainly no wise man wants the Constitution amended by any trickery or any contrivance or any unfair means of that kind."

The Senate then passed the Tennessee resolution, in essentially the same form in which it was reported by the judiciary committee. On July 23, the House concurred in the amendments made by the Senate, and on the same day the resolution was sent to the President for his signature.[1]

The President was in the position of that Democratic congressman who when called upon to vote on the question declared he was paired with himself. The President, like the congressman, favored the resolution and therefore signed it; likewise, he opposed the preamble, and against it sent to Congress a protest, in which he said:[2]

Among other reasons recited in the preamble for the declarations contained in the resolution, is the ratification, by the state government of Tennessee, of "the amendment to the Constitution of the United States abolishing slavery, and also the amendment (the 14th) proposed by the 39th Congress." If, as is also declared in the preamble, "said state government can only be restored to its former political relations in the Union by the consent of the law-making power of the United States," it would really seem to follow that the joint resolution which at this late day has received the sanction of Congress, should have been passed, approved, and placed on the statute books before any amendment to the Constitution was submitted to the legislature of Tennessee for ratification. Otherwise the inference is plainly deducible that while, in the opinion of Congress, the people of a state may be too strongly disloyal to be entitled to representation, they may nevertheless, during the suspension of their " former, proper, practical relations to the Union," have an equally potent voice with other and loyal states in propositions to amend the Constitution, upon which so essentially depend the stability, prosperity, and very existence of the nation.[3]

[1] *Globe*, p. 4056.   [2] *Ibid.*, pp. 4102, 4103.
[3] All the Tennessee representatives and senators were admitted to their seats during the last few days of the first session of the 39th Congress.

In this passage President Johnson alluded to what has been called the "vital flaw in the consistency of the congressional plan."[1]

Three of the four matters which at the outset of this chapter it was proposed to examine, have now been discussed. No separate analysis of the fourth—the opinions of the politicians—seems to be necessary, as those opinions have been sufficiently indicated in giving an account of congressional action on the fourteenth amendment, the restoration bill, and the resolution for admitting Tennessee to her place in the Union. A brief summary by way of answering the questions suggested in the first paragraph of this chapter may now be given.

First, was the fourteenth amendment an offer to the South? The action of Congress on the restoration bill plainly suggests a negative answer, while a majority of the Republican politicians, if inclined at all to regard the admission of Tennessee as a precedent, did so only on condition that the remaining states would show the other evidences of loyalty which Tennessee had displayed. On the other hand there certainly were some Republicans who really did mean to promise to admit the southern representatives whenever their state legislatures should ratify the amendment. Granting that these conservatives with the addition of the Democrats were sufficiently numerous to carry out the promise, the second question remains, was the offer *magnanimous*?

In the opinion of most northern people the southern leaders certainly deserved the punishment accorded them in the third section of the fourteenth amendment, and it is doubtful if those men themselves or the southern people would have complained, had the provisions of that section

[1] Dunning, *Essays*, p. 117.

been enacted into law by Congress. Such a course would have been just. But to ask men who were conscious of no wrongdoing to place a stigma upon themselves, was not even just; it was the reverse of magnanimous. Moreover, when southern political philosophy taught that representation should be according to population, it seems hardly *generous* to have asked the southern people to act the lie by ratifying the fourteenth amendment, and virtually saying that they believed in the principles of section 2, when, as a matter of fact, they could not have done so, since that section was meant to reduce their power in the National Government by thirty or forty per cent. It must be remembered that the fourteenth amendment was not in the nature of a treaty, nor of terms dictated by a conqueror to the conquered. The later Reconstruction act of March 2, 1867, if the supplementary act of March 23 had never been passed, would have been in the nature of "terms" of peace, and as such, the southern communities, no longer recognized as *states,* might conceivably have acted upon it if they had been left to themselves to decide the matter. On the other hand, the fact that the fourteenth amendment was submitted, for instance, to Georgia as well as New York, and in the same way, could only mean that Georgia, theoretically at least, was recognized as a state in the Union, and the equal of New York. Both states were to ratify the amendment on its merits. The matter of political expediency was not supposed to be concerned in the question at all.

This was the view which southerners held of it, and hence they believed that if they should ratify it, they would be stultifying themselves. Therefore all ten of the rebel state legislatures almost unanimously rejected the amendment during the winter of 1866-67.

Third, was there any constructive statesmanship in the

fourteenth amendment? Though the nationalizing of civil rights had already been accomplished by the Civil Rights act, it may be granted that under the circumstances it was wise to incorporate the principles of that act into the Constitution.

Section 2, however, has proved so impracticable that its enforcement, though frequently discussed, has never been attempted. Section 3 was originally intended to be passed as an ordinary act of Congress, and it was certainly a mistake to raise a temporary punitive bill to the dignity of a constitutional amendment. As for section 4, it was entirely unnecessary, and since it was designed to catch votes, especially those of the soldiers, it deserved to be classified as mere political buncombe.

It seems clear, however, that in the opinion of the majority of Congress and of the northern people, it was necessary to require additional guarantees from the southern states as to their future loyalty. Since that was so, the Stewart proposition of universal amnesty and impartial suffrage ought by all means to have been adopted. It appeared then to the nonpartisan thinking people, and certainly appears now, to have been the most statesmanlike solution of the problem that was suggested. It embraced real generosity and magnanimity to the southern people, and at the same time made provision against the disfranchisement of American citizens simply because of their color. Such a provision was just, for of all the restrictions that have ever been placed upon the right to vote, that of color is the least defensible. This Stewart scheme of reconstruction bore the earmarks of real statesmanship, but the majority of the Republicans in Congress were unfortunately not statesmen, but partisans, and therefore the proposition was not adopted.

In the fourth place, were the southern legislatures blameworthy for not adopting the amendment? As already said, they could not have ratified sections 2 and 3 without stultifying themselves. But, it has been said, they should have done so as a matter of political expediency. To this argument the members of the legislatures responded that even if they should so humiliate themselves, they had no assurance that their senators and representatives would be admitted to their places in Congress. Moreover, the southern people were, till within a few days of the passage of the first Reconstruction act, incredulous that they would be reduced to a position in their own states inferior to their former slaves. After the 1866 elections, they regarded the fourteenth amendment as inevitable, and negro suffrage as a possibility, but it does not appear that they ever seriously considered that they would again be placed under military rule, their state governments overthrown, and new governments established in which apostates to their cause, northern adventurers and negroes would have the controlling influence. And even if they could have foreseen such a result of their refusal to accept the amendment, it is doubtful if fear would have caused them to have acted differently. The only time the southern people were ever really frightened was immediately after the collapse of the Confederacy. After that, they were successively dismayed, disgusted, and angered, or all three at the same time, but they never again were afraid. It might have been expedient for the southern states to have ratified the fourteenth amendment, but it is hardly fair to consider them culpable for not doing so. Those writers who attempt to shift upon the South a part of the blame for the evils of reconstruction are hardly justified.[1] The southern people in the decade of 1860-1870 have a big load of blame to bear, without being

[1] Nearly all the older writers did so, and Professor Woodburn, in his *Life of Thaddeus Stevens*, leaves an impression of the same purpose.

burdened with any part of the responsibility for the Reconstruction acts.

What then was the fourteenth amendment if it was not a plan of reconstruction? An editorial in the *New York Herald* of June 12, 1866, gives an excellent answer to the question.

This congressional proposition for the amendment of the Constitution, as modified by the Senate, is an ingeniously contrived party platform for the coming fall elections. . . . . There is nothing here obnoxious to public opinion in the way of negro suffrage, while the alternative suggested will be satisfactory to the North. There are no vindictive penalties here against rebels and traitors, but conditional exclusions, which cannot be resisted successfully before the people who put down the rebellion. The same may be said of the propositions touching the national debt, the debts of the rebellion, and the four millions of liberated southern slaves. Upon this platform the Republican party adhering to Congress can carry our approaching northern state elections as they did last year if there be no other sharply defined issues.

The *Herald* was right. Johnson had no chance against Congress before the people on the issue of the fourteenth amendment.

The *Herald* recognized that the radicals did not regard the fourteenth amendment as a finality. It therefore suggested to the President that the only way to defeat their schemes of confiscation, negro suffrage, and possibly impeachment, was to unite with those conservatives, like Bingham and Fessenden, who did consider that amendment a finality, advise the southern states to ratify it, reorganize his cabinet with able men from the conservative faction in the most important places, and withdraw the attention of the country from domestic politics by adopting a strong foreign policy, especially toward France and England. Such a course would have been excellent politics, and had Johnson been a Disraeli or a Bismarck he might have accepted the suggestion. But since he was only Andrew Johnson—a first-rate stump speaker, a second-rate statesman, and a third-rate politician, he did nothing of the kind, and the *Herald* owners went over to the opposition, as did all Republicans who were not in some way connected with the administration, and who had not already done so.

In the political campaign that ensued, the fourteenth amendment was spoken of by Republican politicians, as a finality in reconstruction, or a mere step toward " complete justice," partly according to the temperament of the speaker, but principally according to the nature of the constituency which he represented. Even radicals in doubtful states like New York, Indiana, and Ohio, referred to that amendment as the " magnanimous offer " of a generous people to the South, and assured their constituents that if it were ratified by the rebel states, they would surely be restored. On the other hand, their brothers in Massachusetts and New England generally, and in radical western states like Michigan, Wisconsin, and Iowa, paid scant respect to it, and denied that Congress intended it to be a finality.[1] Though there were a great many causes contributory to the triumph of the radicals in the fall elections of 1866, perhaps none was more potent than this automatic, adjustable, congressional " plan." It was indeed an excellent " plan " for winning a political campaign, but as a " plan " for reconstructing rebel states, it was destined soon to go askew.

[1] My authority for this generalization is derived from a careful reading of numerous speeches made during the campaign, and reported in the New York newspapers.

CHAPTER VIII.

The Reconstruction Act

On November 15, 1866, *The Independent*, which more than any other journal expressed the views of the extreme radicals, said: "This journal, if it should call for a list, could get more names of Republicans than our fifty-six columns could print, all subscribed to the solemn declaration that the Republican party stands unpledged to make the pending amendment the basis of reconstruction, but, on the contrary, is bound in honor to a reconstruction on the one and only basis of equal rights."

In the preceding chapter the attempt has been made to show that so far as the party as an organization was concerned, the foregoing statement was correct. Individuals, and even party conventions in some of the states, had certainly made the assertion that the rebel states would be readmitted should they ratify the fourteenth amendment. It is possible that they would have been admitted, but had the Republican party or even a respectable minority of it, been sincerely desirous of effecting restoration on the basis of the fourteenth amendment they certainly could have done so, even in the face of the fact that by the time the second session of the 39th Congress met, it was evident that that amendment would be rejected by all the rebel states.[1] The fact that only an

[1] When Congress met on December 3, three of the rebel states had already rejected the fourteenth amendment, and the other seven did so during the next two months. Flack, pp. 191–204.

exceedingly small number of Republicans were sincerely attached to their so-called plan of reconstruction made it easy for Stevens and Sumner to take the lead, and as Mr. Horace White has said, "cross the Rubicon with the whole army."[1] As Caesar was doubtless glad to have an excuse for crossing the real Rubicon, the radicals in the second session of the 39th Congress were just as happy to have an excuse for crossing the figurative Rubicon. Their excuse, of course, was the failure of the rebel states to ratify the fourteenth amendment, but some of their members did not need this provocation in order to come to a decision in regard to crossing the proverbial stream.

One of these latter was Charles Sumner. On December 4, he gave notice to the Senate that at an early date he would introduce resolutions defining the true principles of reconstruction, by which the illegality of the existing governments in the rebel states, and the exclusion of such states from representation in Congress and from voting on constitutional amendments, would be declared.[2]

On the same day, Broomall, a satellite of Thaddeus Stevens, introduced in the House a resolution instructing the committee on territories "to enquire into the expediency of reporting a bill providing territorial governments for the several districts of country within the jurisdiction of the United States, formerly occupied by the once existing states of Virginia, North Carolina, etc. and giving to all adult male inhabitants, born within the limits of the United States, or duly naturalized, and not participants in the late rebellion, full and equal political

---

[1] *Life of Lyman Trumbull*, p. 291.
[2] *Globe*, 2nd sess. 39th cong., p. 7.

rights in such territorial governments."[1] The resolution was adopted by a strict party vote. Many additional resolutions and bills looking towards the enfranchisement of the negroes and the dismantling of the Johnson governments were introduced during the first week of the session.

Since the Memphis and New Orleans riots,[2] the argument that the negroes and the loyal whites in the South were being terribly persecuted had grown in popularity, and it was urged daily on the floor of Congress that the governments in the southern states should be placed in their control, so that they could protect themselves from the unrepentant rebels. Hardly a Republican dared lift his voice against the rising enthusiasm for universal negro suffrage and the reconstruction of the existing governments in the South. When, after a committee of the legislature of North Carolina, for instance, on December 6, gave as one of the reasons for rejecting the fourteenth amendment, that its ratification would not facilitate the restoration of the state,[3] Spalding of Ohio, a friend and follower of Bingham, in order to assure the southern states that Congress was sincere in offering the fourteenth amendment as a plan of reconstruction, on December 10 proposed a resolution declaring the intention of Congress to admit their senators and representatives upon ratification of that amendment.[4] But the house was unwilling to give any such assurance, and Spalding's resolution was unceremoniously referred to the joint committee on reconstruction without debate, and was never

[1] *Globe*, p. 11.

[2] See Rhodes, vol. v, p. 611 *et seq*. Also see *infra*, p. 398.

[3] Flack, p. 200. See also Hamilton, *Reconstruction in North Carolina*.

[4] *Globe*, p. 48.

heard of again. Even Blaine, who at that time was considered among the conservatives, and who later declared that the southern states would have been restored to their places in the Union had they adopted the fourteenth amendment,[1] on December 10 declared that the people had pronounced with unmistakable emphasis in favor of the amendment with the *superadded and indispensable* prerequisite of manhood suffrage.[2] Continuing, he said:

The objection in the popular mind of the loyal states to the constitutional amendment as a basis of final adjustment is not directed to what that amendment will effect, but to what it will *not effect*. And among the objects of prime importance which it will not effect is the absolute protection of the two classes in the South to whom the Government owes the most, viz. the loyal white men and the loyal black men . . . The obligation on the Federal Government to protect the loyalists of the South is supreme, and it must take all needful means to assure that protection. Among the most needful is the gift of free suffrage, and *that must be guaranteed.*

When Blaine wrote his book some fifteen years after this speech was made, he was evidently not very proud of his party's reconstruction record and was anxious to shift responsiblity for its blunders. It is clear from his own speech that his statement in his book, if not entirely untrue, is at least questionable.

During the whole of the second session of the 39th Congress there were in Washington a large number of southern loyalists who were telling all sorts of stories about the indignities and dangers to which they and the colored people were subjected by their rebel neighbors.

[1] Blaine, *Twenty Years of Congress*, vol. ii, pp. 243-245.
[2] *Globe*, p. 53.

They demanded of Congress protection, which meant that they, and not the rebels, should be placed in control of the southern governments. In order to accomplish the result which these loyalists desired, Thaddeus Stevens, after consulting freely with some of them, introduced on December 19 a bill designed for that purpose.[1] It was not debated, however, until January 1867, by which time it had been amended to read as follows:[2]

Whereas the eleven states which lately formed the government called the "Confederate States of America," have forfeited all their rights under the Constitution, and can be reinstated in the same only through the action of Congress:

Sec. I. Be it enacted by the Senate and House of Representatives of the United States of America in Congress assembled, that the eleven states lately in rebellion, except Tennessee, may form valid state governments in the following manner:

Sec. II. And be it further enacted, that the state governments now existing *de facto* though illegally formed in the midst of martial law, and in many instances the constitutions were adopted under duress, and not submitted to the ratification of the people, and therefore not to be treated as free representatives, yet they are hereby acknowledged as valid governments for municipal purposes until the same shall be duly altered and their legislative and executive officers shall be recognized as such.

Sec. III. And be it further enacted, that each of the ten states which were lately in rebellion, and have not been admitted to representation in Congress, shall hold elections on the first Tuesday of May, 1867, to choose delegates to a convention to form a state government. The convention shall consist of the same number of members as the most numerous branch of the legislature of said state before the rebellion. It shall meet at the former capital of said state on the first Monday

---

[1] *House Journal*, 2nd sess. 39th cong., p. 102.
[2] *Globe*, p. 250 *et seq.*

in June of said year, at twelve noon, with power to adjourn from time to time, and shall proceed to form a state constitution, which shall be submitted to the people at such a time as the convention shall direct, and if ratified by a majority of the legal voters shall be declared the constitution of the state. Congress shall elect a commission for each of said states, to consist of three persons, who shall elect, or direct the mode of selecting, the election officers for the several election districts, which districts shall be the same as before the rebellion, unless altered by said convention. The officers shall consist of one judge and two inspectors of elections, and two clerks; the said officers, together with all the expenses of the election, shall be paid by the United States, and said expense shall be repaid by said state or territory. Each of said officers shall receive five dollars per day for the time actually employed, Each of the members of said commission shall receive three thousand dollars per annum, and their clerks two thousand dollars. The commissioners shall procure all the necessary books, stationery, and boxes, and make all regulations to effect the objects of the act. The President of the United States and the military commander of the district, shall furnish so much military aid as the said commissioners shall deem necessary to protect the polls and keep the peace at each of said election districts. If by any means no election should be held in any of the said late states on the day herein fixed, the election shall be held on the third Monday of May, 1867, in the manner herein prescribed. Returns of all such elections shall be made to the said commissioners, whose certificates of election shall be *prima facie* evidence of the fact.

Sec. IV. And be it further enacted that the persons who shall be entitled to vote at both of said elections shall be as follows: all male citizens above the age of twenty-one years who have resided one year in said state and ten days within the election district.

Sec. V. And be it further enacted that the word citizen as used in this act, shall be construed to mean all persons (except Indians not taxed) born in the United States or duly naturalized. Any male citizen above the age of twenty-one years shall be competent to be elected to act as delegate to said convention.

Sec. VI. And be it further enacted that all persons who on the 4th day of March, 1861, were of full age, who held office, either civil or military, under the government called the "Confederate States of America" or who swore allegiance to said government are hereby declared to have forfeited their citizenship and to have renounced allegiance to the United States, and shall not be entitled to exercise the elective franchise or hold office until five years after they shall have filed their intention or desire to be reinvested with the right of citizenship, and shall swear allegiance to the United States and renounce allegiance to all other governments or pretended governments; the said application to be filed and oath taken in the same courts that by law are authorized to naturalize foreigners: Provided, however, that on taking the following oath, the party being otherwise qualified, shall be allowed to vote and hold office:

"I, A. B., do solemnly swear that on the 4th of March, 1864, and at all times thereafter, I would willingly have complied with the requirements of the proclamation of the President of the United States issued on the 8th of December, 1863, had a safe opportunity of so doing been allowed me; that on the said 4th of March, 1864, and at all times thereafter, I was opposed to the continuance of the rebellion, and to the establishment of the so-called Confederate government; and voluntarily gave no aid or encouragement thereto, but earnestly desired the success of the Union, and the suppression of all armed resistance to the Government of the United States; and that I will henceforth faithfully support the Constitution of the United States, and the Union of the states thereunder."

Sec. VII. And be it further enacted that no constitution shall be presented to or acted on by Congress which denies to any citizen any right, privileges, or immunities which are granted to any other citizen in the state. All laws shall be impartial, without regard to language, race or former condition. If the provisions of this section should ever be altered, repealed, expurged, or in any way abrogated, this act shall become void, and said state lose its right to be represented in Congress.

Sec. VIII. And be it further enacted, that whenever the foregoing conditions shall be complied with, the citizens of said state may present said constitution to Congress, and if the same shall be approved by Congress said state shall be declared entitled to the rights, privileges, immunities, and be subject to all the obligations and liabilities of a state within the Union. No senator or representative shall be admitted into either House of Congress until Congress shall have declared the state entitled thereto.

The foregoing was a substitute for the old restoration bill that had been presented by the joint committee at the same time the fourteenth amendment was reported,[1] but its terms resembled much more closely Stevens' reconstruction bill which he had introduced on May 28. His reason for offering it as a substitute for the original restoration bill was to keep it from being referred to the joint committee without debate. Under the rule of the House everything relating to reconstruction was so referred, and Bingham made the point of order that this bill should go the same route. The Speaker, with whom Stevens had no doubt conferred, overruled Bingham on the ground that it was a substitute for a bill that the committee itself had offered, and could be recommitted only by special vote of the House.[2] A few days later Bingham moved that it be so disposed of,[3] but such disposition of it was exactly what Stevens did not wish as he thought recommitting it would be the same as killing it outright. Consequently, the House engaged in a gen-

[1] See *supra*, p. 117.
[2] *Globe*, p. 250 *et seq.*
[3] *Ibid.*, p. 500.

eral debate nominally on the question of recommittal, but actually the principal points made in the speeches were on the merits of the bill.

Before Stevens' bill was finally recommitted he accepted three amendments to it which should be noted before proceeding with an analysis of the debate. Sections 2 and 7 were stricken out,[1] and a new section was added which suspended the writ of habeas corpus in the ten rebel states and placed them under martial law.[2] Section 2 was withdrawn because some radicals believed it would weaken their position if they should recognize the Johnson governments even for municipal purposes. The martial law clause was added so that the loyalists would be protected until the new governments should be established. Section 7 was omitted because it was generally agreed on all sides that its principles were untenable.

Before proceeding with the discussion of the speeches it would seem necessary to explain why a bill which never became law should be treated at such length. In the first place, this bill heretofore has not been given the position justified by its proportionate importance in the development of congressional reconstruction; and inasmuch as this is a more or less detailed history of congressional reconstruction, it would seem proper to give the measure the emphasis it deserves. Secondly, though it differs somewhat in its machinery from that instituted in the supplementary Reconstruction act of March 23, the practical operation of the former would doubtless have been about the same as that of the latter. Though the consideration of the March 23d act does not fall within the province of this essay, nevertheless, it logically belongs in the category of the joint committee's accomplishments, and a discussion of what were practically

---

[1] *Globe*, pp. 536, 816.   [2] *Ibid.*, p. 594.

its principles seems properly to come within the scope of a history of that committee.

When on January 3, Stevens' bill came up for discussion he made an energetic speech in behalf of its adoption.[1] He desired that the House at an early date should come to some conclusion as to the rebel states. This, he argued, was becoming more and more necessary every day; and the late decision of the Supreme Court of the United States had rendered urgent immediate action by Congress upon the question of the establishment of governments. The late decision to which Stevens referred was in the case of *ex parte* Milligan, wherein the court held "that military commissions and the other incidents of martial law were unconstitutional save where flagrant war made the action of the ordinary courts impossible."[2] This decision Stevens characterized as more infamous than the Dred Scott decision, and far more dangerous to the lives and liberties of the loyal men of the country. It unsheathed the dagger of the assassin and placed the knife of the rebel at the throat of every man who dared proclaim himself loyal to the Union. He declared that the rebels were murdering the loyal whites daily, and daily putting in secret graves not only hundreds but thousands of the colored people and that unless Congress proceeded at once to adopt some means for their protection, he and his colleagues would be liable to the just censure of the world for their negligence and cowardice.

Congress must not allow the revolution through which the country had been passing to subside until the nation

---

[1] *Globe*, p. 250 *et seq*.

Dunning, *Reconstruction*, p. 89. For a complete discussion of the case, see *Essays*, p. 45 *et seq*.

had been erected into a perfect republic. But little had been done toward establishing the government on the true principles of liberty and justice. Though the material shackles of four million slaves had been broken, they had not been given the privilege of participating in the formation of the laws of the government. They needed civil weapons to enable them to defend themselves against oppression and injustice.

He restated his theory of conquered provinces, denied that there was any understanding that if the amendment were adopted the southern states would be admitted, and said in regard to negro suffrage: "If it be just it should not be denied; if it be necessary, it should be adopted; if it be a punishment to traitors, they deserve it."

On January 16 Bingham made a speech denouncing the contention of Stevens and a great many other radicals that Congress was not bound by the terms of the fourteenth amendment in making a final settlement of the reconstruction question.[1] Furthermore he asserted that a large number of Union members, especially those from New York and Ohio, owed their re-election to the 40th Congress to the fact that their state conventions had placed the acceptance by the rebel states of the amendment as the final condition of restoration.

He denounced Stevens' conquered province theory, and while he admitted that Congress could legislate for the rebel states before they were represented, he was certain they were still in the Union. He thought their position was somewhat analogous to that of Rhode Island and North Carolina in 1789; these two states were not represented in Congress, but nobody denied their power to ratify the Constitution because of that fact.

[1] *Globe*, pp. 500-505.

So it was with the rebel states; they had the power to ratify the fourteenth amendment, and by doing so ought to become automatically entitled to representation. He then attacked the bill in detail, and so completely demolished section 7, that, as we have seen, Stevens was forced to withdraw it, even though he said it was dear to his heart. Bingham sharply criticized the clause which had for its purpose the decitizenizing of the rebels, and so conclusively did he prove that Congress had no power to expatriate American citizens that, though Stevens did not withdraw the clause, it found no place in the later Reconstruction acts.

In conclusion he said: "Stand by the great amendment for equal right and equal protection. There is strength in it; the strength that abides in an inviolable justice. There is peace in it; that peace that comes of laws which are just to all and oppressive of none."

Some one reminded Bingham that all the southern states which had taken action on the amendment, had rejected it. To this he replied: "It does not follow that they will not yet accept it." But it was hardly to be expected that Bingham's plea for mercy would have much weight, when the majority of those to whom it was addressed habitually spoke of the rebels in terms of which the following is typical:

> I would not advocate banishment for them, for I would not even poison the air of Australian convicts with their presence . . . . It rests upon us to decide at an early day whether we are to allow rebels to come and take their seats here unwashed, unrepentant, unpunished, unpardoned, unhung, (laughter) or whether we will heed the voice of our friends, fleeing from the South for their lives; whether we will listen to the supplication of four million black people, all true to the great prin-

ciples which we here seek to establish. For one I urge the earliest action.[1]

Eldridge, a Democrat of Wisconsin, said it was idle to attempt any resistance to a caucus measure of the majority.[2] It was appalling to those who from early childhood had been accustomed to revere and love the Constitution, to feel that it was in the keeping of a party having the power and determination to destroy it. Never in the history of the country had there been a measure or movement fraught with such fatal and fearful consequences to the Republic as the one under consideration. Referring to that part of Stevens' speech in which he had expressed the hope that the revolution begun without the consent of Congress would not end until all the incongruities and despotic provisions of the Constitution should be corrected, Eldridge said there could be no mistaking Stevens' object; it was to avoid or get rid of some of the provisions of the Constitution.

Eldridge saw in the movement that was then going on in Congress, of which the pending bill was only a part, three purposes. In the first place, there was a determination either to abolish the Supreme Court, or at least circumvent it in such a way that it would be powerless to perform its functions. This he had gathered from the speeches of the gentlemen of the majority, wherein they denounced the Supreme Court as an institution as well as its recent decisions.[3] In the second

---

[1] Grinnel, *Globe*, p. 537.   [2] *Globe*, pp. 561–564.

[3] Eldridge was referring to the Milligan, Cummings and Garland decisions, especially the first. See *supra*, p. 363. In the two last-named cases the Court held that a state and a Federal test oath, designed to exclude rebel clergymen and attorneys from exercising their functions, were unconstitutional as *ex post facto* laws. See Dunning, *Essays*, p. 121.

place, he saw a well organized effort on foot which seemed to be gaining force every day, either to depose the President entirely or at least to make of his office a mere sinecure. The third and final purpose of the majority, and to which the others were largely contributory, was to turn ten sovereign states into territories or hold them as conquered provinces.

He declared that the states and their governments were not destroyed by attempted secession. All the attempts to take them out of their relations to the other states of the Union were failures and every step in that direction was an illegal and void act. The moment the rebellion was put down, the people of each state had the right to their government as before the war. On the part of the Confederates the struggle was to separate and divide; on the North's part to prevent separation and division, and preserve the states in the Union. The southern people sought to avoid the laws of the Federal Government; the northern people to enforce them.

They claimed the right to secede when they felt disposed; we avowed secession a monstrous heresy, and that the Union was formed in perpetuity. They seized their arms and appealed to the God of battles for the justice of their cause; we accepted the wager of battle and pressed them so closely that in desperation they cried, for the purpose of rallying their dispirited forces, that we meant to subjugate them. As victory wavered in the balance we solemnly declared: "That, banishing all feelings of mere passion or resentment, we will recollect only our duty to the whole country; that this war is not waged upon our part in any spirit of oppression, nor for the purpose of conquest or subjugation; but to defend and maintain the supremacy of the Constitution and to preserve the Union, with all the dignity, equality, and rights of the several states unimpaired; that as soon as these objects are accomplished the war ought to cease."

Eldridge then declared that the only other object of the war which later developed after the above declaration was made was the abolition of slavery. Therefore, according to the laws of nations about which Stevens so persistently talked, when the war was concluded the only right which the conquerors had over the conquered was to enforce those declared objects of the war. As seen above these objects had been two fold: (1) the maintenance of the Union; (2) the abolition of slavery. Any scheme of reconstruction that proposed to include other than these two objects was contrary both to the law of nations, and to the Constitution of the United States. It was unconstitutional because the sovereign powers of Congress are named in the Constitution, and that document itself was created by a certain political people, and therefore Congress had no right to create in the individual states a new political people. That is to say, that Congress itself was created by the old political people of all the states, and to attempt to change that people in the states was to invade their liberty, because the political people in each state had always had the right to add to or detract from their own number.

The disorders in the South, the frequent riots and numerous murders during the last half of 1866, together with the ill-tempered and not infrequently lying speeches by vindictive and malignant politicians both in and out of Congress, had caused many thinking men to fear the country was hurrying toward a renewal of civil strife. Eldridge was one of these and the following remarks seem to show that he sincerely deprecated the extremely partisan and revengeful course that was being pursued by the Republicans:

I hope, I devoutly pray these troublous times may have an end without further sacrifice of fraternal blood; that our constitutional rights and liberties may not be lost in this fanatical revolution. Let sectional hatred and all revenge be buried in oblivion. Reconciliation is the only restoration. Malignant passion has counseled long enough; let it slumber. Is it not enough to enslave ten million people, and hold them in a state of conquest for two years? Congress has an opportunity such as no other body of men ever had before, such as I fear it will never have again, by a word to speak peace, reconciliation, and amity to a suffering and unhappy country. A brave and unarmed people lie conquered at your feet, bound in spirit and oppressed with many sorrows. They have surrendered all for which they contended on the battle field and more than you demanded before they gave to you their arms. Let not the pride of victory, passion, revenge make you unjust and change your victory into defeat.

In concluding, he reminded his opponents that generosity had never lost the conqueror anything, but that cruel and unwise exactions had often renerved many an arm and renewed many a struggle. "Better than that subjugation and oppression should continue, follow the example of the monster Duke of Alva: take twenty thousand to the block and be satisfied. Two hundred thousand may not satisfy the people for wrong and injustice long continued."

Whatever else may be said against reconstruction as actually carried out by Congress, most writers have concurred in the opinion that it was a grand result in history that our great civil war was not followed by any confiscations or executions or any considerable number of imprisonments. In connection with Eldridge's intimation that it would have been better to execute a few of the leading rebels than to initiate measures of subjugation and oppression of the whole mass of the southern people, the question may properly be asked, was he not right? Of course it is impossible to give a satisfactory answer to the question, but it may well be doubted if either the confiscation of the large estates in the South and the division of them among the negroes, or the execution of a few of the leading traitors, or both, would have left such bitterness in the breasts of the southerners as was actually left by the Reconstruction acts and their aftermath. It was certainly true that at the close of the war these leading traitors did not hope much better for themselves than a halter, and their countrymen at that time would not have been greatly disposed to regret such a fate to these authors of all their woes. As for the negro he would have been benefited a great deal more by forty acres and a mule than he was by the ballot, and the former would have been conceded to him by his white neighbors with a great deal more grace than was the latter. Moreover, if he had forty acres and a mule, sooner or later he would have obtained the ballot, and under such circumstances as would have been of value both to himself and his country. It is notorious that the negro's disfranchisement in the South at the present time is not due nearly so much to his color as to his economic dependence. Wherever he is the possessor of so much as forty acres of land he can have the ballot if he wants it. As Thaddeus Stevens at one time expressed it: "Seek ye first for the negro a little land, and all other things will be added unto him."

In general the Democrats and those Republicans who opposed Stevens' bill based their arguments principally on legal and constitutional technicalities, whereas its advocates placed theirs almost entirely on practical considerations. Had the opponents of the bill met their adversaries on their own ground, it is apparent that they could have made out a much stronger case against the bill than they did. The Constitution had been so stretched during the preceding five or six years that men were not inclined to pay much attention to pleas that that sacred document was being violated. As for state integrity and equality the great majority of people in the North in 1867 regarded South Carolina and Virginia as quite different in relation to the Union from Massachusetts and New York, and no amount of constitutional theorizing could make them change their opinion.

There were in Congress, however, about a half dozen representatives, mostly from Kentucky, who though of pro-slavery antecedents and southern sympathies, had remained steadfast in their loyalty to the Union. They and their fellow citizens had been kept in line by Lincoln's wise "border state policy," and as one of them said, had the National Government dared announce at the beginning that the war was waged for any purpose other than to save the Union, it could not have recruited a dozen regiments in all the border states.[1] Though these border state people had reluctantly accepted the abolition of slavery as an accomplished fact, they regarded the negro in much the same light as did the white people in the ex-confederate states, and neither had nor pretended to have any illusions concerning the political capacity of the black race. They looked upon this attempt to put the southern state governments in the hands of people who held their positions by reason of negro suffrage as an unmixed evil and an attack upon civilization itself. They met Stevens and his extreme radical henchmen on their own ground of practical considerations and foretold with remarkable accuracy what the result of the radical experiment would be. Replying to the stock

---

[1] Ward, *Globe*, appendix, p. 61.

argument of the radicals that the people of ten rebel states could not be safely trusted with a voice in the Government because of their "disloyalty," one of these Kentuckians said that the radicals in employing that argument overlooked one very important truth—the people of the South did not make war upon our republican form of government nor seek to destroy it; they only sought to make two republics out of one. They were then and always had been as much attached to the American system of free representative government as those persons who were abusing them for disloyalty.[1]

Another Kentuckian, Hise, discussed the meaning attached to the word *loyalty* by the majority party.[2] It meant loyalty to them, loyalty to their dominion, submission to their will, undisputed recognition of their power and authority, and a promise for its perpetual continuance. Freedom meant to make slaves of the southern people by placing and maintaining their state governments in the control of the negroes, and through their agency hold the southern whites in submission. "The negroes are your friends, and they and the felons and jailbirds are to be admitted to the right of suffrage and allowed to hold office in those states by your bill, should it be passed and carried into execution."[3] In addition to the classes mentioned the membership of the proposed conventions would be composed of camp followers, sutlers and army contractors, all reckless and

---

[1] Ward, *Globe*, appendix, p. 61.   [2] *Globe*, appendix, pp. 66-69.

[3] Hise had good reason to speak of "jailbirds and felons," for on January 7, Stevens had moved to amend his bill so as to disqualify from voting in the new governments only those criminals convicted of treason. *Globe*, p. 324. In defence of this extraordinary amendment he said that otherwise the negroes would be deprived of the ballot for every little insignificant offense, and even new offenses would be created for the purpose of disfranchising them.

unprincipled adventurers from the North who had overrun the South to plunder both the white man and the negro. The governments of the southern states would be committed to them, and by them would be sent "loyal" representatives to Congress. "My God, what a representation it will be!"

Such then would be the practical effect of the radical idea of loyalty, should Stevens' bill embodying that idea become law. As a matter of fact, the term loyalty was inapplicable to this country. It signified submission to a feudal superior, whereas here where all were equal, no such thing as legal or obligatory loyalty to any man or party could be required of an American citizen. All were bound to obey the Constitution and to submit to the laws, but the rights of free discussion had always existed. The whole superstructure of both the state and Federal governments were built upon the declared right of the people to alter, abolish, overturn, and reconstruct their political institutions at pleasure.

In concluding his argument Hise said the bill as a whole was a miserable scheme of public policy to destroy the political force and influence of the southern states as members of the Union. And yet it was devised by a party whose adherents were loudest in their professions of devotion to free government, and of love of liberty.

These men claim to be the special advocates of human liberty and equal rights. They say they must put their friends, *their loyal friends*, in possession of the state governments, and then they will send loyal delegations to Congress. Oh, yes, they will send loyal delegations! So this bill, if executed, will establish corrupt and despotic local governments for all those states. It will place in office the most ignorant and degraded portion of the population, who would rule and ruin without honesty or skill the actual property holders and native inhabitants, making insecure life, liberty, and property Those states would still be held in their Federal relations subject to the most rapacious, fierce, and unrelenting despotism that ever existed—that of a vindictive and hostile party majority of a Congress in which they have no voice or representation, and for that very reason they will be oppressed by that irresponsible majority.

The last important speech made on the bill was that of Henry J. Raymond, who, though he had formerly supported President Johnson and participated in the Philadelphia convention, had not severed his connection entirely with the Republican party.[1] His speech is of interest in that he gave what, at this distance, seems to be the best interpretation of the meaning of the 1866 elections that was given by any speaker in the House. He said he had concurred in the policy of the President, and was still of the opinion that had it been carried out fully and promptly by the Republican party, it would have restored peace and healed to a great extent all the troubles of the body politic. Nevertheless, he did not maintain that the President's was the best policy now (January 24, 1867). He defended his change of position by saying that his case was analogous to that of a physican who may prescribe a gargle for a sore throat, but if the prescription should be disregarded until the sore throat has become an inflammation or raging fever, such physician would be wanting in sound judgment should he, for the sake of consistency, continue to prescribe only the original simple gargle. He therefore would dismiss as impracticable that method of settling the controversy which a year earlier he had so earnestly urged. The point then as to whether or not the people were willing that the

[1] *Globe*, pp. 715–720.

rebel states should resume their former position of political power as states in the Union without some security for the future, had been decided in the negative. Moreover, he believed that the people decided that whatever settlement of the reconstruction question should be fixed upon, should be made by the legislative and not by the executive branch of the Government. Further than these two points the people had not pronounced decisively on any specific plan of reconstruction, but to the extent that any decision had been made, it was in favor of the constitutional amendment as a basis of adjustment. Certainly they had not committed themselves in advance to anything and everything which Congress might see fit to do.

Raymond was positive, from a careful and impartial scrutiny of the lines along which the campaign had been waged in most of the states, that the people had not in their verdict indorsed the cardinal principles of the Stevens bill. By cardinal principles he meant those provisions of the bill by which the state governments in the South were to be deprived of all legal authority, the extension of martial law over all that territory, the suspension of the privilege of the writ of habeas corpus, the universal enfranchisement of the blacks, and the partial disfranchisement of the whites. Two reasons, said he, had been given for abolishing the existing state governments: (1) their origin; (2) their failure to protect the rights, liberties, and property of their citizens. He believed they had originated as legally as any such governments could under the circumstances, and that anyhow it was usual all over the world to recognize *de facto* governments, and respect their authority, without enquiring too closely and rigidly into the legality of their origin. He admitted that the existing governments were not protecting the lives and liberties of the loyal people and the negroes as fully as they might. This he regretted, but pointed out that because of the confusion in politics, the great change and disorder in social arrangements, the almost complete failure of the crops, and the consequent stringency in finance and business, such a condition was to be expected, and it was really a wonder that lawlessness was not more prevalent than was actually the case.[1] He doubted if the substitution of military governments for those in existence would work a very beneficial change, because if the Freedmen's Bureau which was already in the South under the authority of the President was not keeping order, it was hardly to be expected that the army under the same authority would do so.

In conclusion he suggested two alternatives as a solution of the reconstruction problem. One was to change the fourteenth amendment by replacing the punitive section three with a section denying the right of secession, and in that form re-submit the amendment for their adoption. He believed that since the punitive section had been the stumbling-block in the way of southern legislatures' adopting the whole amendment, its removal would lead them to reconsider their action. If, however, the majority were unwilling to pursue this course he had no objection to a resolution proclaiming the rebel states out of the Union, and another declaring the amendment officially adopted upon its ratification by the legislatures of three-fourths of the loyal states. The southern states could then be re-admitted after the amendment had become a part of the Constitution, and they would be bound by its provisions.

When Raymond concluded his argument, Stevens rose

---

[1] *Cf.* also speech by Dodge, *Globe*, pp. 627-629.

to say that he saw such diversity of opinion on his side of the House that, if he did not change his mind, he would on the morrow (Jan. 26) relieve the House from any question on the merits of the bill by moving to lay it on the table.[1] Evidently he did change his mind, for he made no such motion. On the 26th, however, he proposed that if Bingham would withdraw his motion to recommit,[2] he would throw the bill into committee of the whole so as to allow five-minute speeches and amendments until the House should be satisfied one way or the other as to the expediency of passing the bill.[3] Ashley, a colleague of Bingham's, urged him to accept Stevens' proposition.[4] He declared all members of his party were pledged to overthrow the existing state governments in the South,[5] and therefore he thought action looking toward that end should be taken at once. To recommit the bill would mean its burial, for he was certain the committee could not agree as to its terms before March 4, when the 39th Congress would expire. Bingham, however, refused to withdraw his motion. The radicals feared that with the assistance of the Democrats, Bingham would have strength enough to carry his motion, so they began to consider what ought to be done when the inevitable should become an accomplished

---

[1] *Globe*, p. 721.

[2] According to parliamentary rules, the only motion relating to a bill that takes precedence of a motion to recommit is one to lay on the table; so unless Stevens could get Bingham to withdraw his motion, the vote on that question had to be taken before any other disposition could be made of the bill.

[3] *Globe*, p. 781. [4] *Ibid.*, pp. 781-785.

[5] He referred to the unanimous Republican vote by which Broomall's resolution had been passed. See *supra*, p. 355. Bingham and the conservatives, however, did not interpret that vote to mean what Ashley thought it meant.

fact. George W. Julian, an old-time abolitionist and extreme radical, in a speech on January 28, pointed out the way.[1] He thought that Stevens had been premature in urging the adoption of a reconstruction bill, and believed that the first thing to be done was to provide protection for the loyalists and negroes in the South by establishing there military governments. After this should be done Congress would then be at leisure to provide for the erection of permanent civil governments founded on the general principles enunciated in Stevens' bill. This was an excellent tactical move on the part of the radicals, for while a great many Republicans were not ready for an out-and-out reconstruction bill, the argument that something must be done for the protection of "our friends in the South" was sufficient to cause them to vote for a bill securing that protection by establishing military law there. Paradoxically enough they were willing to declare the Johnson governments unconstitutionally created and failures in that they did not protect the lives and liberty of negroes and southern loyalists, but they were not prepared, to provide, in terms, for their abolition. In fact it does not appear that the conservatives gave up the expectation that these "illegal governments would serve as the nucleus for the erection of governments really legal" until a disfranchising clause was incorporated into the first Reconstruction act.[2]

Stevens, however, was not willing to accept Julian's suggestion until he had tested his strength both in the House and in the reconstruction committee. This he had an opportunity to do in the House on January 28,

[1] *Globe*, appendix, pp. 77–80.
[2] See *infra*, p. 408.

for on that day the vote was taken on Bingham's motion to recommit. Stevens was sustained by a small majority of the Republicans, but as Bingham had the support of all the Democrats his motion was carried, *yeas* 88, *nays* 65, *not voting* 38.[1] So the first victory lay with the Bingham faction, thanks to the assistance of the Democratic party. Had the members of that party continued to support Bingham as they should have done, most of Stevens' schemes, at least during the 39th Congress, would have come to nought.

The reconstruction committee to which the Stevens bill was recommitted had been reappointed at the beginning of the second session of the 39th Congress. During this session only two meetings of the committee were held, one on February 4th, the other on the 6th. At the first meeting, Stevens' bill was discussed, but no conclusion was reached.[2] Just before this first meeting adjourned, Stevens offered a resolution to the effect that the rebel states be reconstructed on the principles laid down in his bill.

The committee took no vote on this resolution, and Stevens probably saw that he could not bring a majority of the members to adopt the principles of his bill as a basis of future action. Therefore, he reluctantly accepted the idea suggested earlier by Julian of having a bill enacted to establish military governments in the rebel states, and letting reconstruction wait until the more radical 40th Congress should assemble. Having accepted the idea, he became a most energetic champion of the bill that had for its purpose the carrying into effect of Julian's suggestion. Such a bill was introduced into the Senate on February 4th, by Williams,[3] who though

[1] *Globe*, p. 817. [2] See *supra*, pp. 122–124.
[3] *Globe*, p. 975.

formerly of conservative tendencies, had by this time completely identified himself with the radicals. The bill was entitled, "A bill to provide for the more efficient government of the insurrectionary states," and since it became the basis of the committee's action and embodied the military part of the Reconstruction act of March 2, it is here printed as introduced by Williams.[1]

Whereas, the pretended state governments of the late so-called Confederate states of Virginia, North Carolina, South Carolina, Georgia, Mississippi, Alabama, Louisiana, Florida, Texas and Arkansas were set up without the authority of Congress, and without sanction of the people and therefore are of no constitutional validity; and whereas they are in the hands and under the control of the unrepentant leaders of the rebellion, and afford no adequate protection for life or property, but countenance and encourage lawlessness and crime; and whereas it is necessary that peace and good order should be enforced in said so-called states until loyal and republican state governments can be legally formed.

Sec. I. Therefore, be it enacted by the Senate and House of Representatives of the United States of America, in Congress assembled, that each of the so-called states shall constitute a military district, to be subject to the military authorities of the United States as herein enacted and prescribed :—

Sec. II. And be it further enacted that it shall be the duty of the General of the army, under the authority of the Presi-

---

[1] The action of the committee on the bill is meaningless without the original text. It is not preserved in any public document, but fortunately it was printed in the newspapers on February 5. Since it was unusual for newspapers to print a bill that had simply been introduced, it is probable that the radicals who were its champions had it published as a feeler of public sentiment. Most of the radical journals that expressed an opinion thought the bill was justified by existing conditions in the South. For the action of the committee on this bill, see *supra*, pp. 124-129.

dent of the United States, to assign to the command of said districts an officer of the regular army, not below the rank of brigadier-general, and to furnish such officer with a military force sufficient to enable him to perform his duties and enforce his authority within the district to which he is assigned.

Sec. 3. And be it further enacted, that it shall be the duty of each officer assigned as aforesaid to protect all peaceable and law-abiding persons in their rights of person and property, to suppress insurrection, disorder, and violence, and to punish, or cause to be punished, all disturbers of the public peace and criminals; and to this end he may allow the local tribunals to take jurisdiction and to try offenders; or when in his judgment it may be necessary for the trial of offenders he shall have power to organize military commissions or tribunals for that purpose, anything in the constitutions or laws of the so-called states to the contrary notwithstanding. And all legislative or judicial proceedings or processes to prevent or control the proceedings of said military tribunals, and all interference by said pretended state governments with the exercise of military authority under this act shall be void and of no effect.

Sec. 4. And be it further enacted that courts and judicial officers of the United States may issue writs of habeas corpus in behalf of prisoners in military custody only when some commissioned officer on duty in the district where the petition originates shall endorse upon said petition a statement certifying upon honor that he has knowledge or information as to the cause and circumstances of the alleged detention, and that he believes the same to be wrongfully detained, and that he believes the endorsed petition is made in good faith, and that justice may be done, and not to hinder, or delay the punishment of crime; and all persons put under military arrest by virtue of this act shall be tried without unnecessary delay, and no cruel or unusual punishment shall be inflicted.

Sec. 5. And be it further enacted, that no sentence of any military tribunal affecting the liberty or life of any person shall be executed until it is approved by the officer in command of the proper district; and the laws and regulations for the government of the army shall not be affected by this act, except in so far as they conflict with its provisions.[1]

This bill was discussed in the joint committee on February 6th,[2] and after receiving some verbal amendments, was adopted by the committee and reported to the House by Stevens on the same day.[3] He intimated that he would put it on its passage at once, but waited until next day before opening the debate.[4] The Democrats asked for its postponement until February 11, in order to give them some time in which to examine its provisions. Stevens regretted that, due to the lateness of the session, he could not comply with their request, but said that he would allow the minority a reasonable amount of time for its discussion. By "reasonable amount of time," he evidently meant one day, for the concluding words of his speech were: "Tomorrow, God willing, I will demand the vote."

Several reasons may be given for Stevens' anxiety that the bill be passed before the expiration of the 39th Congress. In the first place he felt that it was necessary to commit the members of his party to something more radical than the fourteenth amendment as a final basis of reconstruction. In the second place, just at the time the bill was introduced in the House a conference between the President and the most noted Union generals was being held in Washington, which was supposed both by the radicals and the public press to presage the withdrawal of all the remaining soldiers from the southern states. Stevens hoped the bill would become law before any order looking toward this result could be executed, for he believed it would be easier to put it into opera-

[1] *New York Herald*, Feb. 5, 1867.
[2] See *supra*, p. 124.
[3] *Globe*, p. 1036.
[4] *Ibid.*, p. 1073 *et seq.*

tion, if there were already in the South a nucleus of military force. Finally, Washington was besieged with southern "loyalists," embryonic "scalawags and carpet-baggers," who were telling all sorts of frightful tales about the maltreatment of themselves and the loyal colored people at the hands of the dominant rebels.

It was these stories of cruelty and oppression, augmented by partisan despatches of numerous newspaper correspondents, that truly may be said to have been the *raison d'être par excellence* of this military bill. The radicals never tired of recounting these stories and generally they had plenty of testimony at hand with which to prove the correctness of their assertions. For instance, Henry Wilson, senator from Massachusetts, carried with him at all times a handy little vest-pocket notebook in which he had catalogued a list of all the rebel murders and outrages that had been committed since the passage of the Civil Rights act in April of the preceding year.[1] One of the opponents of the bill gave the following ludicrous but accurate description of this note book, and the use made of it by the ingenious "Natick cobbler:" "The senator from Massachusetts has in his possession a little book for you to look upon, in which there are catalogued all the enormities done and committed upon them [i. e. the freedmen and loyal whites] with an exactitude worthy of the most correct statistician. He can give you the most exact dimensions of crime in the southern states; can tell you how high it soars, how deep it dives, its superficial measure, or its cubic quantity to a hair's breadth."[2]

Some examples of the existing conditions in the South, presented in the lurid language of the radicals, should be

---

[1] *Globe*, pp. 1375–1376.   [2] Cowan, *Globe*, appendix, p. 155.

given in order to understand the outward reason for foisting military government upon ten states of the Union. Stevens, for instance, declared :

Persecution, exile and murder have been the order of the day within all these territories so far as loyal men were concerned, whether white or black, more especially if they happened to be black. We have seen these loyal men flitting about everywhere through your cities, around your doors, melancholy, depressed, haggard, like the ghosts of unburied dead on this side of the river Styx, and yet we have borne it with exemplary patience. We have been deaf to the groans, the agony, which have been borne to us by every southern breeze from dying victims. I am for making one more effort to protect these loyal men from the cruelties of anarchy, from persecutions by the malignant, from vengeance visited upon them on our account. If we fail to do it, we should be responsible to the civilized world for the grossest neglect of duty that ever a great nation was guilty of before to humanity.[1]

Boutwell was a past grand master at playing up the rebel outrage argument. "You might as well expect," said he, "to build a fire in the depths of the ocean as expect to reconstruct loyal civil governments in the South until you have broken down the rebel despotisms which everywhere hold sway in that vast region of the country. To-day there are eight millions and more of people, occupying 630,000 square miles of territory, who are writhing under cruelties nameless in their character, injustice such as has not been permitted to exist in any other country in modern times."[2]

"What," asked another radical, "carried our election in the last campaign? It was the story of the southern refugees told to the people of the North and West.

[1] *Globe*, p. 1076. [2] *Globe*, p. 1122.

They told us they demanded protection. They enlisted the sympathy of northern soldiers by telling that the very guerrillas who hung upon the skirts of our army during the war were now murdering southern soldiers who fought on the Union side, and murdering peaceful citizens, murdering black men who were our allies. We promised the people if we were indorsed we would come back here and protect these our allies. Let us enact this bill as an effectual means of furnishing the necessary protection and thus fulfil our promises to our constituents."[1]

Farnsworth, who had succeeded Washburne on the committee, adduced further testimony to show that "unless the military is clothed with some additional authority in the South, the United States garrisons and troops will have to be withdrawn. Because if a soldier is brutally murdered, and the military arrest the offender, he is taken from their hands by writ of habeas corpus issued by the state courts, and is almost invariably discharged without punishment." Farnsworth further stated that the bill was concurred in by Generals Schofield, Thomas, Sickles, Sheridan and other military men, who declared there was no other method of protecting loyal men, black and white, in the South.

Such were the reasons given by the radicals for the necessity of this bill. The extremists like Stevens did not attempt to justify it on constitutional grounds, and those moderates who supported the bill and who desired to salve their stricken consciences by proving its constitutionality, generally made a mess of it. As one of the Democrats said: "Certainly no man will insult the intelligence of the American people by defending this bill on any principle other than that of the right of the con-

---

[1] Hotchkiss, *Globe*, p. 1100.

querors to take possession of and control conquered territory. It is at war with the Constitution and with every principle of free government." Incidentally, he remarked—and he certainly had history on his side—that it could not be defended even on the conquered province theory, for, "when one country conquers another it does not undertake to dictate to the conquered country what government it shall establish."[1]

Hence it is not necessary to concern ourselves with a consideration of the constitutional arguments against the bill, and it certainly is not worth while to devote any attention to those pseudo-constitutional arguments that were made in its favor. Only two other matters in regard to the enactment of this military measure need detain us. One is an answer to the grossly exaggerated and distorted accounts which, as has already been illustrated, the radicals gave of conditions in the South. Secondly, it is of interest to understand why a few honorable and conservative Republicans in both houses of Congress made such heroic efforts so to amend the bill as to mollify some of its severest provisions. Their motives can be understood only by a close scrutiny of their words uttered in debate, and a detailed analysis of the day-to-day action taken on the bill from its introduction on February 6, to its final passage over the President's veto on March 2.

The first task assigned may be disposed of briefly. There is no doubt that there was considerable disorder in the southern states during the winter of 1866–67, but to say that all the crimes or even a majority of them were in the nature of political persecutions on the part of Confederates against Unionists, black or white, is

[1] Finck, *Globe*, p. 1078.

the rankest absurdity; and the men who made such assertions at the time must have been conscious that they were distorting the facts. In reply to these charges Cowan of Pennsylvania gave an excellent *exposé de motit* of the radicals. He said the southern states had constitutions and laws hardly different from those of the North, and that the vast mass of the people, white and black, were satisfied with them. There were only two reasons assigned by the radicals for the abolition of these constitutions and laws, and the substitution of military despotisms for them. One of these reasons was real, the other pretended; but the latter was paraded in front with great ostentation in order to conceal the former, which nevertheless irresistibly intruded itself and showed to all that if it were out of the way as a cause, the pending measure would never have disgraced the halls of Congress even as a bare proposition.

I will first examine this show reason with which Senators are endeavoring to frighten the country, and upon which all the falsehood and ingenuity of radicalism has been busily engaged for the last nine months. It is, that loyal Union men in those states are not secure in their lives and property, but are butchered by wholesale in great numbers with as little concern as though they were dogs. And who, pray, are those loyal Union men who suffer? Listen, and be instructed. They are negroes, whom it is alleged the southern people murder for pastime, just as a naughty boy would kill flies.

After making the reference to Wilson's note-book mentioned above, Cowan said that ingenious senator could do anything in the world with the facts contained therein except to satisfy one that all of them were not cooked up and exaggerated expressly for the occasion. These facts were testified to by nobody except agents of the Freedmen's Bureau, cotton thieves, and other individuals of an equally interested stripe, who, like the hair worms, only wriggle in muddy water. These fellows, male and female, have found the woes of the negro such an easy and profitable way to fame and consideration that, like the dogs of Lazarus, they live by licking his sores; and to hear and see them we would think the world was exceedingly wicked, wholly on account of the negro and for no other reason.

Now, I aver that all this is sheer fabrication, and not a single negro has been killed in the South because he was a Union man. If killed at all he has been killed for some sufficient reason, other than a political one. I suppose that no one will pretend that any respectable man, however much opposed to the Union cause, would care to commit murder upon a negro because the latter favored it. Emperors, kings, and presidents have been assassinated at times to get rid of them in politics, but why any one would go to such trouble to so little purpose in the case of a negro is beyond my comprehension. I am inclined therefore, to think that in the first place these killings, if done at all, are not done by any but common offenders, and that the causes are to be found anywhere else than in the political sentiments of the parties. Everybody knows the tribal antipathy existing between the lower sort of white men and negroes, and no one expects that it will not be the source of frequent brawls and quarrels, especially since the blacks have now no masters either to advise or protect them. In these conflicts the weaker will go to the wall, not because he is loyal or disloyal, but because he is inferior in every way to his antagonists. And the false and foolish notion of equality which you have lately put into the head of the negro amounts only to a standing invitation to every white man to break that head as soon as it insults him.

This measure is intended for a very different purpose than that of providing for a better administration of the civil and criminal laws in the South. It is not intended to make life and property more secure; but it is designed to overturn the state governments there, to substitute in their stead an irresponsible military despotism, and in the trouble and confusion which will follow the authors hope and expect that new governments may be formed upon the basis of political equality between the two different races which inhabit there, and that there may be a chance when all is finished that the political power of the South may be either paralyzed or transferred to the radicals, and that in the meantime no representatives from there are to be allowed to enter either House of Congress.[1]

In order to offer something to the country to give color to this monstrous project, you affect great concern for the negro in another direction, viz. his political status for the future. You first assert his utter and entire helplessness in the presence of the whites; that he cannot defend himself against wholesale murder, even with the Freedmen's Bureau and its military force at his elbow; that he has not sense enough to contract for himself without the guardianship of the Government officials; that in short he is unfit to cope in the battle of life as a freeman, that he must be coddled and nursed, educated and instructed for a year or so, until he bursts his savage cocoon, when it is supposed he will be able to soar away on painted pinion, a full-grown radical bombyx. Only a year or so at farthest is allowed to convert these semi-barbarian slaves into honest and capable patriots, whose wisdom and virtue are to underlie the revised and improved governments of ten states of this Union. Only a year or so is all you allow for this wonderful transformation. Then will the day of Pentecost be fully come, and three or four million negroes are to be changed, not by the apostolic teaching of divinely-inspired men, but by virtue of amended constitutions and the pedagogic efforts of strong-minded school-marms.

The foregoing were not the words of a copperhead or southern sympathizer, but of a man who had been elec-

---

[1] If Cowan could have foreseen the supplementary Reconstruction act of March 23, he could have made this point much stronger.

ted as a Republican. He had been a consistent supporter of the war and of Lincoln's policies, including his reconstruction policy, and simply adhered to it after Johnson became President. Hence the words of Cowan are entitled to a great deal of respect and credence, and when taken in connection with the known fanaticism and extreme partisanship of the radicals, seem to prove a complete refutation of the radical contention that the ex-confederates were butchering the negroes simply because of their loyalty to the Union. As Elijah Hise pointed out in a speech made on this military bill, the radicals did not appear to understand that in the southern states all the property holders, all the traders and merchants who had capital, including all the best and most reputable citizens, were engaged in the movement for secession.[1] Since the ex-rebels were the substantial men of the community, they were the people who were naturally interested in maintaining good government, upholding law and order, and securing the enjoyment of regulated liberty. It was absurd to say that these men who had a deep stake in the well-being and prosperity of their country and who controlled the state governments, were endangering the life, liberty, or property of the people by unlawful misrule. On the other hand, they were the natural persons to whom Congress should have looked for the preservation of law and order, and the prevention of crime and anarchy. Hise, like Cowan, saw that the scheme of the radicals was to spread broadcast in the North false reports of southern crime and cruelty, in order to have the people of that section sustain them in their plot to destroy the existing governments, and erect in their places "loyal" governments in the control of ex-

---

[1] *Globe*, appendix, p. 96 *et seq*.

slaves, southern vagabonds, and northern adventurers. "And when this is done," said Hise, "I suppose the southern states will be placed in their constitutional relations and allowed representation in the two houses of Congress, provided they send true adherents of the radical leaders and supporters of their measures."

Not all the Republicans in Congress, however, were in the category of those who would turn the ex-rebel state governments over to the negroes, the scalawags and the carpet-baggers. Had the southern legislatures ratified the fourteenth amendment, it is possible the conservatives might have succeeded in thwarting the schemes of the radicals by admitting the southern representatives and thus have brought reconstruction to an end. The failure of the southern states to ratify that amendment, however, took the ground from under their feet. When they pleaded for the Republican party to stand by the fourteenth amendment as a final adjustment, the radicals cried that their plea was childish, for as Garfield expressed it, had not "the last one of the sinful ten [rebel states] with scorn and contempt, flung back into our teeth, the magnanimous offer of a generous nation?"[1] Such was the fact, and it placed Garfield's colleague, Bingham, and the other honest conservatives in a most difficult position. Though at first, when the southern states, one after another, began to reject the fourteenth amendment, these conservatives were inclined to say, "Wait, those states will yet accept it," they soon became fully conscious they were in the midst of a revolution, and as revolutions neither go backward nor stand still, they soon saw it was ineffectual to cry, "Wait!" Neither could they maintain that the fourteenth amendment was already adopted, having been

[1] *Globe*, p. 1103.

ratified by three-fourths of the loyal states; for according to their theory the ten rebel states were still states in the Union, and must be counted in order to make valid the adoption of a constitutional amendment. In combating a bill that practically had for its purpose the dismantling of those states, they were inevitably carried toward the position of Andrew Johnson and the Democrats, that since those ten states were in the Union, they should be represented in Congress, for the Constitution plainly says that no state shall be deprived of equal representation in the Senate without its own consent. The direction in which Bingham and the moderate Republicans were tending, Stevens was not slow to see and point out. "If this Congress so decides," said he, "it will give me great pleasure to join the *io triumphe* of the gentleman from Ohio in leading this House, possibly by forbidden paths, into the sheepfold or goatfold of the President."[1] To be accused of "Andy-Johnsonism" was enough to make the moderate Republicans wince; for so unpopular had Johnson become, and so completely had he been repudiated by the people in the fall elections, that no Republican, who did not wish to become a political martyr, would willingly allow himself to be classed as a Johnson supporter.

Hence the moderates could not do what a year earlier they might have done with impunity—*i. e.*, accept the President's policy and allow the southern representatives to take their seats—for then the majority of Republican voters would not have objected to that course, while now they would have considered it little short of treason. Indeed, even had no direful political consequences threatened to attend such a course, the conservatives certainly had no intention of abandoning the ground of

[1] *Globe*, p. 1214.

the fourteenth amendment and going back to the position of the President. In assisting the radicals to rally the people against Johnson, however, the conservatives had helped to raise a storm which they expected to stop with the bulwark of the fourteenth amendment. But that bulwark had fallen when the southern states failed to support it by ratifying the amendment, and now the storm was rapidly passing beyond their control. The story of the enactment of the first Reconstruction bill is the story of how moderate Republicans lost the last remnant of their former power in directing the course of reconstruction.

As we have seen, Stevens introduced the bill into the House on February 6, 1867. The debate continued until late in the afternoon of the next day, when Bingham rose to make his contribution to the discussion.[1] The tenor of his opening remarks showed that he was bursting to express his resentment because of a violent and uncalled-for attack made on him by Stevens on January 28. On that day Stevens had said among other things that no one could believe anything that Bingham might say.[2] Bingham was a man of delicate sense of honor and was deeply offended that his veracity should thus be publicly questioned. So when he began to speak on February 7, it was evident that he intended to take the opportunity to reply in kind to Stevens' derogatory remarks of the week before. The relations of the two factions of the party in the House were becoming exceedingly strained, and representatives who desired above all things that party harmony should be preserved feared that if Bingham should make a speech in his existing state of irritation the breach would be widened. Therefore, a Repub-

---

[1] *Globe*, p. 1079 *et seq*.   [2] *Globe*, p. 816.

lican member asked that he yield so that a motion might be made for a recess until after dinner. Bingham angrily replied that he would not yield; he knew all about the gag and would not submit to it. The Republicans became frightened, and knowing of no other way to prevent Bingham's expressing himself, made a stampede for the door in such numbers that within two minutes the House was almost deserted. The Speaker, who doubtless was a party to the plot, immediately declared that since there was no quorum a motion to adjourn was in order. Such a motion was immediately made and carried, and Bingham's remarks were postponed until after his associates had had an opportunity to assuage his temper.

Before the recess it was evident that Bingham intended to attack the bill *in toto*. So well, however, had the radical disseminators of southern outrages done their work, that it is not at all likely that even with the assistance of the Democrats, Bingham could have rallied enough Republicans to his side to accomplish the defeat of the bill. Evidently this had been made clear to him during the two hours recess by those Republicans who had formerly supported him in his contest with Stevens on the question of recommitting the latter's original reconstruction bill. Therefore, when Bingham renewed his speech, it is clear that he had decided to change his tactics. He did not say whether he would vote for or against the bill, but declared that if it was to become law, he wanted to make it subject to as little objection as possible. He therefore moved to strike out the preamble and insert in its place the one he had offered in committee.[1] Moreover, he wanted to strike

[1] See *supra*, p. 125.

out the term *so-called* everywhere it occurred before the word *states*, as he had so persistently tried to have done in committee. In the fourth section he proposed to give to the United States courts the power without any exception of issuing writs of habeas corpus for persons indictable and punishable according to Federal law. This amendment he offered in order to remove any cause for conflict between the military and civil authorities of the United States.

Speaking of the reason why he desired to amend the preamble, Bingham said he wished thereby to notify in the most solemn form the men who constituted the majority of the people in the ten lately insurgent states, and who themselves were in open, armed rebellion, that all they had to do, in order to get rid of military government, was to present to the Congress of the United States a republican form of state government in accord with the letter and spirit of the Constitution and laws of the United States, together with a ratification of the pending amendment. When men in those states had fulfilled their obligations by assenting to these conditions, he wished them clearly to understand that then their states would be restored at once to their constitutional relations.

The amendments offered by Bingham, together with his speech, show that instead of having the preamble announce that new " governments, republican in form," were to be established in the South, he wanted to have it announce that the military rule which even he had at last been brought to accept as a temporary expedient, would continue only until the existing state governments should accept the fourteenth amendment. Though such a course would have been in keeping with the party platforms of 1866 and doubtless would have met the expectations of a large majority of the northern people, the incessant ding-donging that had been going on for a year or more in Congress to the effect that the Johnson governments were illegal, and which had become more persistent as the resentment against the President increased, had so permeated the brains of the Republican members of the House, that Bingham soon saw that he could not obtain a very large number of followers to pursue with him the course outlined in this speech of February 7. Consequently in a few days he found himself under the necessity of again changing his tactics.

In the meantime, Stevens was making a desperate effort to get the bill passed without amendment. He regarded it merely as a temporary police measure designed to protect the negroes and loyal whites until a definite plan of reconstruction could be worked out in detail. This task he desired to leave to the more radical 40th Congress which by special act of the 39th had been called to meet immediately upon the expiration of the term of the latter on March 4, 1867. "Stevens then hoped," says his biographer, Professor Woodburn,[1] "to secure the disfranchisement of the rebels, the enfranchisement of the negroes, and a moderate plan of confiscation, and then to delay the restoration of the southern states to their privileges within the Union until they were well ready to participate in governing the country."

In accordance with this plan, and true to his promise to allow only one day's debate on the bill, Stevens on February 8 moved the previous question.[2] His motion was not sustained, however, as Bingham, leading the moderate Republicans, was able, with the assistance of the Demo-

---

[1] *Life of Thaddeus Stevens*, p. 477.
[2] *Globe*, p. 1104.

crats, to inflict a decisive defeat upon his rival, the vote on the motion being 62 to 81. For a week following this vote, the bill was debated in the House, and numerous amendments were proposed, only one of which need concern us here. This was an additional section offered by James G. Blaine on Feb. 12.[1] It read as follows:

Sec—And be it further enacted that when the constitutional amendment proposed as article 14 by the 39th Congress shall have become a part of the Constitution of the United States by the ratification of three-fourths of the states now represented in Congress, and when any one of the late so-called Confederate states shall have given its assent to the same and conformed its constitution and laws thereto in all respects; and when it shall have provided by its constitution that the elective franchise shall be enjoyed equally and impartially by all male citizens of the United States, twenty-one years old and upward, without regard to race, color, or previous condition of servitude, except such as may be disfranchised for participating in the late rebellion; and when said constitution shall have been submitted to the voters of said state, as thus defined, for ratification or rejection; and when the constitution, if ratified by the popular vote, shall have been submitted to Congress for examination and approval, said state shall, if its constitution be approved by Congress, be declared entitled to representation in Congress and senators and representatives shall be admitted therefrom on their taking the oath prescribed by law, and then and thereafter the preceding sections of this bill shall be inoperative in said state.

Of course Blaine's purpose in offering this amendment was to forestall Stevens' scheme of allowing reconstruction to go over to the 40th Congress, when, as everybody thought, a much more radical plan could be carried through. Blaine therefore desired, before the House

[1] *Globe*, pp. 1182, 1183.

should become madly rampant in its radicalism, to have incorporated in this military bill this section enunciating the principles upon which the southern states might expect to be finally reconstructed, and thereby commit his party associates to this comparatively conservative plan. In this purpose Blaine had the support of about fifty or sixty conservative Republicans, including Bingham, who by this time had evidently given up the idea that the southern states upon ratifying the fourteenth amendment might be readmitted without having new governments created within their boundaries.

On the same day (Feb. 12) that Blaine offered this amendment, a bill was passed through the House providing a territorial form of government for the state of Louisiana.[1] It had been drawn up by a special committee that had been appointed to investigate the New Orleans riot of July 30, 1866.[2] It provided for a governor and nine councilors in whom all executive and legislative power was vested. These officers were to be appointed by the President, by and with the advice of the Senate, and all were required to be men of unquestioned loyalty. Moreover, the bill was a regular enabling act and created the machinery with which the governor and his councilors were required to erect a new state government in which the right of suffrage was to be exercised by all *loyal* men without regard to color. By virtue of the fact that this special committee was privileged to report at any time, this radical bill had been slipped in for con-

---

[1] *Globe*, p. 1175.

[2] This was a riot between ex-Confederates on the one hand and negroes and loyal whites on the other. It resulted in more than one hundred and fifty persons, mostly negroes, being killed or seriously wounded, and proved conclusively to the minds of the radicals that the existing government was either incompetent or unwilling to protect the lives of loyal citizens. See Rhodes, vol. v, p. 611 *et seq.*

sideration by the House on February 11, and took precedence of the military bill. Strangely enough, it had been supported by radical and conservative Republicans alike, though Stevens appeared chagrined that it should take precedence of his military bill. The radicals supported it because it embodied about all that they desired should be contained in a general reconstruction bill for the other nine states, and did not object to its being considered a precedent for that purpose. Two reasons may be suggested to explain the support given to it by the conservatives. In the first place, nearly everybody felt that Louisiana, the state where disorder had been most prevalent, should be marked for some special punishment. In the second place, the conservatives seemed to believe, that by holding Louisiana up as an example they might force the other states to agree to the fourteenth amendment and comply with the other conditions laid down in the Blaine amendment.[1] These things the conservatives had reason to hope the rebel states would do, especially as they would be under duress of military law from which they could expect to be rid only by yielding. In case they should yield, the conservatives believed they could thwart the scheme of the radicals of passing a supplementary reconstruction act along the lines of the Louisiana bill. Had the conservative plan been carried through, even though it did contemplate negro suffrage, it would have given the native whites, at least in most of the states, more than an even chance with the carpet-baggers, scalawags, and negroes, of maintaining the control of the machinery of the government. And after all it was not negro suffrage *per se* that proved such a curse to the South, but the turning-over of the state governments to

[1] The New York *Herald*, speaking editorially on February 12 and 13, 1867, corroborates this view of the conservatives' motives.

political adventurers. These adventurers could not have obtained control of these governments through negro suffrage alone, but needed the assistance of at least partial white disfranchisement as well as northern bayonets. By the conservative plan it was not proposed to render them these two additional aids.

The speech of Bingham on February 13 proves the foregoing hypothesis.[1] He favored the formation of governments in the southern states by the voluntary action of the people themselves. He did not oppose the military bill provided the Blaine amendment was added and provided further that the whole were passed in spirit if not in fact as a mere addendum to the old Restoration bill of the joint committee. That is to say, he wanted it thoroughly understood that the military government would be terminated just so soon as the existing state governments should ratify the fourteenth amendment and establish impartial suffrage. "Has it," asked he, "indeed come to this, that gentlemen are not content to secure to the emancipated citizens of the Republic the elective franchise and all the rights of citizens and men? Do you insist that by act of Congress they be secured, even where they are in a minority, in the whole political power of the state? Will you by further legislation compel the majority of white citizens to be their subjects for life?"

Though it is true that none of the other conservative Republicans gave quite so frank an exposé of their motives as did Bingham, they certainly understood what he desired, and by their votes indicated that they subscribed to his policy. Moreover, from the bitterness with which the radicals assailed the Blaine amendment, it is clear

[1] *Globe*, p. 1210 *et seq.*

that they too understood the motives of its sponsors. Stevens attacked the proposition and said that its authors were unmistakably leading the House toward "universal amnesty and universal Andy-Johnsonism."[1] That the conservatives were thwarted in their plans, however, was due not so much to the radicals as to the Democrats. The shortsightedness of those gentlemen and the pettiness of the little game of politics which they attempted to play are pitiable. In apportioning the blame for the mistakes of reconstruction, the thirty-five or forty persons who called themselves Democrats should not be overlooked. Nowhere does their imbecility appear in a worse light than in their votes on this Reconstruction bill.

On February 13, Stevens, by means of the previous question, made a second attempt to force his bill through the House in substantially the same form in which a week earlier he had reported it from the committee. However, the previous question was not seconded, and the Democrats were in great glee, for they had learned nothing by experience. It had been so long since they themselves had tasted the sweets of office that they seem to have forgotten that the cohesive power of public plunder is nearly always sufficient, sooner or later, to bind together the factions of a majority party. Hence they thought that if they could prevent any amendments being made to the bill, its entire defeat would be accomplished. Therefore, instead of rendering whatever assistance they could to the conservatives in their effort to mollify the provisions of the bill, they devoted themselves successfully to accomplishing exactly the opposite result.

After the House had refused to second the previous

[1] *Globe*, p. 1213 *et seq*.

question on Stevens' motion that the bill be passed unamended, it looked as though the Blaine amendment certainly would be adopted. It was then that Bingham made his plea that with the military bill, the House send a proclamation to the southern people that they would be kept under the protection of the Federal army not a day after they should adopt the fourteenth amendment and provide for impartial suffrage.[1] When Bingham completed his speech, Blaine moved that the bill be sent to the judiciary committee with instructions that it be reported back to the House immediately with his amendment added.[2] On this motion he called the previous question and was sustained by a bare majority of 7. An analysis of the vote on the previous question shows that 85 Republicans voted *yea*, and 78 extreme radicals and Democrats voted *nay*. It is not correct to conclude that all of these 85 Republicans who voted in the affirmative on seconding the previous question were so moderate in their views as Bingham. Some of them and even Blaine himself supported the amendment for the sole reason that they thought it bad politics to pass a military bill, which carried with it no provision for terminating its operation.[3] But whatever their motives, it is seen that when this first vote was taken there were enough Republicans supporting the amendment to defeat the coalition between extreme radicals and Democrats. Their margin was exceedingly narrow, however, and be-

---

[1] *Globe*, p. 1210 *et seq.*   [2] *Globe*, p. 1213.

[3] *Globe*, pp. 1182, 1183. This inference is easily drawn from the general tenor of Blaine's speech when he offered the amendment. Blaine definitely stated that there was nothing in the amendment to prevent Congress passing enabling acts for the other nine rebel states similar to the one just passed for Louisiana. However, he said that if these nine states would immediately comply with the conditions named in his amendment, such enabling acts would not be necessary.

fore the vote on the main question could be taken, Stevens obtained recognition from the chair and, contrary to the rules of the House, made a thirty-minute speech against the Blaine amendment.[1] In his frantic appeal to his party associates, whom he saw in a majority of nearly two to one against him, he made use of every weapon known to the art of the party manager.

With a voice choking with tears, and in a spirit of inexpressible sadness and grief, he reproached Congress for sitting idle for months and, though the South had been bleeding at every pore, doing nothing to protect the loyal people there in their persons, liberty or property.

Those of us who have health and spirits, have been sitting here enjoying ourselves, while the South is covered all over with anarchy, murder, and rapine. Though we have declared that the President has usurped authority, and that what he has done is void in the face of law, that Congress alone has power to erect governments and protect the people; yet we sit by and move no hand and raise no voice to effect what we declare to be the duty of Congress.

He then turned his great powers of sarcasm and ridicule against Bingham and reproached him with having caused the defeat of his previous bill. He said he had labored upon that bill in conjunction with loyal men from the South, had altered and rewritten it several times. He had warned the House that if that bill should go back to the committee it must die.

Our vigorous friend from Ohio assured us that it would come back from the committee fresh and blooming, but it has not come and I have been forced to accept a position that I could not help. This bill that now comes in lieu of it en-

---
[1] *Globe*, p. 1213.

counters the same obstacles in precisely the same spirit. There are in it some words difficult to spell; adverbs are improperly placed, gentleman object to its particles and its articles, and my friend from Ohio declared this morning with proper exaltation that he had succeeded in passing through the House a bill which uses the word *states* precisely as the President uses it in his theory as to the right of admission of those claiming to represent the rebel states.

It was in this speech that Stevens denounced the Blaine amendment as a step toward "universal amnesty and universal Andy-Johnsonism," as it let in a vast number of rebels and shut out nobody.

Having appealed to duty, to prejudice, and incidentally to party interest, he made a final appeal to the vanity of his party associates.

If sir, I ought presume upon my age, without claiming any of the wisdom of Nestor, I would suggest to the young gentlemen around me that the deeds of this burning crisis, of this solemn day, of this thrilling moment, will cast their shadows far into the future, and will make their impress upon the annals of our history, and that we shall appear upon the bright pages of that history, just in so far as we cordially, without bickering, without small criticisms, lend our aid to promote the great cause of humanity and universal liberty.

To those of his associates who seemed to fear that the bill was quite as likely to promote oppression as liberty, and to those members who pleaded for forgiveness and mercy toward a conquered foe, Stevens said:

The forgiveness of the gospel refers to private offences, where men can forgive their enemies and smother their feeling of revenge without injury to anybody. But that has nothing to do with municipal punishment, with political sanction of political crimes. When nations pass sentence and decree confiscation for crimes unrepented there is no question of malignity. When the judge sentences the convict he has no animosity. When the hangman executes the culprit he rather pities than hates him. Cruelty does not belong to their vocabulary. Gentlemen mistake, therefore, when they make these appeals to us in the name of humanity. They, sir, who while preaching this doctrine are hugging and caressing those whose hands are red with the blood of our and their murdered kinsmen, are covering themselves with indelible stains which all the waters of the Nile cannot wash out.

This speech may be placed as one of the few ever delivered in Congress that have resulted in the changing of votes. As a direct result of it, sixteen Republicans, who had voted with Blaine and Bingham on seconding the previous question, now voted with Stevens against the motion to commit, so that motion was lost by a vote of 69 to 94.[1] Nearly all the Democrats again voted with Stevens. Had only thirteen of them been able to see that their real interest lay on the Bingham side, the Blaine amendment would have been adopted in spite of Stevens' speech. As has already been said, the Democrats had hoped that by preventing the adoption of that amendment, a sufficient number of moderate Republicans would vote with them against the pure military bill to insure its defeat. In this expectation they were sadly mistaken, for only twenty Republicans had sufficient independence to break away from their party and vote against the passage of the bill, though all of them knew it was unconstitutional, and at least a majority of them did not consider it called for by the necessity of the case.

Both the Louisiana and the Reconstruction bills came up for consideration in the Senate on February 14.[2] The

[1] *Globe*, p. 1215.   [2] *Globe*, pp. 1302-1304.

Republican members of that body were not agreed among themselves as to which bill should be taken up first, and a running debate lasting over an hour was engaged in before the question was decided. Some of the radicals wanted to amend the Louisiana bill so that its provisions would be applicable to all the rebel states, combine it with the military bill, and in that form pass both bills at the same time. This was objected to by the conservatives, and Fessenden said that if the Blaine amendment were added to the military bill no additional legislation concerning reconstruction would seem to be necessary, at least for the present. After Fessenden had spoken, Williams, who, as we have seen, was the author of the bill in the first place, and who now took charge of it in the Senate, offered to amend it by adding the Blaine proposition. With this understanding, it was decided by a close vote to proceed with the consideration of the military bill. However, since the usual time for the adjournment of the Senate had already arrived, the debate on the bill did not begin until the next day.

Over night between February 14 and 15 Williams evidently saw a great light, for when the bill came up he immediately withdrew the Blaine amendment.[1]

In explanation of this action, he said that he had offered the amendment in good faith and that he himself had no objection to it, but that upon conferring with *certain persons* he had found that if the bill were passed with the amendment the concurrence of the House could not be secured. This action drew protests both from the conservative Republicans and from the Democrats. Some of the former said they would not vote for the bill at all, unless the amendment were incorporated in it.[2]

---

[1] *Globe*, p. 1360 *et seq.*   [2] For instance, Stewart, *Globe*, p. 1364.

After two days of debate, it became clear that there were so many differences of opinion among the members of the majority party, that unless they were harmonized at once, no reconstruction bill of any character would be passed during the lifetime of the 39th Congress. Therefore, with a view of securing harmonious action those gentlemen held a party caucus on Saturday morning, February 16.[1] A committee of seven, of which John Sherman was chairman, was appointed to amend the bill in such a way that it would secure the support of a majority of the Republican senators. The result of this committee's deliberations was first reported to the caucus, where it was slightly modified, and then to the Senate a little before midnight of that evening.[2] From now on the bill was known as the Sherman substitute but as a matter of fact it was simply the Williams military bill plus the Blaine amendment, with one slight change in each. In the military part, the President instead of the General of the army was designated as the proper person to appoint the military commanders in each of the five districts into which the ten rebel states were divided. In the caucus, due to the influence of Sumner, the Blaine amendment was modified so as to require the several state conventions to insert universal negro suffrage in their constitutions.[3] Though the Democrats offered several amendments and made many motions to adjourn, saying that it was against their religious scruples to work on the Sabbath, the bill was passed after an all-night session early Sunday morning, February 17, 1867. No analysis of the Senate debate will here be attempted. If it were necessary, a suffi-

[1] *New York Herald*, Feb. 18, 1867.
[2] *Globe*, pp. 1458, 1459.   [3] Rhodes, vol. vi, p. 19.

cient number of extracts from the speeches of moderate Republicans could be cited to show that when this bill was passed the general opinion prevailed that no supplementary reconstruction legislation would be enacted until after the southern states had been given a fair chance to initiate movements looking towards the establishment of governments in harmony with the principles enunciated in the bill. Reverdy Johnson voted for the bill, not because he believed it was either just or necessary, but because as a practical man he saw that in this bill the southern whites were given their last opportunity to retain control of the machinery of their governments. Therefore, he thought that it was the part of wisdom for moderate men to unite in support of the bill before another more harsh in its terms should be brought forward.[1] The best proof, however, that the prevailing opinion in the Senate when the Sherman substitute was passed, regarded it as a finality in reconstruction legislation at least until the southern people had been given a fair chance to act, is furnished by the attitude of Sumner in the Senate and Stevens in the House. Gideon Welles states on the authority of Senator Grimes that when the Sherman substitute was adopted, Sumner was violent, swore savagely, and left the Senate in a rage.[2] Concerning this substitute, Sumner said:

It is reconstruction without any machinery or motive power. There is no provision for the initiation of the new governments. There is no helping hand extended to the loyal people who may seek to lay anew the foundations of civil order . . . . I cannot forget, also, that there is no provision by which each freedman can be secured a piece of land, which has always seemed to me important in the work of reconstruction. But

[1] *Globe*, p. 1969.   [2] *Diary*, vol. iii, p. 47.

all this, though of the gravest character, is dwarfed by that other objection which springs from the toleration of rebels in the copartnership of government . . . . while requiring suffrage for all without distinction of race or color, it leaves the machinery and motive power in the hands of the existing governments, which are conducted by the rebels. . . . . It is true that the suffrage is given to the colored race; but their masters are left in power to domineer and even to organize. With their experience, craft, and determined purpose, there is too much reason to fear that all your safeguards would be overthrown, and the Unionists would continue the victims of rebel power. It is not enough to say that rebels *may be* disfranchised. You must say *they must* be disfranchised. Without this, you surrender everything to them.

And yet it has been said that Sumner was a man without guile and had no vindictive feeling toward the South.[1] Thaddeus Stevens agreed with Sumner, and on Monday, February 18, moved that the Senate amendment be not concurred in by the House, and that a committee of conference be asked for.[2] The Washington correspondent of the New York *Independent*, who was one of the shrewdest observers and interpreters of political sentiment then in Washington, wrote the following to his paper concerning Stevens' motives in opposing the Senate amendments:

A prominent point of difference between a class of Republican senators and another class of radical representatives was this: Stevens and his friends insisted upon the disfranchisement of leading rebels in the preliminary elections, and desired that the election of delegates to constitutional conventions should be held under the guidance and control of loyal men. The Senate was willing to allow the southern people to arrange the pre-

[1] Rhodes, vol. v, p. 554.   [2] *Globe*, p. 1315.

liminary elections as they chose, so long as equal rights were established, and felt no particular anxiety on this point, as the state constitutions must be accepted by Congress before representation would be granted.[1]

Additional light is thrown on the radical motives by a speech of Boutwell, who, in supporting Stevens' motion, said he objected to the substitute offered by the Senate primarily because it proposed to grant universal amnesty.[2] Since there were more rebels than loyal men in most of the southern states, by the bill as amended the reorganization of governments in those states would be transferred to the rebels.

"Though every black man will be secured in the right to vote," said he, "the rebels will have the control of the militia and the polls. Under such circumstances do you expect that the negroes, unaccustomed to political struggles, timid, broken down in spirit by the institution of slavery, can deprive the rebels of the places of power which they now possess?" The answer to his question was obvious, and he concluded by declaring that Congress must extend a helping hand to the loyalists so that they could obtain control of the southern state governments.

One of the radical members from Tennessee[3] said he had understood that the giving of this control to the loyalists was to be the purpose of additional legislation by Congress, but that he found in the bill which had come from the Senate universal amnesty and universal suffrage. "Pass this bill and it is the final stroke, the death-blow to the Union men and the men of color in the South. They will have no protection, their rights will not be recognized."

[1] *Independent*, Feb. 28, 1867.   [2] *Globe*, p. 1316.
[3] Stokes, *Globe*, p. 1317.

The debate went on all day, the conservatives favoring and the radicals opposing the Senate amendment. On the morning of February 19 a vote was taken on a motion to concur in the amendment of the Senate. Though a large majority of the Republicans voted in favor of this motion, it was lost because the Democrats voted solidly with Stevens and his minority of extreme radicals against it.[1] Stevens' motion for a conference committee was then passed, and he, Blaine, and Shellabarger were appointed to represent the House on such a committee.[2] The Senate, however, after some debate refused to consent to a committee of conference, and sent a message to the House that it insisted upon its amendments.[3]

On February 19 the House held a special evening session in order further to consider what should be done about the Senate amendments. It is probable that if the vote on a new motion which was made to concur in the Senate amendments had been taken at this meeting it would have been carried. Dilatory tactics, however, were employed by the Democrats, and with the partial assistance of the radicals they were able to prevent a vote being taken.[4] On the next day Wilson made a motion that the amendments of the Senate be concurred in provided that body accept the following additional amendment:

No person excluded from the privilege of holding office by the proposed amendment to the Constitution of the United States shall be eligible to election as a member of the convention to frame a constitution for any of the rebel states, nor shall any such person vote for members of such convention.[5]

[1] *Globe*, p. 1340.
[2] *Ibid.*, p. 1554.
[3] *Ibid.*, p. 1570 *et ante*.
[4] *Ibid.*, p. 1356 *et seq.*
[5] *Ibid.*, p. 1399.

Shellabarger, who had been acting with the radicals, then offered the following as an additional section:

Until the people of said rebel states shall be by law admitted to representation in the Congress of the United States, any civil governments which shall exist therein shall be deemed provisional only, and in all respects subject to the paramount authority of the United States at any time, to abolish, modify, control, or supersede the same; and in all elections to any office under such provisional governments, all persons shall be entitled to vote, and none others, who are entitled to vote under the provision of the fifth section of this act; and no person shall be eligible to any office under any such provisional governments, who would be disqualified from holding office under the provisions of the said article of said constitutional amendment.[1]

Both the Wilson and the Shellabarger amendments were agreed to, and in its amended form the bill once more passed the House by a vote of 126 to 46.

Though the radicals had not won completely, the conservatives were thoroughly defeated; for as everybody recognized, the adoption of these two penal clauses made it impossible for the existing governments in the South to take the initiative in establishing new governments in harmony with the other provisions of the bill. That they otherwise would have done so is not susceptible of proof, but nevertheless it is highly probable that they would. Thoughtful conservative men, both North and South, were becoming alarmed at the radicalism rampant in Congress, and at the evident intention of at least half the Republicans to put the southern states in the hands of the negroes and the loyal whites.

Therefore, Democrats like Reverdy Johnson, Thomas

---

[1] *Globe*, p. 1400.

A. Hendricks,[1] and Manton Marble[2] of the New York *World*, administration Republicans like Raymond,[3] and conservative Republicans like Stewart[4] and Sherman,[4] advised the southerners to act quickly in compliance with the terms of the bill. Though this advice was given both before and after the adoption of the penal clauses, the disfranchisement of nearly all those southerners who were then and for years past had been at the head of political affairs in the South made it impossible for them to accept this advice and take the lead in forming such governments. Moreover, the Blaine amendment, pure and simple, might have been self-operating, but the addition of the Wilson proviso made it necessary to enact supplemental legislation. In order to carry into effect this disfranchisement of the leading rebels, it would of course be necessary to place the machinery for setting up the new governments in the hands of Federal officials. Under such circumstances it is natural that the resulting governments were controlled by the carpet-baggers, scalawags and negroes. Representative Wilson, who was the author of the disfranchising clause, stated later when he was advocating the supplementary Reconstruction bill, that such a bill would not have been necessary had the Democrats not forced the conservatives to yield the disfranchising clause to the radicals in order that the entire bill be not lost.[5] As the New York *Nation*[6] pointed out, the debt which the radicals owed the Democratic party was almost incalculable.

The Senate concurred in the House amendments on February 20.[7] Though the President might have de-

---

[1] *Globe*, p. 1969 *et seq.*
[2] *N. Y. World*, Feb. 23, 1867.
[3] *N. Y. Times*, Feb. 18 and 20, 1867.
[4] *Globe*, p. 1625 *et seq.*
[5] *Globe*, 1st sess. 40th cong., p. 64.
[6] *Ibid.*, Feb. 21, 1867.
[7] *Globe*, p. 1645.

feated this particular bill with a "pocket" veto, he preferred not to evade the question, and on March 2 sent a message to the House announcing his dissent.[1] The message was received with scant respect, and though the Democrats attempted to sustain the veto by dilatory tactics, their scheme was squelched by Blaine's moving to suspend the rules. This motion was agreed to and the bill was again passed by the necessary two-thirds majority.[2] On the same day the Senate took similar action.[3]

As this was the last piece of legislation with which the joint committee on reconstruction was connected, its enactment into law marks the close of that committee's history.

When the 40th Congress assembled, there was an attempt to resurrect the committee, but it ended in failure. There was no longer any need for a joint committee, as the fear that the two houses would not act in concert, which had brought about its appointment in the first place, had long since ceased to exist. Hence, from this time on the House had its own special committee on reconstruction, while in the Senate matters pertaining to that subject were generally looked after by the judiciary committee.

[1] *Globe*, p. 1729.
[2] *Ibid.*, p. 1733.
[3] *Ibid.*, p. 1976.

www.ingramcontent.com/pod-product-compliance
Lightning Source LLC
Chambersburg PA
CBHW021847230426
43671CB00006B/298